THE EARLY
AMERICAN REPUBLIC
1789–1829

THE EARLY
AMERICAN REPUBLIC
1789–1829

Paul E. Johnson
University of South Carolina

New York   Oxford
OXFORD UNIVERSITY PRESS
2007

Oxford University Press, Inc., publishes works that further Oxford University's
objective of excellence in research, scholarship, and education.

Oxford New York
Auckland Cape Town Dar es Salaam Hong Kong Karachi
Kuala Lumpur Madrid Melbourne Mexico City Nairobi
New Delhi Shanghai Taipei Toronto

With offices in
Argentina Austria Brazil Chile Czech Republic France Greece
Guatemala Hungary Italy Japan Poland Portugal Singapore
South Korea Switzerland Thailand Turkey Ukraine Vietnam

Published by Oxford University Press, Inc.
198 Madison Avenue, New York, New York 10016
http://www.oup.com

Oxford is a registered trademark of Oxford University Press

Library of Congress Cataloging-in Publication Data

Johnson, Paul E., 1942–
    The early American republic, 1789–1829 / by Paul E. Johnson.
      p. cm.
    ISBN-13: 978-0-19-515422-1 (cloth : acid-free paper)
    ISBN-10: 0-19-515422-3 (cloth : acid-free paper)
    ISBN-13: 978-0-19-515423-8 (pbk. : acid-free paper)
    ISBN-10: 0-19-515423-1 (pbk. : acid-free paper)
    1. United States—History—1783–1865.   2. United States—Politics and government—
1789–1815.   3. United States—Politics and government—1815–1861.   4. United States—
Social conditions—To 1865.   I. Title.

E301.J67 2006
973.4—dc22

                                                                                  2005044914

Printing number: 9 8 7 6 5 4 3 2 1

Printed in the United States of America
on acid-free paper

For Lucy, Bill, Patty, and Buddy

CONTENTS

PREFACE

———•◦•———

THIS IS A SHORT HISTORY OF THE UNITED STATES FROM 1789 TO 1829, written for people who know little about the subject or who have forgotten what they once knew. It addresses two big subjects. First, it tells the story of national politics from the presidency of George Washington to the inauguration of Andrew Jackson. In these years, the Founders struggled to make a national republic, then watched as their United States became bigger, more democratic, and more divided than anything they had tried to make. Second, this book describes the beginnings of American market society in these years— years in which large numbers of Americans first began to organize their lives around earning, buying, and selling. Put simply, this is a book about the beginnings of American nationhood, American democracy, and American free-market capitalism. Most of us think that all three are inevitably American: we count a unified nation, representative democracy, and a market economy as the natural order of the United States. It is a principal task of this book to demonstrate that none of these was natural or inevitable in 1790, and that all of them were contested and partial in 1830.

Though it is shaped by these larger concerns, the book is more descriptive than overtly analytic. The first two chapters narrate national politics between 1789 and 1815. The United States in these years was a revolutionary republic in an Atlantic world ruled by kings and aristocrats. The American Revolution rejected not only colonial dependence but monarchy and titled hierarchy as well. All thirteen revolutionary states adopted republican constitutions, and the Constitution of 1789 established a national republic. But consensus on national independence and republican government did not end constitutional argument. The extent to which the governments of the states and of the United States could tax, coerce, and otherwise govern their citizens (and the realities of what citizens would put up with) was not settled. Neither was the degree of sovereignty given up by the states when they ratified the national constitution. There were no clear answers to these questions. Scholars who look for "original intent" in the sparse records of the Constitutional Convention find only that the Founders were republicans who wanted to make a United States. Beyond that, there is much more argument and compromise than there is intent. When scholars move on to the state-ratifying conventions they find more argument, less compromise, and an even muddier picture of what anyone might have intended. And when they move into the first decades of government under the

Constitution, they find again that the Founders were less a pantheon of gods who laid down eternal law than they were a debating society. They accepted the Constitution and argued within (and about) its language and limits, but the Constitution left plenty of room for debate.

That contest would have been heated under any circumstances. It was made more difficult by events in the wider world. A few months after George Washington took office, France began a republican revolution of its own. In 1793 the French beheaded their king and declared an international war of all peoples against all monarchs, a war that persisted through twists and turns and moments of peace until the forces of reaction under Great Britain defeated Napoleon in 1815. American political leaders were bitterly divided between supporters of French republicanism and British reaction. Worse, the warring powers of Europe abused American sovereignty, intervened in American politics, and ultimately drew the United States into their war. It was within that domestic and international maelstrom that Federalists and Jeffersonians made the United States. When the smoke cleared in 1815, the new nation had weathered its first twenty-five years and was an established—though still vaguely defined—democratic republic.

Chapters 3 through 5 leave politics to trace the rise of American market society in the years 1790–1830. During the European wars, Americans experienced a high-water mark of the old colonial export economy. Seaport merchants and financiers, freed from colonial restraints and provided with wartime European markets, made a lot of money exporting American food and raw materials and importing British manufactured goods. But most Americans (in 1790, nearly nine in ten) lived on farms and continued to do what their parents and grandparents had done: they provided for themselves and their neighborhoods and sent produce to the seaports to trade for imported comforts and luxuries. Some, like the rising cotton aristocracy of the South and some of the grain farmers of the mid-Atlantic, engaged in that trade on a large scale. But most farmers, North and South, worked with their families, bartered with neighbors, and sent small surpluses on to long-distance trade. Whatever their levels of engagement, the agriculturalists of the early United States worked within an export-oriented economy in which the financial and industrial center remained outside the country. The political ties with Britain were severed. The neocolonial economic ties were strong and getting stronger.

With the end of war in 1815, Americans began paying less attention to Britain and the North Atlantic and more to the development of their own country. Land purchases and war had removed the European and Indian brakes on western settlement. Southerners planted a Cotton Belt across a thousand-mile swath of the Lower South. Southern economic growth in the years 1790 to 1830 was stupendous, but it took place within the old colonial framework: the South exported cotton and other plantation staples to Great Britain and received manufactured goods, along with bills for shipping, insurance, credit, and other services, from outside the region. The South experienced growth with minimal qualitative change: the planters remained rich and retained political power, the slaves remained slaves, and most white farmers remained at the margins of the plantation economy. The South in 1830 was merely a bigger and busier version of what it had been in 1790.

Development went differently in the North. The seaports had grown during the war years, and saltwater merchants had made great fortunes. Most of that money went into banking, insurance, and urban real estate, but some of it built factories. In the countryside, farmers responded to rising urban markets by increasing their surpluses, often to the point of becoming single-crop commercial farmers. New inland towns and cities rose up to serve a commercializing agriculture, and state governments increased their support for roads, canals, and the infrastructure of a business society. The result, clearly visible by 1830, was a specialized and integrated northern market society. Mixed, semisubsistence agriculture gave way to dairy farms, truck farms, wheat farms, and poultry farms. The farmers sent their food to American workers, who made everything from farm tools to pocket watches to religious pamphlets to ready-made shoes, and to a growing army of clerks and businessmen who managed the wholesaling, retailing, transport, and credit systems of a new market society. Thus, the North experienced the agricultural, industrial, and commercial revolutions as one process, a process that freed them from old colonial limits, that made the northern economy both modern and self-sustaining, and that opened a wide path for the development of the acquisitive individual. Between 1790 and 1830—after 1815 in particular—large numbers of strategically placed northerners began to think and act like a nineteenth-century middle class: they assumed that economic life was based in money, buying, and selling (and not, as had been the case with their grandfathers, in the stewardship of family land), that ambition and individual accumulation were admirable, that careers should be open to diligence and talent, that the goal of life was to get more.

By the 1820s American life chances were governed increasingly by money and ambition, less by inheritance and family land. Some Americans welcomed the change, some did not. But nearly all of them experienced it as a crisis of the rural patriarchy in which they had grown up. Chapter 5 treats cultural developments in these years as responses to this fundamental crisis of authority. The chapter examines religious revivals, reformulations of racial ideology, and redefinitions of republican citizenship for their contributions to the remaking of gender roles, family forms, and public identities. With important exceptions, new formulations of race, religion, and citizenship shored up the entitlements of white men, creating a public life that was more democratic, more individualistic, and more explicitly white and male than had been the United States of 1790.

Chapter 6 returns to politics. In particular, it traces two issues that would occupy American politics from the end of the War of 1812 through the Civil

War. First, Americans argued over the national government's role in economic development—a debate that centered on banking, currency, and credit, on government subsidies for roads and canals, on the tariff, and on the settlement of public land in the West. Second—and this was much more dangerous—they began to argue about slavery. The framers of the Constitution knew that slavery was an issue that could make a United States impossible. They sidestepped differences between the slaveholding southern states and northern states that were outlawing the institution. The leaders of the early republic agreed that slavery was a question for the states and not the national government. The admission of new states, however, was the business of Congress. When Missouri, the first state west of the Mississippi, applied for admission in 1819 as a slave state, slavery entered national politics. Northerners (whose numerical majority increased steadily) and southerners saw for the first time that the question of slavery was central—and dangerous—to the republic.

The ruling Democratic-Republicans (this was the period of one-party government known as the Era of Good Feelings) divided along less ominously sectional lines on issues of economic development: those who called themselves National Republicans favored various forms of federal intervention; Republican fundamentalists favored states' rights and a limited national government. To protect slavery, the union, and the old republic, northern and southern Republicans formed the Democratic Party and elected Andrew Jackson president in 1828. In the 1830s, their National Republican opponents—North and South—would form the Whig Party and fight for an economic nationalism that, they promised, would heal sectional divisions. Politicians within that two-party system fought about federalism and economic development and studiously avoided the explosive question of slavery. The result was mass democracy, an expanding capitalist economy, and an increasingly tenuous nation.

ACKNOWLEDGMENTS

FIRST, I THANK THE COMMUNITY OF SCHOLARS WHO WRITE ABOUT the early republic. They have made a big, solid, and imaginative literature, and I have tried hard to do it justice. The anonymous readers for Oxford University Press saved me from many (but not all) of my mistakes, and offered suggestions that made this a better book. Also at Oxford, Peter Coveny, June Kim, and Barbara Mathieu guided the manuscript with courtesy and skill. I must also thank Patrick Maney and the colleagues and graduate students who made it fun to write this book while working at the University of South Carolina.

Portions of the text are revised from John M. Murrin, et al., *Liberty, Equality, Power: A History of the American People* (4th ed., 2005), and are used with permission of Wadsworth/Thomson Learning

THE EARLY
AMERICAN REPUBLIC
1789–1829

Source: Library of Congress, Prints and Photographs Division (reproduction number LC USZ62-126500).

CHAPTER 1

Federalists

GEORGE WASHINGTON LEFT MOUNT VERNON FOR THE TEMPORARY capital in New York City in April 1789. It was an eight-day journey, and the whole way was lined with grateful citizens of the new republic. Militia companies marched beside the new president. Local dignitaries escorted him from town to town and arranged great banquets in his honor. Crowds cheered, church bells rang, and lines of girls in white dresses waved demurely as Washington passed. At Newark Bay he boarded a white barge decorated with flowers and a red canopy, rowed by thirteen trained pilots in white uniforms. Shore batteries and a Spanish warship anchored in the harbor fired their cannon, and scores of boats surrounded the president's barge, each of them filled with cheering spectators. The boats flew flags, and some carried bands of music. One boat drew near the barge, and a chorus sang an ode composed for Washington's arrival—set to the tune of "God Save the King." The shore was lined with rank upon rank of jubilant New Yorkers. As the president's barge passed the Battery at the southern tip of Manhattan, said a witness, the "successive motion of the hats was like the rolling motion of the sea, or a field of grain." The mayor of the city and the governor of New York greeted Washington at the wharf. A company of militia and two marching bands led him through the crowds on the final half mile of his journey to the president's house.

MAKING A NATIONAL GOVERNMENT

What the Federalists Were Up Against

The Americans who celebrated their new president were less certain about their new national government. It was revolt against centralized authority that had made them an independent people. For many, distrust of government—distant and powerful government in particular—was the first rule of being an American. They had fought their Revolution and persisted through the 1780s under Articles of Confederation that created a weak president and that refused the power to tax or coerce the states or the people at large. The result, according to those who supported the Constitution, had been "local mischiefs"—state governments that failed to pay their debts, that issued bogus paper money, and that squabbled with each other, along with a popular "licentiousness" that ran from selfishness to disobedience to the odd riot and small rebellion—that undermined property, commerce, and social order at home and encouraged contempt for the United States abroad.

George Washington and most who would help him govern had feared that local disorder would destroy the union between the states that had made the Americans independent. They had supported a new Constitution to prevent that. But in translating the Constitution into a working government, they confronted both popular fears and differences among themselves about the amount and kinds of centralized power that they had created. The great question was whether the American Revolution had made a new nation or a federation of thirteen independent republics. Translated into politics and government, this became the problem of "consolidation": the popular fear, voiced loudly during the ratification struggles in the states, that the powers of the new central government to tax, legislate, and protect would wipe out the powers of the states and the liberties of the people and erect a nation-state on old-world models. There were, we will see, members of Washington's administration who wanted to take big steps in that direction. But others in government, along with hundreds of thousands of watchful citizens, were wary of the powerful executives, taxmen, and professional armies that, they thought, the Revolution had banished from America.

The officers of the new government were elected and appointed from among the educated men who had written the Constitution and struggled to get it ratified by the states. They were a postcolonial elite, and they formed a very thin upper crust: planters and large farmers who grew staple crops for shipment out of the country, merchants and financiers who shipped those staples to the old Mother Country and imported manufactured goods into America, and the lawyers who served both. None of them was a manufacturer (there were almost no factories in the United States), and none was primarily a banker (there were only three banks in the new country, all serving the export economy.) These men were committed to making government under the Constitution work. They knew the rules of gentlemanly comportment, of the maintenance of personal honor, and the ethos of public service. They sometimes disagreed on fundamental policies. Some were jealous and ambitious, and a few were merely stupid. But they all knew the importance of acting like a public-spirited gentleman, and most of them had staked their public lives on the success of the American republic.

In 1789, success was not certain. About half of the country's active citizens had opposed adoption of the Constitution, and no one really knew how they would react when their new governors tried to govern them. The overwhelming majority of America's four million people lived on farms, with most of the others in rural villages that served the farms. (Only Boston, New York, Philadelphia, Baltimore, and Charleston had populations over 10,000, and only 1 American in 32 lived in those small cities.) In New England, small, family-owned farms predominated. Yankee farmers satisfied their needs from their own and their neighbors' labor and land and sent small surpluses to seaport towns that shipped them to Europe and the Caribbean. In an emerging grain country that stretched from New York's Hudson Valley through the mid-Atlantic and on into Maryland and Virginia, farmers practiced the same neighborhood-based subsistence economy but shipped large and increasing amounts of wheat, corn, and other grains overseas. In the tidewater areas of the Chesapeake and on into the Carolinas and Georgia the farms were bigger, and they were worked by slaves. These were commercial plantations, growing huge crops of tobacco and rice (and, within a few years, cotton) for shipment overseas. Farmers in the interior of the southern states, including the brave souls who were spilling beyond the Appalachians into Kentucky and Tennessee, raised corn and hogs, hunted and fished, bartered with their neighbors, and sent a trickle of produce over bad roads, down rivers, and—again—onto international markets.

From Maine to Georgia, and from the poorest backcountry settler to the richest plantation grandee, America's farmer-citizens had a few important things in common. First, in striking contrast to the peasant nations of the Old World, most of them owned their own farms, made their own decisions about what to do with their resources, and took great—often belligerent—pride in their independence. The first duty of national government would be to protect the "life, liberty, and property" that British colonial rule had supposedly endangered. Second, though Americans in 1789 were free of colonial political controls, they were still embedded in a colonial economy. From the small farmer with his bushel or two of surplus corn to the plantation master with his shiploads of tobacco or rice, American farmers sent their produce on to international markets. There were simply too few nonfarming Americans to constitute a domestic market for food, too few manufacturers to buy farm-produced raw materials. The Americans sent their produce overseas (the Caribbean, Britain, and continental Europe) and bought their manufactured goods from Britain. The need to protect and nurture that trade had been among the principal motives for making the Constitution, and it would be one of the great tests of Washington's administration.

Not all Americans, of course, were free citizens and farm owners. Half were women, who derived their legal and public identities through their fathers or husbands. One in five were African Americans, nearly all of them slaves. British law had allowed slavery in all of the thirteen colonies. By 1789 some northern states had freed their slaves by statute, and others were preparing to do the same. But most African Americans lived as slaves in the southern states, and they had little reason to cheer the success of an independent, slaveholding United States. Beyond the Appalachians were hundreds of thousands of free and unconquered Native Americans. They occupied more than half of what the maps said was the United States, and they knew the danger posed by an independent republic of land-hungry farmers. Often with the help of European governments, they would provide President Washington with some of his biggest challenges.

The United States in 1789 was not only a new nation but a postcolonial society—a "society" and a "nation" only because it had a constitution and a map. During the next twenty-five years, the republic would expand across space and become—for those who were white and male—more democratic. Americans would become more busy and prosperous as the disruptions of war made Europe hungrier for American food and raw materials. But for all its spatial and economic growth, the United States in 1815 remained a nation of farmers who bought their consumer goods from other countries, who lived their social and emotional lives within their own neighborhoods, and who—to confound those who wished to govern them—were self-conscious republicans who had won their independence through force of arms.

Washington's "Republican Court"

George Washington arrived in New York on April 23 and took the oath of office seven days later. His inaugural address, delivered to his "Fellow Citizens" of the Senate and House of Representatives, tried to reassure Americans about their government without clearing up the confusion. The president spent much of his time telling the people that he had not wanted the presidency, that he doubted his capacities for the job, that he would not accept a salary, that he would rather be back on his farm, that he did not relish the power that the Constitution put in the hands of the president. (In an early draft of the address, he had gone so far as to divulge that he had no children and thus could never sire a royal family.) He did, however, say that "The People of the United States . . . have advanced to the character of an independent nation," a phrase that bypassed the states and constituted "the people" as a "nation." It was a logical next step to assume that their government was "national" as well. In the debates over ratification, "national government" was held up as the result of the Constitution both by its promoters and those who opposed it. "Nation" was a loaded word: the framers had left it out of the Constitution and later in 1789 Congress would rebuke the president for using it. Washington smoothed this over by referring to a "United Government" (a happily noncommittal phrase) that was the result of "tranquil deliberations, and voluntary consent of so many distinct communities," and went on to advise the legislators to act in the public good, without favoritism, factionalism, or regional jealousy, and with "a reverence for the characteristic rights of freemen." The United States under the Constitution, in short, would be a "nation" with a "United Government" (whatever that meant) led by patriots who were both republicans and gentlemen and who respected the rights of free men. Vague, reassuring, and unobjectionable, the inaugural address was a fine performance of manners by America's first citizen and gentleman. As for American hopes and fears about government under the Constitution, they would be answered only in practice.

Reporting for work, President Washington found the Congress embroiled in its first controversy—an argument over the majesty that would attach to his office. Vice President John Adams had asked the Senate to create a title of honor for the president. Adams, along with many of the senators, wanted a resounding title that would reflect the power of the new executive. They rejected "His Excellency" because that was the term used for ambassadors, colonial governors, and other minor officials. Among the other titles they considered were "His Highness," "His Mightiness," "His Elective Highness," "His Most Benign Highness," "His Majesty," and "His Highness, the President of the United States, and Protector of Their Liberties." The Senate debated these more or less royal titles for a full month, then gave up when it became clear that the more democratic House of Representatives would not assent to any of them. (At some point in all this, a wag suggested that the pudgy Vice President Adams be dubbed "His Rotundity.") The legislators settled on simply calling Washington "the President of the United States," and on the austere dignity of "Mr. President." A senator from Pennsylvania expressed relief that the "silly business" was over. Thomas Jefferson, not yet a member of the government, pronounced the whole affair "the most superlatively ridiculous thing I ever heard of."

Jefferson would learn, however, that much was at stake in the argument over titles. The Constitution provided a blueprint for the government of the United States. But it was George Washington's administration that would translate that blueprint into a working state. Members of the government knew that their decisions would set precedents. It mattered very much what citizens called their president, for that was part of the huge constellation of laws, customs, and forms of etiquette that would give the new government either a republican or (as many antifederalists feared) a courtly tone. Many of those close to Washington wanted to protect presidential power from the localism and democracy that, they felt, had nearly killed the republic in the 1780s. Washington's stately inaugural tour, the high salaries being paid to executive appointees, the formal balls and presidential dinners, the observance of the English custom of celebrating the executive's birthday, the talk of putting Washington's image on the national currency—all were meant to bolster the power and grandeur of the new government, particularly of its executive.

Soon after taking office, Washington began holding presidential levees on Tuesday afternoons where guests could meet the president. His wife, Martha, hosted similar receptions on Fridays. These were excruciatingly formal affairs. A witness reported that the levees were "numerously attended by all that was fashionable, elegant, and refined in society; but there was no place for the intrusion of the rabble in crowds, or for the more coarse and boisterous partisan—the vulgar electioneer—or the impudent place hunter—with boots and frock-coats, or round abouts, or with patched knees, and holes at both elbows. . . . Full dress was required of all." When Jefferson became secretary of state and attended official social functions, he often found himself the only democrat at the dinner table. Aristocratic sentiments prevailed, said Jefferson, "unless there chanced to be some [democrat] from the legislative Houses." The battle over presidential titles, as well as the social round of what some called Washington's "republican court" were not "silly business." They were revealing episodes in the argument over how questions of governance that Americans had debated since the 1760s would finally be answered.

For his part, Washington assured the country that he did not want to be king. He complained about the levees and receptions that placed him "in the midst of perpetual fetes." Although he would uphold the dignity and power of the presidency, Washington assured Americans that he would never be anything but a republican public servant. Only George Washington, resting on the immense popular trust and affection that he had won in the Revolution, could have combined regal forms and republican assurances and gotten away with it.

James Madison and the First Congress

James Madison, congressman from Virginia, assumed leadership of the First Congress. Madison's federalist credentials were impeccable. He had helped to call the Constitutional Convention and had written the first draft of the Constitution. Along with Alexander Hamilton and John Jay of New York, he had authored *The Federalist,* the most cogent and widely known argument in favor of ratification. He had returned to Virginia to urge adoption of the Constitution in his home state, then—against the stiff opposition of antifederalists—won election to the First Congress.

Madison was a committed federalist, but he understood the Constitution and the problem of union differently than did many in Washington's administration. Many assumed that having defeated the antifederalists they could go about the business of creating a nation state. As fervently as anyone in government, Madison believed that the enduring success of the Revolution depended on union under the Constitution. But he wanted a *federal* and not a national government: some powers, he said, belonged to the national government, some were reserved to the states, and both must know their responsibilities and limits. Madison also knew that half of the active citizens of the United States had opposed the Constitution. He wanted to help make a national government in ways that observed their worries about "consolidation," the fear that the national government would monopolize power and transform the states into mere provinces, and equally strong worries that national government threatened individual liberties. The situation—as had every situation since the 1770s—demanded that both citizens and their elected governors be "patriotic" (the revolutionaries had called this "virtuous"), eschewing selfishness and local or regional interests in favor of the common good. Only compromise and conciliation would ensure the success of the Constitution, Madison insisted. Anything else would make it fail.

Under Madison's guidance Congress strengthened the national government while trying to reconcile doubtful citizens to the Constitution. First they dealt with foreign commerce—the lifeblood of the American economy. Under the Articles of Confederation, the United States had lacked either a commercial policy or the power to negotiate agreements with other countries. The first step was to write a national tariff on imports. Madison spoke against legislation that would benefit any part of the union and hurt the others, then watched as the first flurry of congressional logrolling created a document that favored the Northeast at the expense of the South and West. Still, the tariff was a milepost: it aroused little popular opposition, it told the international trading community that the United States had a national government with a uniform commercial policy, and it provided 90 percent of the national government's income.

Congress turned next to institutional guarantees of individual liberties that had been demanded by the state-ratifying conventions. Madison proposed nineteen amendments to the House. The ten that survived congressional scrutiny and ratification by the states became the Bill of Rights. They reflected fears raised by a generation of struggle with centralized power—fears that had underlay much of the opposition to the Constitution. The First Amendment guaranteed freedom of speech, press, and religion against federal interference. The Second and Third Amendments, prompted by revolutionary distrust of standing armies, guaranteed the continuation of a militia of armed citizens and stated the specific conditions under which soldiers could be quartered in citizens' households. The Fourth, Fifth, Sixth, Seventh, and Eighth Amendments defined and protected a citizen's rights in court and when under arrest—rights whose violation had been high on the Revolution's list of grievances. The Ninth Amendment stated that the enumeration of specific rights in the first eight amendments did not imply a denial of other rights; the Tenth stated that powers not assigned to the national government by the Constitution remained with the states and the citizenry—though the studied omission of the word "expressly" left a lot of room for interpretation. An amendment that would have extended the First Amendment prohibitions to state legislatures passed the House but was voted down in the Senate; nationalization of the Bill of Rights would wait until the Civil War and the Fourteenth Amendment.

Madison, a committed nationalist, had performed skillfully. Many doubters at the ratifying conventions had called for amendments or a second Constitutional Convention that would weaken the government detailed in the Constitution. The Bill of Rights assured the citizenry that the national government would not attack their liberties, and thus drew popular support to the national government and away from the most committed antifederalists. The Bill of Rights was an historic guarantee of individual liberties. But in the context in which it was written and ratified, it was an even more important guarantee of the power and endurance of the national government.

To fill out the framework of government outlined in the Constitution, Congress then created the executive departments of War, State, and Treasury and guaranteed that the heads of those departments and their assistants would be appointed solely by the president, thus creating the president's Cabinet and protecting it from congressional control. Congress then created the federal courts that were demanded but not specified in the Constitution. The Judiciary Act of 1789 established a Supreme Court with six members, along with thirteen district courts and three circuit courts of appeal. The act made it possible for certain cases to be appealed from state courts to federal circuit courts, which would be presided over by traveling Supreme Court justices, a provision that both increased and dramatized federal power. As James Madison and other members of the intensely nationalist First Congress surveyed their handiwork, they could congratulate themselves on having strengthened national authority and eased popular mistrust of that authority at the same time.

The Political Economy of Alexander Hamilton

Washington filled posts in what would become the Cabinet with familiar faces. As secretary of war, he chose Henry Knox, an old comrade from the Revolution. The State Department went to his fellow Virginian Thomas Jefferson. He chose Alexander Hamilton of New York, his trusted aide-de-camp from Revolutionary days, to head the Department of the Treasury.

Hamilton was the most single-minded nationalist in the new government. He was a brilliant economic thinker, an admirer of the British system of centralized government and finance, and a supremely arrogant and ambitious man. Hamilton opposed the independent powers of the states, and he was openly contemptuous of ordinary citizens. He had left the Constitutional Convention hoping that the new union was just a start, and that the reassuring presence of George Washington would "conciliate the confidence and affection of the people and perhaps enable the government to acquire more consistency than the proposed constitution seems to promise for so extended a country. It may then triumph altogether over the state governments and reduce them to an entire subordination." Hamilton was the arch-consolidationist. He envisioned the United States as a great commercial nation with a powerful and uncontested national state. More than anyone else in the administration, perhaps even more than Washington himself (he later referred to Washington's presidency as "my administration"), Hamilton directed the making of the government of the United States.

Perhaps the greatest single problem to which the new Constitution was addressed was the Confederation's inability to pay its debts and establish a system of government finance. In 1789 Congress asked Secretary of the Treasury Hamilton to report on the public finances. The debt fell into three categories, Hamilton reported. The first was the $11 million owed to foreigners—primarily debts to France incurred during the Revolution. The second and third— roughly $24 million each—were debts owed by the national and state governments to American citizens who had supplied food, arms, and other resources to the revolutionary cause. Congress agreed that both justice and the credibility of the new government dictated that the foreign debts be paid quickly and in full. But the domestic debts raised questions. Those debts consisted of notes issued during the Revolution to soldiers, and to merchants, farmers, and others who had helped the war effort. Over the years, speculators had bought up many of these notes at a fraction of their face value. When word spread that the Constitution would create a government likely to pay its debts, speculators and their agents fanned out across the countryside buying up all the notes they could find. By 1790 the government debt was concentrated in the hands of financiers and speculators—most of them northeasterners—who had bought notes for 10 to 30 percent of their original value. Full payment would bring them enormous windfall profits.

The Revolutionary War debts of the individual states were another source of contention. Nationalists, with Hamilton at their head, wanted to assume the debts of the states as part of a national debt—a move that would concentrate the interests of public creditors and the need for taxation and an expanded civil service in the national government. The state debts had also been bought up by speculators, and they posed another problem as well: many states, including all the southern states with the exception of South Carolina, had paid off most of their notes in the 1780s; many of the other states still had significant outstanding debts. If the federal government assumed the state debts and paid them off at the face value of the notes, many citizens would be taxed to pay debts that they had already paid, and money would flow out of the southern, middle, and western states into the pockets of the northeastern financiers who held fully four-fifths of the combined national debt.

That is precisely what Hamilton proposed in his *Report on Public Credit*, issued in January 1790. He urged Congress to assume the state debts and combine them with the federal government's foreign and domestic debts into a consolidated national debt. He agreed that the foreign debt should be paid promptly and in full, but he insisted that the domestic debt be a permanent, tax-supported fixture of government. Under his plan, the government would issue securities to its creditors and pay an annual rate of interest of 4 percent. Hamilton's funding and assumption plans announced to the international community and to actual and potential government creditors that the United States now had a government that would pay its bills. But Hamilton had domestic plans for the debt as well. A permanent, unified debt would attract the wealthiest financiers in the country as creditors and would render them loyal and dependent on the national government. (Hamilton stated this explicitly: "If all the public creditors receive their dues from one source, their interests will be the same. And having the same interests, they will be united in support of the fiscal arrangements of government.") At the same time, the debt would require a significant enlargement of the federal civil service, national financial institutions, and increased taxes. The national debt, in short, was at the center of Alexander Hamilton's plans for a powerful national state.

As part of that plan, Hamilton asked Congress to charter a Bank of the United States. The government would store its funds in the bank and oversee its operations, but the bank would be run by directors representing private stockholders. The Bank of the United States would print and back the national currency and regulate other banks. The Bank of the United States would be by far the most powerful financial institution in the country (its capital was four times that of the other three American banks combined). It would thus be the principal supplier of loans for commercial and (eventually) manufacturing projects, determining which (whose) projects were funded. Hamilton's proposal also made stock in the bank payable in government securities (the paper that constituted the national debt), thus adding to the value of the securities, giving the bank a powerful interest in the fiscal stability of the government, and binding the holders of the securities even closer to the national government. Those who looked closely saw that Hamilton's Bank of the United States was a carbon copy of the Bank of England—a bulwark of that country's marriage of government and wealth.

The government funded the debt and paid its principal and interest by collecting taxes. Most of the revenue came from the duties on imports. But most in government agreed that a direct, internal tax (one of the great bugaboos of the Revolution) was necessary. Madison and some others favored a tax on salt, which could be spread equitably throughout the country. Hamilton, however, called for a federal excise tax on wines, coffee, tea, and spirits. The tax on spirits would fall most heavily on the whiskey produced in abundance in the interior and on the western fringes of settlement. Its purpose, stated openly by

Hamilton, was not only to produce revenue but to establish the government's power to create an internal tax and collect it in the most remote regions in the republic. We shall see that he got a version of what he wanted: a "Whiskey Rebellion" in the West and an overwhelming display of federal force.

Hamilton completed his economic proposals in 1791 with his *Report on Manufactures.* Here he described the contributions of manufacturing to national strength and independence and proposed bounties to investors who built American factories. The proposal, he said, would help America provide its own necessary manufactured goods. It would also provide opportunities for the capital amassed in international trade, and it would create an internal market for the food and raw materials produced on American farms. Finally, it would forge yet another link between the national government and the nation's more active men of wealth—the only Americans who could afford such capital-intensive gambles. This was one part of Hamilton's system that did not work. The most substantial result was the "National Manufacturing City" at Paterson, New Jersey, where investors built a system of mill raceways and a cotton factory in 1794. The factory closed two years later, and Paterson was nearly a ghost town until the necessities of the War of 1812 and the take-off of American manufacturing in the 1820s made it—with small thanks to Hamilton—a manufacturing city. The United States in 1791 was simply not ready to industrialize: Britain amply supplied the American market with cheap, familiar goods, and none but the most desperate Americans (there were far fewer of these than in the Old World), were willing to give up farm ownership (or the dream of it) for wage labor. Most men of wealth refused to gamble on domestic manufactures; the smart money continued to go into international trade and government securities.

Hamilton's organization of government finance was complete by the end of 1791. Taken separately, the consolidated government debt, the national bank, and the federal excise tax ably solved discrete problems of government finance. Taken together, however, they constituted a full-scale replica of the treasury-driven government of Great Britain. Not everyone in government liked that result.

Opposition

In 1789 every branch of the national government was staffed by supporters of the Constitution. The most radical antifederalists took positions in state governments or left politics altogether. Nearly everyone in federal office was committed to making the new government work. In particular, Alexander Hamilton at the Treasury Department and James Madison in the House of Representatives expected to continue the political and personal friendship they had made while writing the Constitution and working to get it ratified. Yet in the debate over the debt and the national bank, Madison led congressional opposition to Hamilton's proposals. In 1792 Thomas Jefferson joined the opposition, insisting that Hamilton's schemes would dismantle the Revolution. Within a few short years the consensus of 1789 had degenerated into an angry argument over what sort of government would finally result from the American Revolution. This was no mere politician's contest for office. More than twenty-five years later, Jefferson still insisted that the battles of the 1790s had been "contests of principle between the advocates of republican and those of kingly government."

Hamilton presented his national debt proposal to Congress as a solution to specific problems of government finance, not as part of a blueprint for an English-style state. Madison and other southerners opposed it because they did not want northern speculators—many of whom had received information from government insiders—to reap fortunes from notes bought at rock-bottom prices from soldiers, widows, and orphans. Calling Hamilton's plan "public plunder," Madison favored payment plans that discriminated between original holders and speculators—a solution that would ease his ethical scruples and reduce the flow of money out of the South. Most in Congress thought Madison's proposal impractical, and the debt was funded as Hamilton proposed.

Assumption of the state debts was more troublesome. Hamilton had the support of nationalists and of the New York capitalists who would profit most from his debt proposals, but many in government—particularly those from the South—distrusted the centralization, favoritism, and inside deals that federal assumption of the state debts entailed. The assumption bill stalled in Congress. The weeks dragged on, and Hamilton saw his dreams of centralized finance turning into failure. One day, Thomas Jefferson ran into Hamilton outside the president's house in New York. Hamilton, according to Jefferson, did not look good: "sombre, haggard, & dejected beyond despair, even his dress uncouth & neglected." Hamilton begged Jefferson to serve as intermediary between him and Madison and other congressional opponents. Assumption was crucial to the financial strength of the government, he said. To get it, he agreed to move the capital of the United States south to a site on the Potomac River. It was a huge concession. Congress planned to move the national capital to Philadelphia for three years and then select a permanent site. Hamilton intended to tie northeastern "moneyed men" to the federal government. If New York or Philadelphia became the permanent capital, political and economic power might be concentrated there as it was in Paris and London—court cities in which power, wealth, and every kind of excellence were in league against a plundered and degraded countryside. The Philadelphia republican Benjamin Rush condemned the "government which has begun so soon to ape the corruption of the British Court, conveyed to it through the impure channel of the City of New York." Madison and other agrarians considered Philadelphia just as bad. Nor did they favor the current front-runner: a site on the Susquehanna River near York, Pennsylvania. They accepted the assumption of state debts in return for removal of the capital to the South. The compromise went to the heart of revolutionary republicanism. It distanced commercial wealth (Hamilton's well-heeled northeastern army of public creditors) from the federal government, and it put an end to the "republican court" that had formed around Washington. This radically republican move ensured that the capital of the United States would be, except for purposes of government, an unimportant place.

When Hamilton proposed the Bank of the United States, republicans noted its similarity to the Bank of England and voiced deep suspicion. It was at this point that Thomas Jefferson went into open opposition. He wrote a letter to Washington arguing that Hamilton's bank proposal endangered the republic. The Constitution did not grant Congress the right to charter corporations. Indeed, the Constitutional Convention had considered and rejected that power. If Congress incorporated Hamilton's bank, they would open the door to endless transgressions of the constitutional limits on government, and that would certainly revive the popular fears of centralized despotism that had nearly defeated ratification of the Constitution. Hamilton responded (as republicans feared he might) with the first argument for expanded federal power under the clause in the Constitution empowering Congress "to make all laws which shall be necessary and proper" to the performance of its duties. President Washington and a majority in Congress ultimately sided with Hamilton.

Jefferson's strict constructionism (his insistence that the government had no powers beyond those specified in the Constitution) was tied to fears of the de facto constitution that Hamilton's system was making. Jefferson insisted that the federal bank was unconstitutional, that a federal excise tax was certain to arouse public opposition, and that the organization of the debt rewarded speculators and penalized honest citizens. But more important, Jefferson argued, Hamilton used government securities and stock in the Bank of the United States to buy the loyalty not only of merchants and capitalists but of members of Congress. Thirty congressmen owned stock in the Bank of the United States. Many others held government securities or had close ties to men who did. Jefferson charged that Hamilton had created a "corrupt squadron" of "paper men" in Congress—men who did the administration's bidding because they were dependent on the administration for their unearned livelihoods. A generation steeped in the rhetoric of the American Revolution recognized this as the classic means by which the executive (or, worse, the unelected ministers of the executive) corrupted the representatives of the people and transformed them into its own servile tools. "The ultimate object of all this," insisted Jefferson, "is to prepare the way for a change, from the present republican form of government, to that of a monarchy, of which the English constitution is to be the model."

For their part, Hamilton and his supporters (who by now were calling themselves Federalists) insisted that the centralization of power and a strong executive were necessary to the survival of the republic. The alternative was a return to the localism and public disorder of the 1780s and, ultimately, to the failure of the Revolution. The argument drew its urgency from the understanding of both Hamilton and his detractors that the United States was a weak revolutionary republic in a world governed by kings and aristocrats, and that republics had a long history of failure. They all knew that it was still very possible for Americans to lose their Revolution. Until late 1792, however, the argument over Hamilton's centralizing schemes was limited very largely to members of the government. Hamilton and his supporters tried to mobilize the commercial elite on the side of government, while Madison and Jefferson struggled to hold off the perceived monarchical plot until citizens could be aroused to defend their liberties. Then, as both sides began to mobilize popular support, events in Europe came to dominate the politics of the American republican experiment, to place that experiment in even greater jeopardy, and to increase the violence of American politics to the point at which the republic almost failed.

THE REPUBLIC IN A WORLD AT WAR, 1793–1800

Late in 1792 French revolutionaries rejected monarchy and proclaimed the French Republic. They beheaded Louis XVI in January 1793. Eleven days later the French, already at war with Austria and Prussia, declared war on conservative Britain, thus launching a war between French republicanism and British-led reaction that, with one brief outbreak of peace, lasted until the defeat of Napoleon in 1815.

Americans and the French Revolution

Americans could not have escaped involvement even had they wanted to. Treaties signed in 1778 allied the United States with France. Americans had overwhelmingly supported the French Revolution of 1789 and had applauded the progress of French republicanism during its first three years. But gratitude for French help during the American Revolution and American hopes for international republicanism were put to severe tests in 1793, when the French Republic began to execute thousands of aristocrats, priests, and other "counter-revolutionaries," and when the French threatened the sovereignty of nations by declaring a war of all peoples against all monarchies. The argument between Jeffersonian Republicanism and Hamiltonian Federalism was no longer a squabble within the United States government. National politics was now caught up and subsumed within the struggle over international republicanism.

As Britain and France went to war in 1793, President Washington declared American neutrality, thereby abrogating obligations made in the 1778 treaties with the French. Washington and most of his advisors realized that the United States was in no condition to fight a war. They also wanted to stay on good terms with Great Britain. As much as 90 percent of American imports came from Britain, and a similar percentage of the federal revenue came from customs duties on those imports. Thus the nation's commerce and the financial health of the government both depended on good relations with Great Britain. Moreover, Federalist conservatives genuinely sympathized with the British in the war with France. Their cultural ties were to Britain, and their commercial and governmental aspirations rested on friendship with that country. They, of course, valued their hard-won independence, but they regarded the American republic not as something utterly new but as a "perfected" England. Internationally, they viewed Britain as the defender of hierarchical society and ordered liberty against the homicidal anarchy of the French.

Jefferson and his friends saw things differently. They applauded the French for carrying on the republican revolution Americans had begun in 1776, and they had no affection for the "monarchical" politics of the Federalists or for America's continued neocolonial dependence on British trade. The faction led by Jefferson and Madison wanted to abandon the English mercantile system and trade freely with all nations. They often spoke of replacing Britain with France as America's principal trading partner. They did not care if that course of action hurt commercial interests (most of which supported the Federalists) or impaired the government's ability to centralize power in itself. While Federalists looked upon their country as an England cleansed of its corruptions, Republicans considered the American and French Revolutions as parts of a world-historical movement to replace monarchy and aristocracy with popular self-government. Republicans agreed that the United States should stay out of the war. But they sympathized as openly with the French as the Federalists did with the British.

Neutrality

The United States tried to remain neutral throughout the war years from 1793 to 1812. It was not easy. Not only were the Americans divided, but Great Britain and France intervened repeatedly in the internal affairs of the United States. The first of these interventions began in April 1793, when the French Girondists (the revolutionary faction that had declared the war on all monarchies) sent Citizen Edmond Genêt as minister to the United States, with orders to enlist American aid with or without the Washington administration's consent. President Washington declared a strict American neutrality, and Genêt went over his head, commissioning American privateers to harass British shipping and enlisting Americans in intrigues against the Spanish outpost of New Orleans. Genêt then opened France's Caribbean colonies to American shipping, providing American shippers a choice between French free trade and British mercantilism. (Genêt's mission came to an abrupt end in the summer of 1793, when the Girondists fell from power. Learning that he would be guillotined if he returned to France, he accepted the hospitality of Americans, married a daughter of George Clinton, the old antifederalist governor of New York, and lived out the rest of his life as an American country gentleman.)

The British responded to Genêt's free-trade declaration with a promise to seize any ship trading with French colonies in the Caribbean. Word of these Orders in Council—almost certainly by design—reached the Royal Navy before American merchant seamen heard of them, with the result that 250 American ships fell into British hands. The Royal Navy also began searching American ships for English sailors who had deserted or had switched to safer, better-paying work in the American merchant marine. Inevitably, some American sailors were kidnapped into the British Navy. It was a contemptuous and infuriating assault on American sovereignty. Meanwhile the British, operating from Canada and from forts in the Northwest, began promising military aid to the Indians north of the Ohio River. Thus while the French ignored the neutrality of the United States, the English engaged in both overt and covert acts of war.

Western Troubles

The Washington administration faced troubles not only on the high seas but in its own western territories. The United States was a huge country in 1790, at least on paper. In the treaty that ended the War of Independence in 1783, the British ignored Indian claims and ceded all the land from the Atlantic Ocean to the Mississippi River to the new republic, with the exceptions of Spanish Florida (which included the Gulf Coast) and New Orleans. The states then surrendered their individual claims to the federal government, and in 1789 George Washington became president of a nation that stretched nearly 1,500 miles inland. Most white Americans, however, lived on a thin strip of settlement on the Atlantic coast and along the few navigable rivers that emptied into the Atlantic. Some were pushing their way into the wilds of Maine and northern Vermont, and in New York they had set up communities as far west as the Mohawk Valley. Pittsburgh was a struggling new settlement, and two outposts had been established on the Ohio River—at Marietta and at what would become Cincinnati. Farther south, farmers had occupied the Piedmont lands up to the eastern slope of the Appalachians and were spilling through the Cumberland Gap into the new lands of Kentucky and Tennessee.

North of the Ohio River the Shawnee, Miami, Delaware, and Potawatomie nations, along with smaller tribes, controlled nearly all the land shown on the Northwest Ordinance's neatly gridded and largely fictitious map. To the south, Indians the whites called the Five Civilized Tribes still occupied much of their ancestral land: the Cherokees in the Carolinas and northern Georgia, the Creeks in Georgia and Alabama, the Choctaws and Chickasaws in Mississippi, and the Seminoles in southern Georgia and Spanish Florida. Taken together, Indian peoples occupied most of the land that treaties and maps showed as the interior of the United States.

Though many of the woodland tribes were still intact and living on their old lands in 1790, they were in serious trouble. Members of the Iroquois Federation had sided with the British during the Revolution and had lost. The victorious Americans restricted them to reservations in New York and Pennsylvania; many fled to Canada. The once-powerful Cherokees had been severely punished for fighting for the British, and by 1790 had ceded three-fourths of their territory to the Americans. Like the Iroquois, by this time they were nearly surrounded by white settlements.

But in the Old Northwest, the Shawnee, Miami, and other tribes, with the help of the British who still occupied seven forts within what was formally the United States—continued to trade furs and impede white settlement. Skirmishes with settlers brought reprisals, and the Indians now faced not only hostile pioneers but the U.S. Army. They met the challenge well. In the Ohio country, expeditions led by General Josiah Harmar and General Arthur St. Clair failed in 1790 and 1791—the second ending in an Indian victory in which 630 soldiers died.

Upper Canada (what is now Ontario) in the 1790s was thinly settled and protected by few soldiers. British Canadians depended on the native peoples of the Northwest as trading partners and as a buffer between them and an unfriendly United States. The British occupied seven forts south of the Great Lakes, in territory that belonged to the United States under the treaty that ended the Revolutionary War. The situation in the Northwest came to a head in the summer and fall of 1794. The Shawnee and allied tribes, emboldened by their two victories over American armies, plotted with the British and talked of driving all settlers out of their territory. Thus while the British harassed American commerce on the ocean, they and their Indian allies made things dangerous for settlers and soldiers south of the Great Lakes.

It was also in early 1794 that Americans west of the Appalachians directly challenged their new government. Frontier whites, sometimes with the encouragement of English and Spanish officials, grew increasingly contemptuous of a national government that could neither pacify the Indians nor guarantee their free use of the Mississippi River. President Washington heard that two thousand Kentuckians were armed and ready to attack the Spanish at New Orleans—a move that would have started a war with Spain. Settlers in Georgia were making unauthorized forays against the Creeks. Worst of all, settlers up and down the frontier refused to pay the Federalists' excise tax on whiskey, a direct refusal of federal authority. In western Pennsylvania, mobs tarred and feathered excise officers and burned the property of distillers who paid the tax. In July 1794, five hundred militiamen near Pittsburgh marched on the house of General John Neville, one of the most hated of the federal excise collectors.

Neville, his family, and a few federal soldiers fought the militiamen, killing two and wounding six before they abandoned the house to be looted and burned. Two weeks later, six thousand "Whiskey Rebels" met at Braddock's Field near Pittsburgh, threatening to attack the town.

In 1794 President Washington faced serious international and domestic threats. The British demanded that Americans trade internationally only within the British system. At the same time, native peoples and white settlers in the West—the vast region that Washington, unlike other Federalists, saw as the site of America's future greatness—were defeating American armies and refusing to pay American taxes. Faced with a crisis of his "United Government," Washington did what he could: he secured the Northwest by force and capitulated to the British on the high seas.

In summer 1794 President Washington sent a third army, under General "Mad Anthony" Wayne, into the Northwest. Wayne defeated the Indians at Fallen Timbers, near present-day Toledo. The battle was fought almost within the shadow of a British-occupied fort, and the victorious Americans marched around the fort insulting the English soldiers inside. Wayne's victory forced the Treaty of Greenville, in which Native Americans ceded two-thirds of what are now Ohio and southeastern Indiana. It was at this point that the British decided to abandon their forts in the Old Northwest.

A month after Wayne's victory, Washington ordered 12,000 federalized militiamen from eastern Pennsylvania, Maryland, Virginia, and New Jersey to quell the Whiskey Rebellion in western Pennsylvania. The president promised amnesty to rebels who pledged to support the government and prison terms to those who did not. As the army marched west from Carlisle, they found defiant liberty poles but no armed resistance. Arriving at Pittsburgh, the army arrested 20 suspected rebels—none of them leaders—and marched them back to Philadelphia for trial. In the end, only two "rebels," both of them feeble-minded, were convicted. President Washington pardoned them and the Whiskey Rebellion was over. In two quick strokes Washington had asserted federal authority over the farthest reaches of the United States by defeating the Indians, discouraging the British, and convincing settlers that they had a national government that could levy and collect taxes.

Jay's Treaty

While he sent armies against Indians and frontiersmen, President Washington sent John Jay, chief justice of the Supreme Court, to negotiate a commercial treaty with Britain. Much was at stake. From the beginnings of independence, Americans had argued for freedom of the seas; now they argued for their rights as neutrals to trade with anyone. Britain, however, remained a mercantilist nation committed to using commerce to strengthen His Majesty's government. It was also embroiled in a worldwide war with republican France and could not imagine allowing trade that benefited its enemies. The British excluded American ships from both British and French islands in the Caribbean (a lucrative market for American food). They defined food as military supplies, and thus banned American exports to France and French-held territory, and they allowed American trade with Britain only within the rules of the British mercantile system. Put very simply, the British allowed American ships to trade internationally only if they functioned as a de facto British merchant marine. Finally, the British continued to kidnap American sailors and occupy the northwestern forts.

Madison, Jefferson, and the republicans in Congress insisted on neutral rights and wanted to fight the British with (at least) trade restrictions of their own—perhaps even to substitute France for England as America's chief trading partner. Federalists knew, however, that the success of their government and the well-being of their own neomercantilist financial community depended on trade with Great Britain, and John Jay went to London committed to making a deal. Armed with news of Wayne's victory at Fallen Timbers, Jay won a promise from the British to remove their troops from American territory in the Northwest. But on every other point he agreed to British terms. Jay's Treaty made no mention of the impressment of sailors or other violations of American maritime rights, nor did it refer to the old issue of British payments for slaves carried off during the Revolution. (Jay himself hated slavery and was glad not to negotiate this point.) The treaty did allow small American ships (boats under 70 tons) back into the West Indies but only on terms that the Senate would reject. On the North Atlantic, it reopened the massive trade of American farm products for British manufactures—with the British treated as a most-favored nation. Jay's Treaty avoided war with Britain and revived American commerce. At the same time, it sacrificed American sovereignty and neutral rights and made the United States a wartime commercial ally of Great Britain. Given the power of Great Britain, it was the best that Americans could expect. Washington, obliged to choose between an unpopular treaty and an unwinnable war, passed Jay's Treaty on to the Senate, which in June 1795 ratified it by a bare two-thirds majority.

It was during the fight over Jay's Treaty that dissension within the government was first aired in public. The seaport cities and much of the Northeast reacted favorably to the treaty. It ruled out war with England and cemented an Anglo-American trade relationship that strengthened both Hamilton's national state and the established commercial interests that supported it. Moreover, there was little enthusiasm for the French Revolution in the Northeast—particularly in New England, with its long history of colonial wars with France. Southern republicans, on the other hand, saw Jay's Treaty as a blatant sign of the designs of Britain and the Federalists to subvert republicanism in both France and the United States. The Virginia legislature branded the treaty unconstitutional, and anti-treaty congressmen demanded to see all documents relating to Jay's negotiations. Washington responded by telling them that their request could be legitimate only if the House was planning to initiate impeachment proceedings—thus tying approval of the treaty to his enormous personal prestige.

On March 3, 1796, Washington released the details of a treaty that Thomas Pinckney had negotiated with Spain. In the treaty, Spain recognized American neutrality and set the border between the United States and Spanish Florida on American terms. Most important, Pinckney's Treaty put an end to Spanish claims to American territory east of the Mississippi and gave Americans the unrestricted right to navigate the Mississippi River and transship produce at the Spanish port of New Orleans. Coupled with the victory at Fallen Timbers and the British promise to abandon their Northwest posts, Pinckney's Treaty satisfied the most pressing demands of western settlers. Along with Washington's prestige, Pinckney's negotiations helped turn the tide in favor of the unpopular Jay's Treaty. With a diminishing number of hotheads willing to oppose Washington, western representatives joined the Northeast and increasing numbers of southerners to ratify Jay's Treaty.

Washington's Farewell

George Washington refused to run for reelection in 1796, setting a two-term limit that was observed by every president until Franklin Roosevelt. Washington could be proud of his accomplishments. He had presided over the creation of a national government and—in the face of serious arguments—kept it together for its first seven years. He had secured the most distant and least governable settlements by ending British, Spanish, and Indian military threats and by securing free use of the Mississippi River for western produce. Those policies, together with the federal invasion of western Pennsylvania, had made it evident that the government could and would control its farthest regions. Washington had also avoided war with Great Britain—though not without overlooking assaults on American sovereignty. As he was about to leave government he wrote, with substantial help from Alexander Hamilton, his farewell address. In it he warned against long-term "entangling alliances" with other countries. America, he said, should stay free to operate on its own in international affairs—an ideal that many felt had been betrayed in Jay's Treaty. Washington also warned against internal political divisions. Of course, he did not regard his own Federalists as a "party"—they were simply friends of the government. But he saw the Democratic-Republicans (the term that Jefferson and his supporters were adopting) as a self-interested, irresponsible "faction," thus branding them, in the language of eighteenth-century republicanism, as public enemies. Washington's call for national unity and an end to partisanship was in fact a parting shot at the Republican opposition.

Washington's retirement opened the way to the fierce competition for public office that he had feared. In 1796 Americans experienced their first contested
presidential election. The Federalists chose as their candidate John Adams, the
starchy conservative from Massachusetts who had served as vice president.
The Democratic-Republicans nominated Thomas Jefferson. According to the
gentlemanly custom of the day, neither candidate campaigned in person. Jefferson stayed home at Monticello and showed little overt interest in the campaign. Adams retired to his farm near Boston. But friends of the candidates, the
growing number of newspaper editors who enjoyed their patronage, and even
certain European governments ensured that the election would be intensely
partisan and contested.

Though there was significant Federalist and Democratic-Republican support in most states, it was clear that Adams would carry New England and
Jefferson would carry the South. The election, then, would be decided in Pennsylvania and New York. Few states, most of them in the South, chose presidential electors by direct vote in 1796. In most, including the crucial mid-Atlantic
states, state legislatures selected presidential electors. The election of 1796
would be decided in elections to the legislatures of those states, and in subsequent intriguing within those bodies. John Beckley, clerk of the House of Representatives, devised the Republican strategy in Pennsylvania. He secretly circulated a list of well-known and respected candidates for the state legislature
who were committed to Jefferson's election as president. Discovering the Republican slate only when it was too late to construct a similar list, the Federalists lost the elections. In December, Beckley delivered all but one of Pennsylvania's electoral votes to Jefferson. In New York, however, there was no John
Beckley. Adams took the state's electoral votes and won the national election.
The distribution of electoral votes revealed the bases of Federalist and Republican support: Adams received only two electoral votes south of the Potomac.
Jefferson received only eighteen (all but five of them in Pennsylvania) north of
the Potomac.

The voting was over, but the intriguing was not. Alexander Hamilton, who
since his retirement from the Treasury in 1795 had directed Federalist affairs
from his New York law office, knew that he could not manipulate the independent and almost perversely upright John Adams. So he secretly instructed
South Carolina's Federalist electors to withhold their votes from Adams. That
would have given the presidency to Adams' running mate, Thomas Pinckney,
relegating Adams to the vice presidency. (Before the ratification of the Twelfth
Amendment in 1804, the candidate with a majority of the electoral votes became president, and the second-place candidate became vice president.) Like
some of Hamilton's other schemes, this one backfired. New England electors
heard of the plan and angrily withheld their votes from Pinckney. As a result,
Adams was elected president and his opponent Thomas Jefferson became vice

president. Adams won the election. But he took office with a justifiable mistrust of many members of his own party, and with the leader of the opposition as his second in command. It was not an auspicious beginning.

Troubles with France, 1796–1800

An international crisis was in full swing as Adams entered office. The French looked upon Jay's Treaty as an alliance between Britain and the United States. They recalled their envoy in 1796 and broke off relations with the Americans. The French hinted that they intended to overthrow the reactionary government of the United States but would postpone taking action in the hope that a friendlier Thomas Jefferson would replace "old man Washington" in 1797. Then, during the crucial elections in Pennsylvania, they stepped up their seizures of American ships trading with Britain, giving the Americans a taste of what would happen if they did not elect a government friendlier to France. When the election went to John Adams, the French gave up on the United States and set about denying Britain its new de facto ally. In 1797 France expelled the American minister and refused to carry on relations with the United States until it addressed French grievances. The French ordered that American ships carrying "so much as a handkerchief" made in England be confiscated without compensation and announced that American seamen serving in the British navy would be summarily hanged if captured.

President Adams wanted to protect American commerce from French depredations. But he did not want a war with France, and he agreed that French grievances (including Jay's Treaty and the abrogation of the French-American treaties of 1778) were legitimate. He decided to send a mission to France, made up of three respected statesmen: Charles Cotesworth Pinckney of South Carolina, John Marshall of Virginia, and Elbridge Gerry of Massachusetts. But when these prestigious delegates reached Paris, they were left cooling their heels in the outer offices of the Directory—the revolutionary committee of five that had replaced France's beheaded king. At last three French officials (the correspondence identified them only as "X, Y, and Z") discreetly hinted that France would receive them if only they paid a bribe of $250,000, arranged for the United States to loan $12 million to the French government, and apologized for unpleasant remarks that John Adams had made about France. The delegates refused, saying "No, not a sixpence," and returned home. There a journalist transformed their remark into "Millions for defense, but not a cent for tribute."

President Adams asked Congress to prepare for war, and the French responded by seizing more American ships. Thus began, in April 1798, an undeclared war between France and the United States in the Caribbean. The French navy was busy with the British in the North Atlantic, but French privateers inflicted costly blows on American shipping. With the British providing powder and shot for American guns, the U.S. Navy chased French privateers in the

Caribbean, while many Americans (nearly all of them Federalists) worried about a French invasion of the United States.

The Crisis at Home, 1798–1800

The troubles with France precipitated a crisis at home. The disclosure of the XYZ correspondence, together with the quasi-war in the Caribbean, produced a surge of public hostility toward the French and, to some extent, toward their Republican friends in the United States. The elections of 1798 produced solid Federalist majorities in Congress. Federalists wanted to unite the country in the face of war. Many of them, led again by Alexander Hamilton, wanted to use the crisis to destroy the Democratic-Republicans. Without consulting President Adams, the Federalist-dominated Congress passed a number of wartime measures. The first was a federal property tax—graduated, spread equally between sections of the country, and justified by military necessity, but a direct federal tax nonetheless. Congress then passed four laws known as the Alien and Sedition Acts. The first three were directed at immigrants: they extended the naturalization period from five to fourteen years and empowered the president to detain enemy aliens during wartime and deport those he deemed dangerous to the United States. The fourth law—the Sedition Act—set jail terms and fines for persons who advocated disobedience to federal law or who wrote, printed, or spoke "false, scandalous, and malicious" statements against "the government of the United States, or the President of the United States [note that Vice President Jefferson was not included], with intent to defame . . . or to bring them or either of them, into contempt or disrepute."

President Adams never used the powers granted under the Alien Acts. But the Sedition Act resulted in the prosecution of fourteen Republicans, most of them journalists. Newspapers were the principal means of spreading news from the capital and mobilizing popular support. Jeffersonians were building a network of intensely partisan papers, and Federalists, suspecting foreign plots and internal subversion, had decided to throw the opposition into jail. William Duane, editor of the Philadelphia *Aurora*, was indicted when he and two Irish friends circulated a petition against the Alien Act on the grounds of a Catholic church. James Callendar, editor of a Jeffersonian newspaper in Richmond, was arrested, while another prominent Republican went to jail for statements made in a private letter. Jedediah Peck, a former Federalist from upstate New York, was arrested when he petitioned Congress to repeal the Alien and Sedition Acts. Matthew Lyon, a scurrilous and uncouth Republican congressman from Vermont, had brawled with a Federalist representative in the House chamber. He went to jail for his criticisms of President Adams, Federalist militarism, and what he called the "ridiculous pomp" of the national administration.

The Sedition Act was unpopular, and it helped to undermine the Adams administration. It backfired in other ways as well: far from closing down the Jeffersonian newspapers, it fostered the growth of new ones. Republican leaders screamed that the Alien and Sedition Acts violated the guaranteed freedoms of the First Amendment, a sure sign of encroaching monarchism. (Indeed, the British government had begun a mass roundup of English republican radicals at the same time, reinforcing the sinister "Englishness" of Federalist policies.) Virginia authorized construction of an armory in Richmond, began stockpiling weapons, and prepared to call up the militia. Elsewhere, opposition to the Sedition Act ranged from popular attempts to obstruct the law to fist fights in Congress.

Unable to stop the Federalists in the national government, national leaders of the Democratic-Republicans turned to the states for help. Southern states, which had provided only 4 of the 44 congressional votes for the Sedition Act, took the lead. Jefferson drafted resolutions for the legislature of Kentucky. Madison did the same for the Virginia legislature. These so-called Virginia and Kentucky Resolves restated the constitutional fundamentalism that had guided Republican opposition to the Federalists through the 1790s. Jefferson's Kentucky Resolves reminded Congress that the Alien and Sedition Acts gave the national government powers not mentioned in the Constitution and that the Tenth Amendment reserved such powers to the states. He also argued that the Constitution was a "compact" between sovereign states, and that state legislatures could "nullify" federal laws they deemed unconstitutional. Jefferson's defense of civil liberties anticipated constitutional theories that states-rights southerners would use to defend slavery after 1830. Historians have found ways to apologize for Jefferson's words, but this much is clearly true: faced with a repressive national government that he knew was contemptuous of both the people and the Constitution, Jefferson in 1798 was willing to threaten disunion.

Federalists took another ominous step when they implemented President Adams' request that Congress create a military prepared for war. Adams wanted a stronger navy, both because the undeclared war with France was being fought on the ocean and because Adams agreed with other Federalists that America's future as a commercial nation required a respectable naval force. Hamilton and others (who were becoming known as "High Federalists") preferred a standing army. At the urging of Washington and against his own judgment, Adams appointed Hamilton inspector general. As such, Hamilton would be de facto commander of the army. Congress authorized a 20,000-man force and Hamilton proceeded to raise it. Congress also provided for a much larger army to be called up if there was a declaration of war. When he expanded the officer corps in anticipation of such an army, Hamilton excluded Republicans and commissioned only his political friends. High Federalists talked openly of using a standing army to enforce the Alien and Sedition Acts and put down an impending rebellion in the South. Beyond that, there was little need for such a force. The war was being fought at sea, and most Americans believed that the citizen militia could hold off any land invasion until an army was raised. The Republicans, President Adams himself, and many other Federalists now became convinced that Hamilton and his High Federalists were determined to destroy their political opponents, enter into an alliance with Great Britain, and impose Hamilton's statist designs on the nation by force. By 1799 Adams and many of his Federalist friends had come to believe that Hamilton and his supporters were dangerous, antirepublican militarists.

Adams was both fearful and angry. First the Hamiltonians had tried to rob him of the presidency, and then had passed the Alien and Sedition Acts, the direct tax, and plans for a standing army without consulting him. None of this would have been possible had it not been for the crisis with France. Adams, who had resisted calls for a declaration of war, began looking for ways to declare peace. In a move that he knew would split the Federalists and probably cost him reelection in 1800, he opened negotiations with France and stalled the creation of Hamilton's army while the talks took place. At first the Senate refused to send an envoy to France. The senators relented when Adams threatened to resign and leave the presidency to Vice President Jefferson. In the agreement that followed, the French cancelled the obligations the United States had assumed under the treaties of 1778. But they refused to pay reparations for attacks on American shipping since 1793—the very point over which many Federalists had wanted to declare war. Peace with France cut the ground from under the more militaristic and repressive Federalists and intensified discord among the Federalists in general, and it helped to quiet some of the more rabid Democratic-Republicans. It also damaged Adams' chances for reelection.

The Election of 1800

Thomas Jefferson and his Democratic-Republicans approached the election of 1800 better organized and more determined than they had been four years earlier. Moreover, events in the months preceding the election worked in their favor. The Alien and Sedition Acts, the direct tax of 1798, and the Federalist military build-up were never popular. Even when peace with France was certain, the Federalists continued. The army suppressed a minor tax rebellion led by Jacob Fries in Pennsylvania, prosecutions under the Sedition Act revealed its partisan origins, and the Federalists showed no sign of repealing the tax or abandoning the Alien and Sedition Acts and the new military. Taken together, these events gave credence to the Republicans' allegation that the Federalists were using the crisis with France to consolidate their power, destroy their opposition, and overthrow the American republic. The Federalists' actions, charged the Republicans, were expensive, repressive, unwise, and unconstitutional. They were also the classic means by which despots destroyed liberty. The Federalists countered by warning that the election of Jefferson and his radical allies would release the worst horrors of the French Revolution onto the streets of American towns. Each side believed that its defeat in 1800 would mean the end of the republic.

Jefferson had been fighting central governments for a long time. His revolutionary writings, culminating in the Declaration of Independence, had spelled out his enduring argument in the language of eighteenth-century Anglo-American republicanism. Politics was an unending battle between liberty and power. Liberty without power was anarchy, power without liberty was despotism, and the two encroached upon each other whenever they had the chance. The happiest solution was representative government: the people delegated some of their liberty to governments that protected them and conducted their necessary collective concerns, then relied on their representatives (and ultimately themselves) to keep state power within its limits. The governments of both George III and Alexander Hamilton, according to Jefferson, had become power mad. In the British system, unelected ministers of the king had gobbled up power by dispensing favors: government offices, military commissions, mercantile rewards, and government jobs. Worse, they had corrupted the legislature with such bribes, making the people's representatives dependent on the favors of the executive. With that, liberty had no voice, and power was free to destroy it.

That had happened in Great Britain: Parliament was bought off, and the king's evil ministers plundered the country and extinguished liberty, then looked to their American colonies for more booty. It had happened again, said the Jeffersonians, in the 1790s. Though the Constitution carefully separated the legislature from the executive (the president is elected separately, not selected from Parliament as in Britain; and the Americans forbade plural officeholding—demanding that legislators appointed to executive or judicial office give up their seats in Congress), Jefferson claimed that Hamilton—a classic ambitious and unelected minister—had found ways to corrupt Congress, primarily with the paper that surrounded his funded debt and his national bank. With a bought-off Congress doing his bidding, the Hamiltonians had won their financial program, their taxes, their Sedition Act, and a standing army that could be used as a national police to enforce their destruction of liberty and consolidation of power. As a Virginia Republican put it, a Federalist victory would produce "chains, dungeons, transportation and perhaps the gibbet" for the opposition—in short, violent repression on the model of Great Britain.

For their part, Federalists predicted French-style anarchy and bloodshed should the Democratic-Republicans win. A Connecticut Federalist moaned that "There is scarcely a possibility that we shall escape *Civil War*" following a Republican victory and predicted other bad results: "murder, robbery, rape, adultery, and incest will all be openly taught and practiced, the air will be rent with the cries of distress, the soil will be soaked with blood, and the nation black with crimes." Alexander Hamilton put it succinctly: the election of Jefferson would lead to the "overthrow . . . [of] the Government" by a "Revolution after the manner of Bonaparte."

The Democratic-Republicans were strong in the South and weak in the Northeast; South Carolina was the one southern state in which Adams had significant support. Jefferson knew that in order to achieve a majority of electoral votes he had to win New York, the state that had cost him the 1796 election. Jefferson's running mate, Aaron Burr, arranged a truce in New York between Republican factions led by the Clinton and Livingston families and chose candidates for the state legislature who were both locally respected and committed to Jefferson. In New York City, Burr played skillfully on the interests and resentments of craftsmen and granted favors to merchants who worked outside the British trade that was dominated by Federalist insiders. The strategy succeeded. The Republicans carried New York City and won a slight majority in the legislature; New York's electoral votes belonged to Jefferson. (When it became clear that Jefferson had won the state, Hamilton suggested changing the law so that New York's electors would be chosen by popular vote; John Jay, the Federalist governor of New York, rejected the suggestion.) The election was decided in South Carolina, which after a brisk campaign cast its votes for Jefferson.

When the electoral votes were counted, Jefferson and Burr had won with 73 votes each. Adams had 65 votes, and his running mate Charles Cotesworth Pinckney had 64. (To distinguish between their presidential and vice-presidential candidates—and thus thwart yet another of Hamilton's attempts to rig the election—the Federalists of Rhode Island had withheld one vote from Pinckney.) Jefferson and Burr had tied, though everyone knew that Jefferson was the presidential candidate. But under the Constitution, a Federalist Congress would decide whether Jefferson or Burr was to be president of the United States. Federalists talked of choosing Burr. Jefferson wrote that Democratic-Republicans had decided "to declare openly and firmly, one and all, that the day such an act passed, the Middle States would arm, and that no such usurpation, even for a single day, should be submitted to." One of his supporters put it more bluntly: anyone other than Jefferson "who should thus be appointed President by law and accept the office would instantaneously be put to death." The Republican governors of Pennsylvania and Virginia made plans to call up the militia to prevent the expected usurpation. After six quarrelsome, overheated days and 35 ballots on which most Federalist congressmen voted for Burr (whose part in these proceedings has never been fully uncovered), a compromise was reached: Many Federalists abandoned Burr but turned in blank ballots and thus avoided voting for the hated (but victorious) Jefferson. With that, the "Revolution of 1800" had won its first round.

Source: *We Owe Allegiance to No Crown.* Collection of Richard C. Hume.

CHAPTER 2

Jeffersonians

THOMAS JEFFERSON ENTERED OFFICE WITH HIS SUPPORTERS IN control of both houses of Congress. He used that opportunity to support his vision of what the United States should be. That vision was very different from Hamilton's. Whereas Hamilton dreamed of a commercial nation state peopled by obedient citizens and divided into states that were mere provinces of the center, Jefferson insisted that government existed to protect liberty, not to grasp power for itself. Jefferson envisioned a great agricultural "Empire for Liberty" stretching across the continent: republican states linked by shared values, shared history, a shared agricultural interest, and mutual affection into an ever-expanding national union. Jefferson was not, as many Federalists insisted, an enemy of national government. He knew that union was essential to the success of the republican revolution. (In his inaugural address, he would insist that "We are all Republicans, we are all Federalists." It was both a peace offering and a statement of fundamental belief.) Jefferson's ideal national government would guarantee the republican character of each state and oversee the making of new ones; it would maintain a uniform commercial policy; it would protect the whole and coordinate the waging of necessary wars; and it would guarantee peace between the states. The alternative to union was breakdown into a heap of small, vulnerable republics and, ultimately, the failure of the American Revolution.

Jefferson's vision demanded a general government that was small, republican, and uncorrupted. It also demanded a virtuous (Jefferson and Madison now called this "patriotic" and "public spirited") citizenry. Jefferson wanted Americans to remain a republic of farmers who owned their land and thus, in his political science, enjoyed independence and liberty as natural states. They were dependent on no one, and their only interest was protection of their liberty and land. Jefferson's vision included a modest capital city and seaport towns that mediated foreign trade. But there was no room for factories or great cities. "Let our work-shops remain in Europe," he had said in the 1780s. "The loss by the transportation of commodities across the Atlantic will be made up in happiness and permanence of government."

The health and permanence of Jefferson's yeoman republic had two preconditions: Unoccupied land into which the republic could expand, and a free commerce linking farmers to the markets and consumer goods of Europe. Without new land, a burgeoning rural population would be drawn out of agriculture and into factories and cities—where they would form a dependent, propertyless, and decidedly unrepublic horde. And without commerce, the Americans would degenerate into a nation of self-sufficient hermits and sacrifice the great potential of Jefferson's republic. In 1801, the new president's agenda was clear: he would dismantle the Federalist state, encourage westward expansion, and ensure free trade for American agricultural exports.

THE JEFFERSONIANS IN POWER

On the first Tuesday in March 1801, Thomas Jefferson left his rooms at Conrad and McMunn's boarding house in the half-built capital city of Washington and walked up Pennsylvania Avenue. There were military salutes along the way, but Jefferson forbade the pomp and ceremony that had ushered Washington into office. Jefferson, accompanied by a few friends and a company of artillery from the Maryland militia (and not by the professional military of which Hamilton had dreamed), walked up the street and into the unfinished capitol building. The central tower and the wing that would house Congress were only half completed. Jefferson joined Vice President Burr, other members of the government, and a few foreign diplomats in the newly finished Senate chamber.

Jefferson took the oath of office from Chief Justice John Marshall, a distant relative and political opponent from Virginia. Then, in a small voice that was almost inaudible to those at a distance, he delivered his inaugural address. Referring to the political discord that had brought him into office, he began with a plea for unity, insisting that "every difference of opinion is not a difference of principle. We have called by different names brethren of the same principle. We are all Republicans, we are all Federalists." Jefferson did not mean that he and his opponents should forget their ideological differences. He meant only to invite moderate Federalists into a broad Republican coalition in which there was no room for the designs of Alexander Hamilton and his High Federalist friends, a coalition that could unite true republicans from the South, the mid-Atlantic, and even New England under a united government and shared principles. Grateful that the Atlantic Ocean separated the United States from "the exterminating havoc" of Europe and that his countrymen were the possessors of "a chosen country, with room for our descendants to the thousandth and thousandth generation," he declared that Americans were a free people with no need for a national state built on European models. A people blessed with isolation, bountiful resources, and liberty needed only "a wise and frugal Government, which shall restrain men from injuring one another, shall leave them otherwise free to regulate their own pursuits of industry and improvement, and shall not take from the mouth of labor the bread it has earned. This is the sum of good government, and thus is necessary to close the circle of our felicities."

In particular, Jefferson's "wise and frugal" government would respect the powers of the individual states. It would also defend the liberties ensured by the Bill of Rights. It would be made smaller, and it would pay its debts without incurring new ones, thus ending the need for taxation and cutting the ground from beneath the burgeoning Federalist state. It would rely for defense on "a disciplined militia" that would fight invaders while regulars were being trained—thus getting rid of Hamilton's standing army. It would protect republican liberties from enemies at home and from the nations of Europe. And, Jefferson promised, it would ensure "the encouragement of agriculture, and of commerce as its handmaiden." Beyond the fostering of an agrarian republic and the maintenance of limited, frugal government, Jefferson promised very little. Blessed with peace abroad and the defeat of the High Federalists at home, he believed that the United States could at last enter into its experiment with truly republican government.

The simplicity of Jefferson's inauguration set the social tone of his administration. Later, Jefferson would write a newspaper (anonymously) that "There is no 'court of the U.S.' since the 4th of Mar. 1801. That day buried levees, birthdays, royal parades, and the arrogation of precedence in society by certain self-stiled friends of order, but truly stiled friends of privileged orders." The new president reduced the number and grandeur of formal balls, levees, and dinners. He sent his annual messages to Congress to be read by a clerk rather than delivering them in person, in the manner of English kings and Federalist presidents. He refused to ride about Washington in a carriage, preferring to carry out his errands on horseback. Abandoning the grand banquets favored by his predecessors, Jefferson entertained senators and congressmen at small dinners—dinners that were served at a round table without formal seating, thus abandoning the fine-tuned hierarchy of the Federalists' old arrangements. Jefferson presided over the meals without wearing a wig and dressed in old homespun and a notorious pair of worn bedroom slippers. The casualness (slovenliness, said some of his critics) did not extend to what was served, however. The food was prepared by expert chefs and accompanied by fine wines. And it was followed by brilliant conversation perfected by Jefferson while he was a diplomat and a visitor to the salons of Paris. The president's dinners set examples of the unpretentious excellence through which this cultivated country squire hoped to govern the republic that he claimed to have saved from monarchists.

Jefferson's first order of business was to reduce the size and expense of government. The Federalists, despite their elitism and statist dispositions, had left a surprisingly small federal establishment. Jefferson found only 316 employees who were subject to presidential appointment and removal. Those employees, together with 700 clerks and assistants and 3,000 post office workers, made up the entire federal civil service. Jefferson reduced the diplomatic corps and replaced officeholders who were incompetent, corrupt, or avowedly antirepublican. But the rate of turnover was only about 50 percent during his first term. The replacements were not the violent revolutionaries that Federalists had warned against but Republican gentlemen who matched or exceeded the social status of the departed Federalists. Jefferson altered the politics of the civil service, but he left its size and shape intact.

Jefferson made more substantial cuts in the military. The Federalists had built a sizable army and navy to prepare for war and, if necessary, to put down opposition at home. Legislation passed in March 1802 reduced the army to two regiments of infantry and one of artillery—a total of 3,350 officers and men, most of whom were assigned to western posts far from the centers of white population. The navy experienced similar cutbacks. The goal, Jefferson explained, was to rely mainly on the militia for national defense but to maintain a small, well-trained professional army as well. (The same legislation that reduced the army created the military academy at West Point, thus providing a trained corps of officers in the event that a citizen army became necessary.) At Jefferson's urging, Congress also abolished the direct tax of 1798 and repealed the parts of the Alien and Sedition Acts that had not already run out. Jefferson personally pardoned the 10 victims of those acts who were still in jail and repaid with interest the fines that had been levied on them.

Thus, with a few deft strokes, Jefferson dismantled the repressive apparatus of the Federalist state. And by reducing government expenditures, he reduced the government's debt and the army of civil servants and "paper men" gathered around it. During Jefferson's administration, the national debt fell from $80 million to $57 million, and the government built up a treasury surplus even after paying $15 million in cash for the Louisiana Purchase (see later subsection entitled *Louisiana*). Though some doubted the wisdom of such stringent economy, no one doubted Jefferson's frugality.

The Jeffersonians and the Courts

Jefferson's demands for a "wise and frugal" government applied to the federal judiciary as well as to other branches of government. The Constitution had created the Supreme Court but had left the creation of lesser federal courts to

Congress. The First Congress had created a system of circuit courts presided over by justices of the Supreme Court. Only Federalists had served on the Supreme Court under Washington and Adams, and Federalists on the circuit courts had extended federal authority into the hinterland—a fact that their prosecution of Jeffersonians under the Alien and Sedition Acts had made abundantly clear. Thus Jeffersonian Republicans had ample reason to distrust the federal courts. Their distrust was intensified by the Judiciary Act of 1801, which was passed just before Jefferson's inauguration by the lame-duck Federalist Congress. Coupled with President Adams's appointment of the Federalist John Marshall as chief justice in January, the Judiciary Act assured long-term Federalist domination of the federal courts. First, it reduced the number of associate justices of the Supreme Court from six to five when the next vacancy occurred, thus reducing Jefferson's chances of appointing a new member to the Court. The Judiciary Act also took Supreme Court justices off circuit and created a new system of circuit courts. This allowed Adams to appoint 16 new judges, along with a full array of marshals, federal attorneys, clerks, and justices of the peace. Adams worked until 9 o'clock on his last night in office signing commissions for these new officers. All of them were staunch Federalists.

Republicans disagreed on what to do about the Federalists' packing of the courts. A minority distrusted the whole idea of an independent judiciary and wanted judges elected by popular vote. Jefferson and most in his party wanted the courts shielded from democratic control, but they deeply resented the uniformly Federalist "midnight judges" created by the Judiciary Act of 1801. Jefferson replaced the new federal marshals and attorneys with Republicans and dismissed some of the federal justices of the peace. But judges were appointed for life and could be removed only through impeachment. The Jeffersonians hit on a simple solution: they would get rid of the new judges by abolishing their jobs. Early in 1802, with some of Jefferson's supporters questioning the constitutionality of what they were doing, Congress repealed the Judiciary Act of 1801 and thus did away with the midnight appointees.

With the federal courts scaled back to their original size, Republicans in Congress, led by the Virginia agrarian John Randolph, went after High Federalists who were still acting as judges. As a first test of removal by impeachment they chose John Pickering, a federal attorney with the circuit court of New Hampshire. Pickering was a highly partisan Federalist. He was also a notorious alcoholic and clearly insane. The Federalists who had appointed him had long considered him an embarrassment. The House drew up articles of impeachment and Pickering was tried by the Senate, which removed him from office by a strict party vote.

On the same day, Congress went after bigger game: they voted to impeach Supreme Court Justice Samuel Chase. Chase was a much more prominent public figure than Pickering, and his "crimes" were not alcoholism or insanity but mere partisanship. He hated the Jeffersonians, and he had prosecuted sedition cases with real enthusiasm. He had also delivered anti-Jeffersonian diatribes from the bench, and he had used his position and his formidable legal skills to bully young lawyers with whom he disagreed. In short, Chase was an unpleasant, overbearing, and unashamedly partisan member of the Supreme Court. But his faults did not add up to the "high crimes and misdemeanors" that are the constitutional grounds for impeachment.

Moderate Republicans in the government doubted the wisdom of the Chase impeachment, and their uneasiness grew when Congressman John Randolph took over the prosecution. Randolph led a radical states-rights faction that violently disapproved, among other things, of the way Jefferson had settled a southern land controversy. A corrupt Georgia legislature had sold huge parcels in Mississippi and Alabama to the Yazoo Land Company, which in turn had sold them to private investors—many of them New England speculators. When a new Georgia legislature rescinded the sale and turned the land over to the federal government in 1802, Jefferson agreed to pay off the investors' claims with federal money.

As Randolph led the prosecution of Samuel Chase, he lectured in his annoying, high-pitched voice that Jefferson was double-crossing southern Republicans in an effort to win support in the Northeast. Jefferson was in fact trying to nationalize his support, partly by distancing himself from Randolph and the more extreme southern Republicans. Most Republican senators agreed with Jefferson, and some of them withdrew their support from the impeachment proceedings to isolate and humiliate Randolph and his friends. With Jefferson's approval, many Republicans in the Senate joined the Federalists in voting to acquit Samuel Chase.

Chief Justice John Marshall probably cheered the acquittal of Justice Chase, for it was clear that Marshall was next on the list. Secretary of state under John Adams, Marshall was committed to Federalist ideas of national power, as he demonstrated with his decision in the case of *Marbury v. Madison*. William Marbury was one of the justices of the peace whom Jefferson had eliminated in his first few days in office. He sued Jefferson's Secretary of State James Madison for the delivery of his commission. Although Marbury never got his job, Marshall used the case to hand down a number of important rulings. The first ruling, which questioned the constitutionality of Jefferson's refusal to deliver Marbury's commission, helped convince Republican moderates to repeal the Judiciary Act of 1801. The last ruling, delivered in February 1803, laid the basis for the practice of judicial review—that is, the Supreme Court's power to rule on the constitutionality of acts of Congress. (Some in Jefferson's party argued that that power belonged to state legislatures.) In arguing that Congress could not alter the jurisdiction of the Supreme Court, Marshall stated that the Constitution is "fundamental and paramount law" and that it is "emphatically the province and duty of the judicial department to say what law is."

Some Republicans saw Marshall's ruling as an attempt to arrogate power to the Court. But John Marshall was not a sinister man. As secretary of state under John Adams, he had helped end the undeclared war with France, and he had expressed doubts about the wisdom and necessity, if not the constitutionality, of the Alien and Sedition Acts. Of more immediate concern, while he disliked Congress's repeal of the 1801 legislation, he did not doubt the right of Congress to make and unmake laws and he was determined to accept the situation. Although the decision in *Marbury v. Madison* angered many Republicans, Jefferson and moderate Republicans noted that Marshall was less interested in the power of the judiciary than in its independence. Ultimately, they decided they trusted Marshall more than they trusted the radicals in their own party. With the acquittal of Justice Chase, Jeffersonian attacks on the federal courts ceased.

Louisiana

It was Jefferson's good fortune that Europe remained at peace during his first term and stayed out of American affairs. Indeed the one development that posed an international threat to the United States turned into a grand triumph: the purchase of the Louisiana Territory from France in 1803.

By 1801, a half-million Americans lived west of the Appalachians. Federalists feared the barbarism of the westerners, but Republicans saw westward expansion as the best hope for the republic. Social inequality and the erosion of yeoman independence would almost inevitably take root in the long-settled East, but in the vast lands west of the mountains Jefferson's republic would renew itself, farm by farm, for generations to come. To serve their transcendent historical task, however, settlers between the Appalachians and the Mississippi River needed protection from the Native Americans whom they were displacing and from the intrigues of foreign governments. They also needed access to markets through the river system that emptied into the Gulf of Mexico at New Orleans. "There is on the globe," wrote President Jefferson, "one single spot, the possessor of which is our natural and habitual enemy. It is New Orleans."

In 1801, Spain owned New Orleans and the huge territory north and west of it. Spain also owned the Floridas, giving it possession of the whole Gulf Coast of what is now the United States. Spain was a declining, badly run empire that posed no threat to the United States, and under Pinckney's Treaty American settlers shipped produce from the interior through the port of New Orleans. In the first years of the nineteenth century, however, news of a secret agreement between Spain and France reached the Americans. The French, who had once overseen a loose empire stretching from Montreal through the Great Lakes and Mississippi Valley to New Orleans, had lost their claims in North America in 1763, but regaining a New-World empire had remained a French ambition. In 1800, Napoleon hatched a plan for a new French empire in America with the

sugar island of Santo Domingo (present-day Haiti and the Dominican Republic) at its center. Slaves under Toussant d'Overture had revolted in 1791, ending
slavery and all but the name of French authority in Santo Domingo. Napoleon
wished to reestablish French control over the island, then supply food to the islands from agricultural settlements in Louisiana. Napoleon's new American
empire would be rich, extensive, and self-sufficient. In October 1800—on the
day before signing the agreements that ended the undeclared war between the
United States and France—Spain had secretly ceded the Louisiana Territory
(roughly, all the land west of the Mississippi drained by the Missouri and
Arkansas rivers) to France. Unlike the decaying Spanish authority, Napoleon's
new empire would immediately threaten every American west of the Appalachians, probably putting an end to Jefferson's cherished empire for liberty
in the West.

Late in 1802 the Spanish, who had retained control (but not ownership) of
New Orleans, closed the port to American commerce, giving rise to rumors that
they would soon transfer the city to France. To forestall such a move, President
Jefferson sent a delegation to Paris early in 1803 with authorization to buy New
Orleans for the United States.

By the time the delegates reached Paris, events had dissolved French plans
for a new American empire. To establish that empire, Napoleon needed two
things: he had to reconquer Santo Domingo, and he had to stay out of war with
Great Britain, whose navy could stop French designs in the Caribbean. He
achieved neither of those. The blacks of Santo Domingo fought fiercely to prevent their re-enslavement under the French. With the help of yellow fever, they
defeated Napoleon's army and established the independent Republic of Haiti.
And while his army disintegrated on the island, Bonaparte found himself getting closer and closer to a European war with Britain. Napoleon—reputedly
chanting "Damn sugar, damn coffee, damn colonies"—decided to bail out of
America and concentrate resources in Europe. He astonished Jefferson's delegation by announcing that France would sell not only New Orleans but the
whole Louisiana Territory for the bargain price of $15 million.

The Louisiana Purchase was the great international triumph of Jefferson's
administration: without war, and at nominal expense, it doubled the size of the
United States and ended the last serious attempt to establish a European presence in North America. Yet Jefferson, who had criticized Federalists whenever
they violated the letter of the Constitution, faced a dilemma: the Constitution
did not give the president the power to purchase territory. The chance to buy
Louisiana, however, was too good to pass up. It would assure Americans access
to the rivers of the interior, it would eliminate a serious foreign threat on America's western border, and it would give American farmers enough land to sustain the agrarian republic for a long time to come. Swallowing his constitutional scruples (and at the same time half-heartedly asking for a constitutional
amendment to legalize the purchase), Jefferson told the American delegates to

buy Louisiana. Republican senators, who shared few of Jefferson's doubts, quickly ratified the Louisiana treaty over Federalist objections that the purchase would encourage rapid settlement and add to backcountry barbarism and Republican strength. Most Americans agreed that the accidents of French and Haitian history had given the United States a grand opportunity, and Congress's ratification of the Louisiana Purchase met with overwhelming public approval. For his part, Jefferson was certain that the republic had gained the means of renewing itself through time. He had bought, he claimed in his second inaugural, his great "empire of liberty."

Lewis and Clark

When Jefferson bought the Louisiana Territory in 1803, he knew that he was giving future generations of Americans a huge fund of land on which to perpetuate their rural republic. About the land itself, however, he knew almost nothing. Only a few French trappers and traders had traveled the plains between the Mississippi and the Rocky Mountains, and no white person had seen the territory drained by the Columbia River. In 1804, Jefferson sent an expedition under Meriweather Lewis, his private secretary, and William Clark, brother of the Indian fighter George Rogers Clark, to explore the new territory. To prepare for the expedition, Lewis studied astronomy, zoology, and botany; Clark was already an accomplished mapmaker. Lewis and Clark kept meticulous journals of one of the epic adventures in American history.

In May 1804, Lewis and Clark and forty-one companions boarded a keelboat and two large canoes at the village of St. Louis. They poled and paddled 1,600 miles up the Missouri River, passing through rolling plains dotted by the farm villages of the Pawnee, Oto, Missouri, Crow, Omaha, Hidatsa, and Mandan peoples. The villages of the lower Missouri had been cut off from the western buffalo herds and reduced to dependence by mounted Sioux warriors who had begun to establish their hegemony over the northern plains.

Lewis and Clark traveled through Sioux territory and stopped for the winter at the prosperous, heavily fortified Mandan villages at the big bend of the Missouri River in Dakota country. In the spring they hired Toussaint Charbonneau, a French fur trader, to guide them to the Pacific. Though Charbonneau turned out to be useless, his wife, a teenaged Shoshone girl named Sacajawea, was an indispensable guide, interpreter, and diplomat. With her help, Lewis and Clark navigated the upper Missouri, crossed the Rockies to the Snake River, and followed that stream to the Columbia River. They reached the Pacific in November 1805 and spent the winter at what is now Astoria, Oregon. Retracing their steps the following spring and summer, they reached St. Louis in September 1806. They brought with them many volumes of drawings and notes, along with assurances that the Louisiana Purchase had been worth many, many times its price.

THE REPUBLIC AND THE NAPOLEONIC WARS, 1804–1815

As Jefferson stood for reelection in 1804, he could look back on an astonishingly successful first term. He had dismantled the government's power to coerce its citizens, and he had begun to wipe out the national debt. The Louisiana Purchase had doubled the size of the republic at remarkably little cost. Moreover, by eliminating France from North America it had strengthened the argument for reducing the military and the debts and taxes that went with it. Jefferson was more certain than ever that the republic could preserve itself through peaceful expansion. The "wise and frugal" government he had promised in 1801 was becoming a reality.

The combination of international peace, territorial expansion, and inexpensive, unobtrusive government left the Federalists without an issue in the 1804 election. They went through the motions of nominating Charles Pinckney of South Carolina as their presidential candidate and then watched as Jefferson captured the electoral votes of every state but Delaware and Connecticut. As he began his second term in 1805, Jefferson could assume that he had ended the Federalist threat and had united the republic around his republican principles. Unhappily, there were other threats just around the corner.

The Dilemmas of Neutrality

In the spring of 1803, a few weeks after closing the deal for Louisiana, Napoleon Bonaparte declared war on Great Britain. This eleven-year war, like the wars of the 1790s, dominated the national politics of the United States. Most Americans wanted to remain neutral. Few Republicans supported Bonaparte as they had supported the French revolutionaries of 1789, and none but the most rabid Federalists wanted to intervene on the side of Great Britain. But neither France nor Britain would allow Americans to remain neutral.

At the beginning, both Britain and France, whose rural economies were disrupted by war, encouraged the Americans to resume their role as neutral carriers and suppliers of food. For a time, Americans made huge profits. Between 1803 and 1807 U.S. exports—mostly foodstuffs and plantation staples—rose from $66.5 million to $102.2 million. Re-exports—goods produced in the British, Spanish, and French islands of the Caribbean, picked up by American vessels, and then reloaded in American ports onto American ships bound for Europe—rose even faster: from $13.5 million to $58.4 million.

In 1805, France and Great Britain began systematically to interfere with that trade. In 1805 the Royal Navy under Lord Nelson destroyed the French and Spanish fleets at the Battle of Trafalgar. Later that year Napoleon's armies won a decisive victory over Austria and Russia at the Battle of Austerlitz and won effective control of Europe. The war reached a stalemate: Napoleon's army occupied Europe, the British navy controlled the seas.

Britain decided to use its naval supremacy to blockade Europe and starve the French into submission. In the Essex Decision of 1805, the British ministry dusted off what was known as the Rule of 1756, which stated that a European country could not use a neutral merchant marine to conduct its wartime trade with its colonies unless that trade was legal during peace. Translated into the realities of 1805, the Essex Decision meant that the Royal Navy could seize American ships engaged in the re-export trade with France and her Caribbean colonies. In the spring of 1806 Congress, angered by British seizures of American ships, passed a Non-Importation Act forbidding the importation of British goods that could be bought elsewhere or manufactured in the United States. A month after that, Britain blockaded long stretches of the European coast. Napoleon responded with the Berlin Decree, which outlawed all trade with the British Isles. The British answered with an Order in Council that demanded that neutral ships trading with Europe stop first for inspection and licensing in a British port. Napoleon responded with the Milan Decree, which stated that any vessel that obeyed the British decrees or allowed itself to be searched by the Royal Navy was subject to seizure by France. Beginning in 1805 and ending with the Milan Decree in December 1807, the barrage of European decrees and counter-decrees meant that virtually all American commerce with Europe was outlawed by one or the other of the warring powers.

Given British naval supremacy, French decrees were effective only against American ships that entered ports controlled by France. The Royal Navy, on the other hand, maintained a loose blockade of the North American coast and stopped and searched American ships as they left the major seaports. Hundreds of ships were seized, along with their cargoes and crews. Under British law, the Royal Navy during wartime could impress any British subject into service. The British were certain that many British subjects, including legions of deserters from the Royal Navy, were hiding in the American merchant marine. They were right. The danger, low pay, bad food, and draconian discipline on British warships encouraged many British sailors to jump ship and take jobs on American merchantmen. Many of the British warships that stopped American merchant ships on the high seas were undermanned; the sailors their officers commandeered often included Englishmen who had taken out U.S. citizenship (an act the British did not recognize) and, inevitably, native-born Americans. An estimated 6,000 American citizens were impressed into the Royal Navy between 1803 and 1812.

The kidnapping of American sailors, even more than maritime seizures of American property and other violations of American neutral rights, enraged the citizens of the United States and brought the country close to war in the summer of 1807. In June the American naval frigate *Chesapeake,* which was outfitting in Norfolk, Virginia, signed on four English deserters from the British navy, along with some Americans who had joined the British navy and then deserted. The British warship HMS *Leopard* was also docked at Norfolk, and some of the deserters spotted their old officers and taunted them on the streets. The *Leopard* left port and resumed its patrol of the American coast. On June 21 the English warship caught the *Chesapeake* off Hampton Roads and demanded the return of the British deserters. When the captain refused, the British fired on the *Chesapeake,* killing three Americans and wounding eighteen. The British then boarded the *Chesapeake,* seized the four deserters, and later hanged one of them. The *Chesapeake* limped back into port.

The *Chesapeake* affair set off huge anti-British demonstrations in the seaport towns and angry cries for war throughout the country. President Jefferson responded by barring British ships from American ports and American territorial waters and ordering state governors to prepare to call up as many as 100,000 militiamen. The United States stood at the brink of full-scale war with the most powerful nation in the world.

Embargo

President Jefferson wanted to avoid war. War inevitably brought high taxes, government debt, the repression of dissent, and the creation of a bloated military and civil service—precisely the evils that Jefferson had vowed to eliminate. Worse, war carried the danger of defeat and thus the possible failure of the United States.

Jefferson had one more card to play: he could suspend trade with Europe altogether and thus keep American ships out of harm's way. For many years, Jefferson had assumed that U.S. farm products and the U.S. market for imported goods had become crucial to the European economies. He could use trade as a means of "peaceable coercion" that would both ensure respect for American neutral rights and keep the country out of war. "Our commerce," he wrote just before taking office, "is so valuable to them, that they will be glad to purchase it, when the only price we ask is to do us justice." Convinced that his farmer's republic could survive without European luxuries more easily than Europe could survive without American food, Jefferson decided to give "peaceable coercion" a serious test. Late in 1807, he asked Congress to suspend all U.S. trade with foreign countries.

Congress passed the Embargo Act on December 22. It was clear within months that peaceable coercion would not work. The British found other markets and other sources of food. They encouraged smuggling between Canada and the United States. In addition, American merchant ships that had been at sea when the embargo went into effect stayed away from their home ports and functioned as part of the British merchant marine. A loophole in the Embargo Act allowed U.S. ships to leave port to pick up American property stranded in other countries, and an estimated 6,000 ships set sail under that excuse. Hundreds of others, plying the coastal trade, were "blown off course" and found themselves thrust into international commerce. For his part, Napoleon seized

American ships in European ports, explaining that, since the embargo kept all American ships in port, those trading under American flags must be British ships in disguise.

The embargo hurt American commerce badly. In 1807 American exports had stood at $108 million. In 1808 they dropped to $22 million. The economy slowed in every section of the country, but it ground to a halt in the cities of the Northeast. While the ocean-going merchant fleet rotted at anchor, unemployed sailors, dockworkers, and other maritime workers and their families sank to levels of economic despair that had seldom been seen in British North America. Northeastern Federalists branded Jefferson's embargo a "Chinese" solution to the problems of commerce and diplomacy. Commerce, they argued, was the great civilizer: "Her victories are over ferocious passions, savage manners, deep rooted prejudices, blind superstition and delusive theory." Federalists accused Jefferson of plotting an end to commerce and a reversion to rural barbarism, and they often took the lead in trying to subvert the embargo through smuggling and other means. In Connecticut, the Federalist governor flatly refused Jefferson's request to mobilize the militia to enforce the embargo.

The Federalists made gains in the elections of 1808. James Madison, Jefferson's old ally and chosen successor, won the presidency with 122 electoral votes to 47 for his Federalist opponent, C. C. Pinckney. And although Republicans retained control of both houses of Congress, Federalists made significant gains in Congress and won control of several state legislatures. Federalist opposition to the embargo, and to the supposed southern, agrarian stranglehold on national power that stood behind it, was clearly gaining ground.

Toward War

When President Madison took office in the spring of 1809, it was clear that the embargo had failed to coerce the British. On the contrary, it had created misery in the seaport cities, choked off the imports that were the principal source of federal revenue, and revived Federalist opposition to Republican dominance. Early in 1809, Congress passed the Non-Intercourse Act, which retained the ban on trade with Britain and France but reopened trade with other nations. It also gave President Madison the power to reopen trade with either Britain or France once they had agreed to respect American rights. Neither complied, and the Non-Intercourse Act proved nearly as ineffective as the embargo.

In 1810 Congress passed Macon's Bill No. 2, a strange piece of legislation that rescinded the ban on trade with France and Britain but then authorized the president to reimpose the Non-Intercourse Act on either belligerent country if the other agreed to end its restrictions on U.S. trade. Napoleon decided to test the Americans. In September 1810, the French foreign minister, the Duc de

Cadore, promised, with vague conditions, that France would repeal the Berlin and Milan Decrees. Though the proposal was a clear attempt to lead the United States into conflict with Great Britain, Madison felt he had no choice but to go along with it. He accepted the French promise and proclaimed in November 1810 that the British had three months to follow suit. "It promises us," he said of his proclamation, "at least an extrication from the dilemma, of a mortifying peace, or a war with both the great belligerents."

In the end, Madison's proclamation led to war. The French repealed only those sections of the Berlin and Milan Decrees that applied to the neutral rights of the United States. The British refused to revoke their Orders in Council and told the Americans to withdraw their restrictions on British trade until the French had repealed theirs. The United States would either have to obey British orders (thus making American exports and the American merchant marine a part of the British war effort—a neocolonial situation utterly repugnant to most Americans)—or go to war. When Congress reconvened in November 1811, it voted military measures in preparation for war with Great Britain.

The Republicans controlled both houses of Congress in 1811–1812: 75 percent of the House and 82 percent of the Senate identified themselves as members of President Madison's party. But they were a divided majority. The Federalist minority, which was united against Madison, was joined on many issues by northeastern Republicans who followed the pro-British, Federalist line on international trade, and by Republicans who wanted a more powerful military than other Republicans would allow. Also opposed to Madison were the self-styled Old Republicans of the South, led by John Randolph. Thus it was a deeply divided Congress that met the war crisis.

In this confused situation, a group of talented young congressmen took control. Nearly all of them were Republicans from the South or the West: Richard M. Johnson and Henry Clay of Kentucky, John C. Calhoun and William Lowndes of South Carolina, George M. Troup of Georgia, Peter B. Porter from the Niagara district of New York, and others. Called the "War Hawks," these men were ardent nationalists who were more than willing to declare war on England to protect U.S. rights. Through their organizational, oratorical, and intellectual power, they won control of Congress. Henry Clay, only 34 years old and serving his first term in Congress, was elected Speaker of the House. More vigorous than his predecessors, Clay controlled debate, packed key committees, worked tirelessly behind the scenes, and imposed order on his fellow congressmen. When John Randolph, one of the most feared members of the House, brought his dog into the House chamber (as he had done for many years), Speaker Clay pointedly ordered the dog removed. Earlier speakers had not dared give such an order.

In the winter and spring of 1811–1812, the War Hawks led Congress into a declaration of war. In November they voted military preparations, and in April they enacted a 90-day embargo—not to coerce the British but to get American ships safely into port before war began. (As in 1807, the embargo prompted seaport merchants to rush their ships to sea.) On June 1, Madison sent a war message to Congress. This was to be the first war declared under the Constitution, and the president stayed out of congressional territory by not asking explicitly for a declaration of war. He did, however, present a list of British crimes that could be interpreted in no other way: the enforcement of the Orders in Council, even within the territorial waters of the United States; the impressment of American seamen; the use of spies and provocateurs within the United States; and the wielding of "a malicious influence over the Indians of the Northwest Territory." Madison concluded that war had in fact begun: "We behold . . . on the side of Great Britain a state of war against the United States; and on the side of the United States, a state of peace toward Great Britain."

Congress declared war on June 18. The vote was far from unanimous: 79 to 49 in the House of Representatives, 19 to 13 in the Senate. All 30 Federalists voted against the declaration. So did one in five Republicans, nearly all of them from the Northeast. Thus the war was declared by the Republican Party, more particularly by the Republicans of the South and West. The Northeast, whose commercial rights were supposedly the issue at stake, opposed the declaration.

A War with Canada and Indians

War Hawks declared a war to defend the sovereignty and maritime rights of the United States. The war that they planned and fought, however, bore the stamp of southern and western Republicanism. Federalists and many northeastern Republicans expected a naval war. After all, it was on the ocean that the British had committed their atrocities, and some remembered U.S. naval successes against France in the quasi-war of 1798–1800 and predicted similar successes against Great Britain. Yet when Madison asked Congress to prepare for war, the War Hawks led a majority that strengthened the army and left the navy weak. Reasoning that no U.S. naval force could challenge British control of the seas, they prepared instead for a land invasion of British Canada.

The decision to invade Canada led the Federalists, along with many of Randolph's Old Republicans, to accuse Madison and the congressional majority of planning a war of territorial aggression. Some members of Congress did indeed want to annex Canada to the United States. But most saw the decision to invade Canada as a matter of strategy. Lightly garrisoned and with a population of only half a million (many of them French, and most of the others American emigres whose loyalties were doubtful), Canada seemed the easiest and most logical place in which to damage the British. Canada was an increasingly valuable colony of Great Britain. The American embargoes, coupled with Napoleon's control of Europe, had impaired Britain's ability to supply her plantation colonies in the West Indies, and Canadian farmers had begun to fill the gap. Thus Canada was both valuable and vulnerable, and American policymakers reasoned that they could take it and hold it hostage while demanding that the British back down on other issues.

There was a second, more important reason for attacking Canada: it was from there that the British provided aid and encouragement to the Indian peoples of the Northwest. These peoples had gone through an epic of cultural disintegration and renewal since their defeat at Fallen Timbers and the signing of the Treaty of Greenville. Confined to a smaller territory but still dependent on the European fur trade, the natives of the Northwest fell into competition with settlers and other Indians for the diminishing supply of game. The Creeks, Choctaws, and other tribes of the Old Southwest faced the same problem: even when they chased settlers out of their territory, the settlers managed to kill or scare off the deer and other wildlife, thus ruining the old hunting grounds. When the Shawnee sent hunting parties farther west, they were opposed by western Indians. The Choctaws also sent hunters across the Mississippi, where they found new sources of furs, along with the angry warriors of the Osage and other peoples of Louisiana and Arkansas. The Indians of the interior now realized that the days of the fur trade, on which they depended for survival, were numbered.

Faced with shrinking territories, the disappearance of wildlife, and diminished opportunities to be traditional hunters and warriors, many Indian societies sank into despair. European diseases (smallpox, influenza, measles) attacked peoples who were increasingly sedentary and vulnerable. Old internal frictions grew nastier. In the Old Southwest, full-blooded Indians came into conflict with mixed-blood Indians—who often no longer spoke the native language and who wanted their people to adopt white ways. Murder and clan revenge plagued the tribes, and depression and suicide became more common. The use of alcohol, which had been a scourge on Indian societies for two centuries, increased. Indian males spent more time in their villages and less on the hunt, and by most accounts they drank more and grew more violent.

Out of this cultural wreckage emerged visionary leaders who spoke of a regenerated native society and the expulsion of all whites from the old tribal lands. One of the first was Chief Alexander McGillivray, a mixed-blood Creek who had sided with the British during the Revolution. Between 1783 and 1793, McGillivray used his father's ties to a Scots trading firm and his mother's ties to clan loyalties to make himself rich and powerful, and he tried to unite the Creeks under a national council that could override local chiefs and form alliances with other tribes and with Spanish Florida. McGillivray's connections with whites and his dismissal of old Creek ways cut into his authority, and his premature death in 1793 ended his dreams of unity.

The Cherokees north and east of the Creeks did succeed in making a unified state. Angered by the willingness of the old chiefs to be bribed and flattered into selling land, and by the departure of tribe members to remote locations in the Appalachians or to government land in Arkansas, a group of young chiefs staged a revolt between 1808 and 1810. Previously, being a Cherokee had meant loyalty to one's clan and kin group and adherence to the tribe's ancient customs. Now it meant remaining on the tribe's ancestral land (migration across the Mississippi was regarded as treason) and unquestioning acceptance of the laws, courts, and police controlled by the national council. By 1810 the Cherokee had transformed themselves from a defeated and divided tribe into a nation within a nation.

Among the many prophets who emerged during these years, the one who came closest to military success was Tenskwatawa, a fat, one-eyed, alcoholic Shawnee who had failed as a warrior and medicine man. When he went into a deep trance in 1805, people thought he was dead and prepared his funeral. But he awoke and told them he had visited heaven and hell and had received a prophetic vision. First, all Indians must stop drinking and fighting among themselves. They must also return to their traditional food, clothing, tools, and hairstyles and must extinguish all their fires and start new ones without using European tools. All who opposed the new order (including local chiefs, medicine men, shamans, and witches) must be put down by force. When all that had been done, God (a monotheistic, punishing God borrowed from the Christians) would restore the world that Indians had known before the whites came over the mountains.

Tenskwatawa's message soon found its way to the Delawares (who attacked the Christians among their people as witches) and other native peoples of the Northwest. When converts flooded into the prophet's home village, he moved to Prophetstown (Tippecanoe) in what is now Indiana. There, with the help of his brother Tecumseh, he created an army estimated by the whites at anywhere between 650 and 3,000 warriors and pledged to end further encroachment by whites. Tecumseh, who took control of the movement, announced to the whites that he was the sole chief of all the Indians north of the Ohio River; land cessions by anyone else would be invalid. Tenskwatawa's prophecy and Tecumseh's leadership had united the Indians of the Old Northwest in an unprecedented stand against white encroachment.

Tecumseh's confederacy posed a threat to the United States. A second war with England was looming, and Tecumseh was receiving supplies and encouragement from the British in Canada. He was also planning to visit the southern tribes in an attempt to bring them into his confederacy. The prospect of unified resistance by the western tribes in league with the British jeopardized every settler west of the Appalachians. In 1811 William Henry Harrison, the territorial governor of Ohio, led an army toward Prophetstown. With Tecumseh away, Tenskwatawa ordered an unwise attack on Harrison's army and was beaten at the Battle of Tippecanoe.

Although Canada was the focus of U.S. military strategy, maritime rights and national honor, along with the British-fed Indian threat west of the Appalachians, were the central issues in 1812. As John C. Calhoun, who was instrumental in taking the nation to war, concluded, "The mad ambition, the lust of power, and commercial avarice of Great Britain have left to neutral nations an alternative only between the base surrender of their rights, and a manly vindication of them."

The American Offensive, 1812–1813

The United States opened its offensive against Canada in 1812, with disastrous results. The plan was to invade Upper Canada (Ontario) from the Northwest, thus cutting off the Shawnee, Potawatomi, and other pro-British tribes from their British support. When General William Hull, governor of Michigan Territory, took a poorly supplied, badly led army of militiamen and volunteers into Canada from a base in Detroit, he found that the British had outguessed him. The area was crawling with British troops and their Indian allies. With detachments of his army overrun and his supply lines cut, he retreated to the garrison at Detroit. Under siege, he heard that an Indian force had captured the garrison at Fort Dearborn. British General Isaac Brock, who knew that Hull was afraid of Indians, sent a note into the fort telling him that "the numerous body of Indians who have attached themselves to my troops will be beyond my controul the moment the contest commences." Without consulting his officers, Hull surrendered his army of 2,000 to the smaller British force. Though Hull was later court-martialed for cowardice, the damage had been done: the British and their Indian allies occupied many of the remaining American garrisons in the Northwest and transformed the U.S. invasion of Upper Canada into a British occupation of much of the Northwest.

The invasion of Canada from the East went no better. In October, a U.S. force of 6,000 faced 2,000 British and Indians across the Niagara River separating Ontario from western New York. The U.S. regular army crossed the river, surprised the British, and established a toehold at Queenston Heights, a few miles downriver from Niagara Falls. While the British were preparing a counterattack, New York militiamen refused to cross the river to reinforce the regular troops. Ohio militiamen had behaved the same way when Hull invaded Canada, and there had been similar problems with the New York militia near Lake Champlain. Throughout the war citizen soldiers proved that Jefferson's confidence in the militia could not be extended to the invasion of other countries. The British regrouped and slaughtered the outnumbered, exhausted U.S. regulars at Queenston Heights.

As winter set in, it was clear that Canada would not fall as easily as the Americans had assumed. Indeed, the invasion, which U.S. commanders had thought would knife through an apathetic Canadian population, had the opposite effect: the attacks by the United States turned the rag-tag assortment of American loyalist emigres, discharged British soldiers, and American-born settlers into a self-consciously British Canadian people. Years later, an Englishwoman touring Niagara Falls asked a Canadian ferry boatman if it was true that Canadians had thrown Americans off Queenston Heights to their death on the rocky banks of the Niagara River. "Why yes," he replied, "there was a good many of them; but it was right to show them that there was water between us, and you know it might help to keep the rest of them from coming to trouble us on our own ground."

At the same time, Tecumseh's Indian confederacy, bruised but not broken in the Battle of Tippecanoe, fought for the British. On a trip to the southern tribes Tecumseh found the traditionalist wing of the Creeks—led by prophets who called themselves Red Sticks—willing to join him. The augmented confederacy provided stiff resistance to the United States throughout the war. The Red Sticks chased settlers from much of Tennessee. They then attacked a group of settlers who had taken refuge in a stockade surrounding the house of an Alabama trader named George Mims. In what whites called the Massacre at Fort Mims, the Red Sticks (reputedly with the collusion of black slaves within the fort) killed at least 247 men, women, and children. In the Northwest, Tecumseh's warriors, fighting alongside the British, spread terror throughout the white settlements.

A wiser U.S. army returned to Canada in 1813. They raided and burned the Canadian capital at York (Toronto) in April and then fought inconclusively through the summer. An autumn offensive toward Montreal failed, but the Americans had better luck on Lake Erie. The barrier of Niagara Falls kept Britain's salt-water navy out of the upper Great Lakes, and on Lake Erie the British and Americans engaged in a frenzied shipbuilding contest through the first year of the war. The Americans won. In September 1813 Commodore Oliver Hazard Perry cornered the British fleet at Put-in-Bay and destroyed it. Control of Lake Erie enabled the United States to cut off supplies to the British in the Northwest, and a U.S. army under William Henry Harrison retook the area and continued on into Canada. On October 5, Harrison caught up with a force of British and Indians at the Thames River and beat them badly. In the course of that battle Richard M. Johnson, a War Hawk congressman acting as commander of the Kentucky militia, killed Tecumseh. Proud militiamen returned to Kentucky with pieces of hair and clothing and even swatches of skin torn from Tecumseh's corpse. Their officers reaped huge political rewards: the Battle of the Thames would eventually produce a president of the United States (Harrison), a vice president (Johnson), three governors of Kentucky, three lieutenant governors, four U.S. senators, and about twenty congressmen. There is no more telling evidence of how seriously the settlers of the interior had taken Tecumseh.

The following spring General Andrew Jackson's Tennessee militia, aided by Choctaw, Creek, and Cherokee allies, attacked and slaughtered the Red Sticks who had fortified themselves at Horse Shoe Bend in Alabama. With the Battles of the Thames and of Horse Shoe Bend, the military power of the Indian peoples east of the Mississippi River was broken.

THE BRITISH OFFENSIVE, 1814

The British defeated Napoleon in April 1814, ending the larger war of which the War of 1812 was a part. Both the British and Americans began thinking about peace. But at the same time, the British concentrated their resources on the American war. The British had already blockaded much of the American coast and had shut down ports from Georgia to Maine. During the summer of 1814, they began to raid the shores of Chesapeake Bay and marched on Washington, D.C. As retribution for the torching of the Canadian capital at York, they chased the army and politicians out of town and then burned down the Capitol and the president's mansion. In September the British attacked the much larger city of Baltimore, but they could not blast their way past the determined garrison that commanded the harbor from Fort McHenry. This was the battle that inspired Francis Scott Key to write "The Star-Spangled Banner," a poem later set to the tune of an English drinking song. (It became the national anthem in the 1930s.) When a British offensive on Lake Champlain stalled during the autumn, the war reached a stalemate: Britain had prevented the invasion of Canada and had blockaded the American coast, but neither side could take and hold the other's territory.

The British now shifted their attention to the Gulf Coast, particularly to New Orleans, a city of vital importance to the trade and communications networks of the trans-Appalachian United States. Peace negotiations had begun in August and the British wanted to capture and hold New Orleans as a bargaining chip. A large British amphibious force sailed up the mouth of the Mississippi and camped eight miles south of New Orleans. There they were met by an American army made up of regulars, Kentucky and Tennessee militiamen, clerks, workingmen, and free blacks from the city, and about a thousand French pirates—all under the command of Andrew Jackson of Tennessee. Throughout late December and early January, unaware that a peace treaty had been signed on December 24, the armies exchanged artillery barrages and the British probed and attacked American lines. Then, on January 8, the British launched a frontal assault. A formation of 6,000 British soldiers marched across open ground toward 4,000 Americans concealed behind breastworks. With the first American volley, it was clear that the British had made a mistake. Veterans of the bloodiest battles of the Napoleonic Wars swore that they had never seen such withering fire; soldiers in the front ranks who were not cut down threw themselves to the ground and surrendered when the shooting stopped. The charge lasted half an hour. At the end, 2,000 British soldiers lay dead or wounded. American casualties numbered only seventy. Fought nearly two weeks after the peace treaty was signed, the Battle of New Orleans had no effect on the outcome of the war or on the terms of peace. But it salved the injured pride of Americans and made a national hero and a political power of Andrew Jackson.

WAR'S END

While most of the nation celebrated Jackson's victory, events in Federalist New England went very differently during the closing months of the war. New Englanders had considered themselves the victims of Republican trade policies, and their congressmen had voted overwhelmingly against going to war. The New England states seldom met their quotas of militiamen for the war effort, and some Federalist leaders had openly urged resistance to the war. The British had encouraged that resistance by not extending their naval blockade to the New England coast, and through the first two years of the war New England merchants and farmers had traded freely with the enemy. In 1814, after the Royal Navy had extended its blockade northward and begun to raid the towns of coastal Maine, some Federalists talked openly about seceding and making a separate peace with Britain. In an attempt to undercut the secessionists, moderate Federalists called a convention at Hartford to air the region's grievances. The Hartford Convention, which met in late December 1814, proposed amendments to the Constitution that underscored New England's position as a self-conscious minority within the Union. First, convention delegates wanted the three-fifths clause, which led to overrepresentation of the South in Congress and the Electoral College, stricken from the Constitution; they wanted to deny naturalized citizens—who were strongly Republican—the right to hold office; they wanted to make it more difficult for new states—all of which sided with the Republicans and their southern leadership—to enter the Union; and finally, they wanted to require a two-thirds majority of both houses for a declaration of war—a requirement that would have prevented the War of 1812.

The Federalist leaders of the Hartford Convention, satisfied that they had headed off the secessionists, took their proposals to Washington in mid-January. They arrived to find the capital celebrating the news of the peace treaty and Jackson's stunning victory at New Orleans. When they aired their sectional complaints and their constitutional proposals, they were branded as negative, selfish, and unpatriotic. Although Federalists continued for a few years to wield power in southern New England, the Hartford debacle ruined any chance of a nationwide Federalist resurgence after the war. Andrew Jackson had stolen control of American history from New England. He would do it again in the years ahead.

The treaty that Washingtonians celebrated ended the war and did little else. Britain's defeat of Napoleon had spurred British and American efforts to end a war that neither wanted, and the Treaty of Paris accomplished nothing more than that. In August 1814 peace talks began in the Belgian city of Ghent. Perhaps waiting for the results of their 1814 offensive, the British opened with proposals that the Americans were certain to reject. They demanded the right to navigate the Mississippi River. Moreover, they wanted territorial concessions and the creation of the permanent, independent Indian buffer state between the American Northwest and Canada that they had promised their Indian allies. The Americans ignored these proposals and talked instead about impressment and maritime rights. As the autumn wore on and the war reached stalemate, both sides began to compromise. The British knew that the Americans would grant concessions in the interior only if they were thoroughly defeated, an outcome that most British commanders thought impossible. For their part, the Americans realized that the British maritime depredations were byproducts of the struggle with Napoleonic France. Faced with peace in Europe and a senseless military stalemate in North America, negotiators on both sides began to withdraw their demands. The Treaty of Ghent, signed on Christmas Eve 1814, simply put an end to the war. The border between Canada and the United States remained where it had been in 1812, Indians south of that border—defeated and without allies—were left to the mercy of the United States, and British maritime violations were not mentioned. The makers of the treaty simply stopped a war that neither side could win, trusting that a period of peace would resolve the problems created by two decades of world war.

Conclusion

In 1816, Thomas Jefferson was in retirement at Monticello, satisfied that he had defended liberty against the Federalists' love of power. The High Federalist attempt to militarize government and jail their enemies had failed. Their direct taxes were repealed. Their debt and their national bank remained in place but only under the watchful eyes of true republicans. And their attempt to ally the United States with the antirepublican designs of Great Britain had ended in what many called the "Second War of American Independence." Jefferson's republic of republics was at last free to spread itself across the continent.

Yet for all his successes, Jefferson in 1816 saw that he must alter his dreams of agrarianism. Throughout his political life, Jefferson envisioned American farmers trading agricultural surpluses for European manufactured goods—a relationship that would ensure rural prosperity, prevent the growth of cities and factories, and thus sustain the landed independence on which republican citizenship rested. Westward expansion, he had believed, would ensure the yeoman republic for generations to come. By 1816 that dream was in need of revision. The British and French had "cover[ed] the earth and sea with robberies and piracies," disrupting America's vital export economy whenever it suited their whims. Put simply, "to be independent for the comforts of life we must fabricate them ourselves." This called for big changes: "we must now place the manufacturer by the side of the agriculturalist." As Jefferson wrote, his countrymen were transforming the yeoman republic into a market society unlike anything he had envisioned.

CHAPTER 3

―――→•◦•←―――

Northern Transformations

IN 1790 AMERICAN SOCIETY APPROXIMATED JEFFERSON'S IDEAL: the United States was a nation of farmers who provided for themselves and sent surpluses overseas to be traded for manufactured goods. To put it in a less bucolic way, Americans remained on the colonial periphery of North Atlantic capitalism. They sent timber, cured fish, wheat, tobacco, rice, and money to Europe (primarily Great Britain), and Europe (again, Britain was the big player) sent manufactured goods—along with bills for shipping, insurance, banking, and tariff duties—back to America. In the 25 years following adoption of the Constitution this old relationship fed significant economic growth in the United States, as European wars increased the demand for American produce and American shipping. Americans sent growing mountains of food and raw materials overseas, and they decorated their homes with comforts and small luxuries produced in British factories.

Beginning in the 1790s and accelerating dramatically with the peace of 1815, northern farmers changed that relationship: by 1830 the primary engine of northern economic development was no longer the North Atlantic trade; it was the self-sustained internal development of the northern United States. Northeastern businessmen noted that rural markets were expanding, that imports were unreliable, and that a crowded countryside produced people eager to work for wages, and they began to invest in factories. New factory towns, together with the old seaports and new inland towns that served a commercializing agriculture, provided the country's first significant domestic market for food. Governments of the northern states built roads and canals that linked farmers to distant markets, and farmers turned to cash-crop agriculture and bought necessary goods (and paid mortgages and crop loans) with the money they made. By 1830 a large and growing portion of New England, the mid-Atlantic, and the Northwest had transcended colonial economics to become an interdependent, self-sustaining market society.

The pioneering sociologist Max Weber made a distinction between capitalism and the *spirit* of capitalism. Economic exchange and the desire for profit, Weber noted, have existed in all societies. Only a few, however, have organized capitalism into an everyday culture. Historians have coined the term "market revolution" to describe the transformation of the North from a society with markets to a market society—a society in which the market was implicated in the ways in which northerners saw the world and dealt with it. This chapter describes that revolution in the North up to 1830. Chapter 4 describes the very different patterns of change in the South in the same years.

POSTCOLONIAL SOCIETY, 1790–1815

Farms

In 1782 J. Hector St. John de Crèvecoeur, a French soldier who had settled in rural New York, explained America's agrarian republic through the words of a fictionalized farmer. First of all, he said, the American farmer owns his own land and bases his claim to dignity and citizenship on that fact. He spoke of "the bright idea of property" and went on: "This formerly rude soil has been converted by my father into a pleasant farm, and in return, it has established all our rights; on it is founded our rank, our freedom, our power as citizens, our importance as inhabitants of [a rural neighborhood] . . ." Second, he said, farm ownership endows the American farmer with the powers and responsibilities of fatherhood. "Often when I plant my low ground," he said, "I place my little boy on a chair which screws to the beam of the plough—its motion and that of the horses please him; he is perfectly happy and begins to chat. As I lean over the handle, various are the thoughts which crowd into my mind. I am now doing for him, I say, what my father did for me; may God enable him to live that he may perform the same operations for the same purposes when I am worn out and old!"

Crèvecoeur's farmer, musing on liberty and property, working the ancestral fields with his male heir strapped to the plough, was concerned with proprietorship and fatherhood, not with making money. He shared those concerns with most northern farmers. Their first concern was to provide food and common comforts for their households. Their second was to achieve long-term security and the ability to pass their farms on to their sons. The goal was to create what rural folks called a "competence": the ability to live up to neighborhood standards of material decency while protecting the long-term independence of the household. Farmers thought of themselves first as fathers, neighbors, and stewards of family resources, and they avoided financial risk. Weather, bad crop years, pests, and unexpected injuries or deaths provided enough of that without adding the uncertainties of cash-crop agriculture and international commodity prices. In this situation most farmers practiced what scholars call "safety-first," "subsistence-plus," or simply "mixed" agriculture. They raised a variety of animals and plants and did not concentrate on a single cash crop. Most farms in the New England and middle states were divided into corn and grain fields, pasturage for animals, woodlands for fuel, a vegetable garden, and perhaps a dairy cow. These complicated farms were a hedge against the uncertainties of rural life. Farm families ate most of what they grew, bartered much of the rest within their neighborhoods, and gambled surpluses on long-distance trade.

West Indian and European markets for American meat, grain, and corn had been growing since the mid-eighteenth century. They expanded dramatically between 1793 and 1815, when war disrupted farming in Europe. Many northern farmers, though they seldom abandoned mixed agriculture, expanded production to take advantage of these overseas markets. The prosperity and aspirations of hundreds of thousands of farmers rose, and their houses were sprinkled with tokens of comfort and gentility. The same markets, however, sustained traditions of household independence and neighborly cooperation. Farmers continued to provide for their families from their own farms and neighborhoods, and they risked little by increasing their surpluses and sending them overseas. They profited from world markets without becoming dependent on them.

Production for overseas markets after 1790 did, however, alter relationships within farm families—usually in ways that reinforced the independence of the household and the power of its male head. Farm labor in postrevolutionary America was carefully divided by sex. Men worked in the fields, and production for markets both intensified that labor and made it more exclusively male. In the grain fields of the middle states, for instance, the long-handled scythe was replacing the sickle as the principal harvest tool. Women could use the sickle efficiently, but the long, heavy scythe was designed to be wielded by men. At the same time, farmers completed the substitution of ploughs for hoes as the principal cultivating tools—not only because ploughs worked better but because rural Americans had developed a prejudice against women working in the fields, and ploughs were male tools. By the early nineteenth century visitors to the long-settled farming areas (with the exception of some mid-Atlantic German communities) seldom saw women in the fields. In his travels through

France, Thomas Jefferson spoke harshly of peasant communities where he saw women doing field labor.

At the same time, household responsibilities multiplied and fell more exclusively to women. Farm women's labor and ingenuity helped create a more varied and nutritious rural diet in these years. Bread and salted meat were still the staples. The bread was the old mix of Indian corn and coarse wheat ("rye and Injun," the farmers called it), with crust so thick that it was used as a scoop for soups and stews. Though improved brines and pickling techniques augmented the supply of salt meat that could be laid by, farmers' palates doubtless told them that it was the same old salt meat. A variety of other foods were now available, however. By the 1790s, improved winter feeding for cattle and better techniques for making and storing butter and cheese kept dairy products on the tables of the more prosperous farm families throughout the year. Chickens became more common, and farm women began to fence and manure their kitchen gardens, planting them with potatoes, turnips, cabbages, squashes, beans, and other vegetables that could be stored in the root cellars that were becoming standard features of farmhouses. By the 1830s a resident of Weymouth, Massachusetts, claimed that "a man who did not have a large garden of potatoes, crooked-necked squashes, and other vegetables . . . was regarded [as] improvident." He might have added poultry and dairy cattle to the list, and he might have noted—as he did not—that all were more likely to result from the labor of women than from the labor of men.

Neighborhoods

Rural communities were far more than accumulations of independent farm-owning households. The struggle to maintain household independence involved most farm families in elaborate networks of neighborly cooperation, and long-term, give-and-take relationships with neighbors were essential economic and social assets. Few farmers possessed the tools, the labor, and the food they would have needed to be truly self-sufficient. They regularly worked for one another, borrowed oxen and plows, and swapped one kind of food crop for another. Women traded ashes, herbs, butter and eggs, vegetables, seedlings, baby chicks, goose feathers, and the products of their spinning wheels and looms. The regular exchange of such goods and services was crucial to the workings of rural neighborhoods. Some undertakings—house and barn raisings and husking bees, for example—brought the whole neighborhood together, transforming a necessary chore into a pleasant social event. The gossip, drinking, and dancing that took place on such occasions were fun. They were also—like the exchanges of goods and labor—social rituals that strengthened the neighborly relations within which farmers created a livelihood and passed it on to their sons.

Few of these neighborhood transactions involved money. Indeed, in 1790 no paper money had yet been issued by the states or federal government, and the widespread use of Spanish, English, and French coins testified to the shortage of specie. In New England, farmers kept careful accounts of neighborhood debts. In the South and West, farmers used a "changing system" in which they simply remembered what they owed; they regarded the New England practice as a sign of Yankee greed and lack of character. Yet farmers everywhere relied more on barter than on cash. "Instead of money going incessantly backwards and forwards into the same hands," observed a French traveler in Massachusetts in 1790, Americans "supply their needs in the countryside by direct reciprocal exchanges. The tailor and the bootmaker go and do their work at the home of the farmer . . . who most frequently provides the raw material for it and pays for the work in goods. They write down what they give and receive on both sides, and at the end of the year they settle a large variety of exchanges with a very small quantity of coin." George Holcomb, a farmer in New York's Hudson Valley, left a record of his neighborly transactions over a few days in 1812: "Today Wm. Dixon paid me eight dollars and I lent the same to Samuel Holcomb and today I wanted about two thirds of it for Wm. Dixon and he paid me in three trees of timber that I went and chopped and got home at night . . . this evening I went to Mr. Zach Chapman to a party, Mr. Foley came and dressed flax for half a cord of wood I drew him last winter to the school house." In a short time, George Holcomb dealt with neighbors and relatives, with cash and bartering, and with a local economy that mixed cut wood, schoolhouse provisions, dressed flax, and a party. He conducted his economic life within an elaborate network of neighborly and family obligations and not by buying, selling, and calculating.

Country storekeepers and village merchants handled relationships between farmers and long-distance markets, and they were as much a part of their neighborhoods as of the wider world. In most areas, farmers brought produce—often a mixed batch of grain, vegetables, ashes, goose down, and so on—to the storekeeper, who arranged its shipment to a seaport town. Some paid cash for produce, but most simply credited the farmer's account. Farmers also bought store goods on credit, and when bad crop years or bad luck made them unable to pay, storekeepers tended to wait for payment without charging interest. Indeed, in many instances the store was incorporated into the relations of local exchange. Hudson River merchants paid the same prices for local goods that were to be sold locally over long periods of time—a price that reflected their relative value within the local barter economy. When sent to New York City, the prices of the same goods floated up and down with their value on international markets. Storekeepers also played a role in local networks of debt, for it was common for farmers to bring their grain, ashes, butter, and eggs to the store, and to have them credited to the accounts of neighbors to whom they were in debt—thus turning the storekeeper into a broker within the complicated web of neighborhood obligations.

Standards of Living

In 1790 most farmhouses in the older rural areas were small, one-story struc-
tures, and few farmers bothered to keep their surroundings clean or attractive.
They repaired their fences only when they became too dilapidated to function.
They rarely planted trees or shrubs, and housewives threw out garbage for
chickens and pigs that foraged near the house.

Inside, there were few rooms and many people. Beds stood in every room,
and few family members slept alone. Growing up in Bethel, Connecticut, the
future show-business entrepreneur P. T. Barnum shared a bed with his
brother and an Irish servant. Guests shared beds in New England taverns until
the 1820s. The hearth remained the source of heat and light in most farmhouses. Between 1790 and 1810, more than half the households in central
Massachusetts, an old and relatively prosperous area, owned only one or two
candlesticks, suggesting that one of the great disparities between wealthy
families and their less affluent neighbors was that the wealthy could light
their houses at night. Another disparity was in the outward appearance of
houses. The better-off families painted their houses white as a token of pris-
tine republicanism. But their bright houses stood apart from the weathered
grey-brown clapboard siding of their neighbors in stark and unrepublican
contrast.

Increased income from foreign markets did, of course, result in improvement. Farmers bought traditional necessities such as salt and pepper, gun-
powder, tools, coffee and tea, but these were now supplemented with an increasingly alluring array of little luxuries such as crockery, flatware, finished
cloth, mirrors, clocks and watches, wallpaper, and the occasional book. At
mealtimes, only the poorest families continued to eat with their fingers or with
spoons from a common bowl. By 1800 individual place settings with knives
and forks and china plates, along with individual chairs instead of benches, had
become common in rural America.

Inheritance

Northern farmers between 1790 and 1815 were remarkably like Jefferson's yeo-
man-citizen ideal: prosperous, independent, living in rough equality with
neighbors who shared the same status. Yet even as rural Americans acted out
that vision, its social base was disintegrating. Overcrowding and the growth of
markets caused the price of good farmland to rise sharply throughout the older
settlements. Most young men could expect to inherit only a few acres of exhausted land or to move to wilderness land in the backcountry. Failing those,
they could expect to quit farming altogether. Crèvecoeur's baby boy—who in
fact ended up living in Boston—was in a more precarious position than his seat
on his father's plough might have indicated.

In Revolutionary America, fathers had been judged by their ability to support and govern their households, to serve as good neighbors, and to pass land on to their sons. After the war, fewer farm fathers were able to do that. Those in the old settlements had small farms and large families, which made it impossible for them to provide a competence for all their offspring. Fathers felt that they had failed as fathers. And their sons, with no prospect of an adequate inheritance, were obliged to leave home. Most fathers tried to provide for all their heirs (generally by leaving land to their sons and personal property to their daughters). Few left all their land to one son, and many stated in their wills that the sons to whom they left the land must share barns and cider mills—even houses—on farms that could be subdivided no further. Such provisions fitted a social system that guaranteed the independence of the household head through complex relations with kin and neighbors. But they were also an indication that that system had reached the end of the line.

Outside New England, farm tenancy was on the increase. In parts of Pennsylvania and in other areas as well, farmers often bought farms when they became available in the neighborhood, rented them to tenants to augment the household income, and gave them to their sons when they reached adulthood. The sons of poorer farmers often rented a farm in the hope of saving enough money to buy it. Some fathers bought tracts of unimproved land in the backcountry—sometimes on speculation, more often to provide their sons with land they could make into a farm. Others paid to have their sons educated, or arranged an apprenticeship to provide them with an avenue of escape from a crowded countryside. As a result, more and more young men left home. The populations of the old farming communities grew older and more female, whereas the populations of the rising frontier settlements and seaport cities became younger and more male. The young men who stayed home often had nothing to look forward to but a lifetime as tenants or hired hands.

The Seaport Cities

When the first federal census takers made their rounds in 1790, they found 94 percent of Americans living on farms and in rural villages. The remaining 6 percent lived in 24 towns with a population of more than 2,500 (a census definition of "urban" that included many communities that were, by modern standards, very small). Only five places had populations over 10,000: Boston (18,038), New York (33,131), Philadelphia (42,444), Baltimore (13,503), and Charleston (16,359). All five were seaports—testimony to the key role of international commerce in the economy of the early republic.

The little streams of produce that left farm neighborhoods joined with others on the rivers and the coastal shipping lanes, and they piled up as a significant national surplus on the docks of the seaport towns. When war broke out between Britain and France in 1793, the overseas demand for American foodstuffs, and thus the production of American farms, increased. The warring European powers also needed shipping to carry products from the Caribbean islands to Europe. America's saltwater merchants, free from the old colonial restrictions, responded by building one of the great merchant fleets in the world, and American overseas trade entered a period of unprecedented growth. Ocean trade during these years was risky and uneven, subject to the tides of war and the strategies of the belligerents. French seizures of American shipping and the resulting undeclared war of 1798–1800, the British ban on America's re-export trade in 1805, Jefferson's nonimportation of 1806 and his embargo of 1807, and America's entry into the war in 1812 all disrupted the maritime economy and threw the seaports into periods of economic collapse. But by 1815 wartime commerce had transformed the seaports and the institutions of American business. New York City had become the nation's largest city, with a population that grew from 33,131 in 1790 to 96,373 in 1810. Philadelphia's population had risen to 53,722 by 1810; Boston's to 34,322; and Baltimore's to 46,555. Economic growth in the years 1790 to 1815 was most palpably concentrated in these cities.

Seaport merchants in these years amassed the private fortunes and built the financial infrastructure that would soon take up the task of commercializing and industrializing the northern United States. Old merchants like the Brown brothers of Providence and Elias Hasket Darby of Salem grew richer, and newcomers like the immigrant John Jacob Astor of New York City built huge personal fortunes. To manage those fortunes, new institutions emerged. Docking and warehousing facilities improved dramatically. Bookkeepers were replaced by accountants familiar with the new double-entry system of accounting, and insurance and banking companies were formed to handle the risks and rewards of wartime commerce.

The cities prospered in these years. The main thoroughfares and a few of the side streets were paved with cobblestones and lined with fine shops and townhouses. But in other parts of the cities, visitors learned that the boom was creating poverty as well as wealth. There had been poor people and depressed neighborhoods in the eighteenth-century seaports, but not on the scale that prevailed between 1790 and 1820. A few steps off the handsome avenues were narrow streets crowded with ragged children, browsing dogs and pigs, with garbage and waste filling the open sewers. Epidemics became more frequent and deadly. New York City, for example, experienced six severe bouts of yellow fever between 1791 and 1822. Each time, the disease entered through the seaport and settled in the slums. Life expectancy in Boston, reputedly the healthiest city in America, was three to five years lower than in the surrounding countryside.

The slums were evidence that money created by commerce was being distributed in undemocratic ways. Per capita wealth in New York rose 60 percent between 1790 and 1825, but the wealthiest 4 percent of the population owned over half of that wealth. The wages of skilled and unskilled labor rose in these years, but the increase in seasonal and temporary employment, together with the recurring interruptions of foreign commerce, cut deeply into the security and prosperity of ordinary women and men. Added to the old insecurities of sickness, fire, accident, aging, and any number of personal misfortunes, these ate up the gains made by laborers, sailors, and most artisans and their families.

Meanwhile, the status of artisans in the big cities was undergoing change. In 1790, artisans were the self-proclaimed "middling classes" of the towns. They demanded and usually received the respect of their fellow citizens. When a clerk in Boston refused to attend dancing classes that one of the town's master saddlers had joined, a newspaper scolded him (a mere "stockjobber's lackey") for considering himself the social superior of the saddler and other "reputable mechanics." Skilled manual workers constituted about half the male workforce of the seaport cities, and their respectability and usefulness, together with the role they had played in the Revolution, had earned them an honorable status.

That status rested in large part on their independence. In 1790 most artisan workshops were household operations with at most one or two apprentices and hired journeymen—wage earners who looked forward to owning their own shops one day. Timothy Dwight, the conservative president of Yale College, observed that there were few of those "amphibious beings" in America who remained journeymen (wage earners) for life. Most master craftsmen lived modestly (on the borderline of poverty in many cases) and aspired only to support their household in security and decency, and to do so by performing useful work. They identified their way of life with republican virtue. Jefferson himself proclaimed them "the yeomen of the cities."

The patriarchal base of that republicanism, however, was eroding. With the growth of the maritime economy, the nature of construction work, shipbuilding, the clothing trades, and other specialized crafts changed. Artisans were being replaced by cheaper labor and undercut by subcontracted "slop work" performed by semiskilled rural outworkers. Perhaps one in five master craftsmen entered the newly emerging business class. The others took work as laborers or wage-earning craftsmen. By 1815, most young craftsmen in the seaports could not hope to own their own shops. About half of New York City's journeymen that year were over thirty years old; nearly a quarter were over forty. Most were married, and half headed a household that included four or more dependents. In short, they had become wage earners for life. In the seaports between 1790 and 1815, the world of artisans like Paul Revere, Benjamin Franklin, and Thomas Paine was passing out of existence. Wage labor was taking its place.

The loss of independence undermined artisan husbands and fathers. Few wage earners could support a family without the earnings of a wife and children. Working-class women took in boarders and did laundry and found work as domestic servants or as peddlers of fruit, candy, vegetables, cakes, or hot corn. They sent their children out to scavenge in the streets. The descent into wage labor and the reliance on the earnings of women and children were at variance with the republican, patriarchal assumptions of fathers.

TRANSPORTATION

After 1815 dramatic improvements in transportation—more and better roads, steamboats, canals—tied old communities together and penetrated previously isolated neighborhoods and transformed them. Most of these improvements were the work of state governments. They made the transition to a market society physically possible.

Transportation in 1815

In 1815 the United States was a rural nation stretching from the old settlements on the Atlantic coast to the trans-Appalachian frontier, with transportation facilities that ranged from primitive to nonexistent. Americans despaired of communicating, to say nothing of doing business on a national scale. In 1816 a Senate committee reported that $9 would move a ton of goods across the 3,000-mile expanse of the North Atlantic. The same $9 would move the same ton of goods only 30 miles inland. A year later, the cost of transporting wheat from the new settlement of Buffalo to New York City was three times greater than the selling price of wheat in New York. Farming for profit made sense only for farmers near urban markets or with easy river access to the coast.

West of the Appalachians, transportation was almost entirely undeveloped. Until the 1820s, most northwesterners were southern yeomen who settled near tributaries of the Ohio–Mississippi River system—a network of navigable streams that reached the sea at New Orleans. Frontier farmers floated their produce downriver on jerry-built flatboats. Boatmen making the trip from Louisville to New Orleans spent a full month navigating dangerous rivers through unsettled territory. At New Orleans, northwestern produce was trans-shipped to New York and other eastern ports. Most boatmen knocked down their flatboats, sold the lumber, then walked home to Kentucky or Ohio over the difficult and dangerous Natchez Trace.

Transporting goods *into* the western settlements was even more difficult. Keelboatmen like the legendary Mike Fink could navigate upstream—using eddies and back currents, sailing when the wind was right but usually poling their boats against the current. Skilled crews averaged only fifteen miles a day, and the trip from New Orleans to Louisville took three to four months. Looking for better routes, some merchants dragged finished goods across Pennsylvania and into the West at Pittsburgh, but transport costs made these goods prohibitively expensive. Consequently, the trans-Appalachian settlements—home to one in five Americans by 1820—remained marginal to the market economy. By 1815 New Orleans was shipping about $5 million of western produce annually—an average of only $15 per farm family in the interior.

Improvements

In 1816 Congress resumed construction of the National Road (first authorized in 1802) that linked the Potomac River with the Ohio River at Wheeling, Virginia—an attempt to link west and east through the Chesapeake. The smooth, crushed-rock thoroughfare reached Wheeling in 1818. At about the same time, Pennsylvania extended the Lancaster Turnpike to make it run from Philadelphia to the Ohio River at Pittsburgh. These ambitious roads into the West, however, had limited effects. The National Road made it easier for settlers and a few merchants' wagons to reach the West. But the cost of moving bulky farm produce over the road remained very high. Eastbound traffic on the National Road consisted largely of cattle and pigs, which carried themselves to market. Farmers continued to float their corn, cotton, wheat, salt pork, and whiskey south by river boat and thence to eastern markets.

It was the steamboat that first made commercial agriculture feasible in the West. Tinkerers and mechanics had been experimenting with steam-powered boats for a generation or more when an entrepreneur named Robert Fulton launched the *Clermont* on an upriver trip from New York City to Albany in 1807. Over the next few years Americans developed flat-bottomed steamboats that could navigate rivers even at low water. The first steamboat reached Louisville from New Orleans in 1815. Two years later, with seventeen steamboats already working western rivers, the *Washington* made the New Orleans–Louisville run in twenty-five days, a feat that convinced westerners that two-way river trade was possible. By 1820, sixty-nine steamboats were operating on western rivers. The 60,000 tons of produce that farmers and planters had shipped out of the interior in 1810 grew to 500,000 tons in 1840. The steamboat had transformed the interior from an isolated frontier into a busy commercial region that traded farm and plantation products for manufactured goods.

In the East, state governments created rivers where nature had made none. In 1817 Governor DeWitt Clinton, after failing to get federal support, talked the New York legislature into building a canal linking the Hudson River with Lake Erie—thus opening a continuous water route between the Northwest and New York City. The Erie Canal was a near-visionary feat of engineering. Designed by self-taught engineers and built by gangs of Irish immigrants, local farm boys, and convict laborers, it stretched 364 miles from Albany to Buffalo. Although "Clinton's Ditch" passed through carefully chosen level ground, it required a complex system of eighty-three locks, and it passed over eighteen rivers on stone aqueducts. Construction began in 1819, and the canal reached Buffalo in 1825. It was clear even before then that the canal would repay New York state's investment of $7.5 million many times over and that it would transform the territory it served.

The Erie Canal would direct the trade of the whole Great Lakes watershed into New York City. But its first and most powerful effects were on western New York, which had been a raw frontier accessible to the East only over a notoriously bad state road. By 1830 the New York corridor of the Erie Canal, settled largely from hill-country New England, was one of the world's great grain-growing regions, dotted with market towns and new cities like Syracuse, Rochester, and Buffalo.

The Erie Canal was an immense success, and legislators and entrepreneurs in other states joined a canal boom that lasted for twenty years. When construction began on the Erie Canal there were fewer then 100 miles of canal in the United States. By 1840 there were 3,300 miles, nearly all of it in the Northeast and Northwest. Northwestern states, Ohio in particular, built ambitious canal systems that linked isolated areas to the Great Lakes and thus to the Erie Canal. Northeastern states followed suit. A canal between Worcester and Providence linked the farms of central Massachusetts with Narragansett Bay. Another canal linked the coal mines of northeastern Pennsylvania with the Hudson River at Kingston, New York. In 1835 Pennsylvania completed a canal from Philadelphia to Pittsburgh.

Time and Money

The transportation revolution brought a dramatic reduction in the time and money that it took to move heavy goods. Turnpikes cut the cost of wagon transport, but goods traveled most cheaply on water. In 1816 freight rates on the Ohio–Mississippi system had been 1.3 cents per ton mile for downriver travel and 5.8 cents for upriver travel; steamboats cut both costs to a bit more than a third of a cent. The Erie Canal and the Ohio canals reduced the distance between East and West and carried goods at about a cent per ton-mile. By 1830 farmers in the Northwest and western New York could grow wheat and sell it at a profit on the New York market.

Improvements in speed were nearly as dramatic. The overland route from Cincinnati to New York in 1815 (by keelboat upriver to Pittsburgh, then by wagon the rest of the way) had taken a minimum of fifty-two days. Steamboats traveled from Cincinnati to New Orleans, then passed goods on to coasting ships that finished the trip to New York City in twenty-eight days. By 1840, upriver steamboats carried goods to the terminus of the Main Line Canal at Pittsburgh, which delivered them to Philadelphia, which sent them on to New York

City for a total transit time of eighteen to twenty days. At about the same time, the Ohio canal system enabled Cincinnati to send goods north through Ohio, across Lake Erie, over the Erie Canal, and down the Hudson to New York City—an all-water route that reduced costs and made the trip in eighteen days. Similar improvements occurred in the densely settled and increasingly urbanized Northeast. By 1840 travel time between the big northeastern cities had been reduced to from one-fourth to one-eleventh of what it had been in 1790. It was these improvements in speed and economy that made a northern market economy possible.

By 1840 improved transportation had made a market revolution. Foreign trade, which had driven American economic growth up to 1815, continued to expand. The value of American exports in 1815 had stood at $52.6 million, whereas imports totaled $113 million. Both rose dramatically in the years of the market revolution: exports (now consisting more of southern cotton than of northern food crops) continued to increase, and the flow of imported manufactured goods increased as well. Yet the growth in foreign trade represented vast reductions in the *proportion* of American—particularly northern—market activity that involved other countries. Before 1815 Americans had exported about 15 percent of their total national product; by 1830 exports accounted for only 6 percent of a vastly increased national production. The reason for this shift was that after 1815 the United States developed self-sustaining domestic markets for farm produce and manufactured goods. The great engine of economic growth—particularly in the North and West—was not the old colonial relationship with Europe but a self-sustaining domestic market.

Markets and Regions

Henry Clay and other proponents of the American System (see Chapter 6) dreamed of a market-driven economy that would transcend sectionalism and create a unified United States. But until at least 1840 the market revolution produced greater results within regions than between them. The farmers of New England traded food for finished goods from Boston, Lynn, Lowell, and other towns in what was becoming an urban, industrial region. Philadelphia sold its manufactures to and bought its food from the farmers of the Delaware Valley. Although the Erie Canal created a huge potential for interregional trade, until 1839 most of its eastbound tonnage originated in western New York. In the West, market-oriented farmers fed such rapidly growing cities as Rochester, Pittsburgh, and Cincinnati, which in turn supplied the farmers with locally manufactured farm tools, furniture, shoes, and other goods. Farther south, the few plantations that did not produce their own food bought surpluses from farmers in their own region. Thus, until about 1840, the market revolution was more a regional than an interregional phenomenon. Yet it was clear to politicians, and to anyone else who looked at a map, that the New England, mid-Atlantic, and Northwestern states were on their way to becoming an integrated market society—a society that did not include southern plantations that grew for export. It was not what Henry Clay had had in mind.

COMMUNICATIONS

Among the items that traveled along the new transportation network was information—newspapers, books, magazines, business communications, personal letters, and travelers who carried news. They reached a public that was remarkably literate and well informed. The literacy rate in the preindustrial United States was among the highest ever recorded. In 1790 approximately 85 percent of adult men in New England and 60 percent of those in Pennsylvania and the Chesapeake could read and write. The literacy rate was lower among women— about 45 percent in New England—but on the rise. By 1820 all but the poorest white Americans, particularly in the North, could read and write. The increases in literacy (increases not only in functional literacy but in the numbers of people who practiced reading as an everyday activity) were greatly encouraged by the schools established by local and state governments. Between 1800 and 1825 in New York state, the proportion of the population enrolled in school rose from 37 percent to 60 percent. For the nation as a whole, that figure stood at 35 percent in 1830—low by New York's or today's standards but higher than in any other country at the time.

The rise of a reading public was accompanied by a print revolution: enterprising men (and a few women) learned how to make their livings by providing cheap Bibles and English novels, almanacs, newspapers, and other printed matter to a public that not only could but did read. Readers were encouraged by their republican governments. The national government in particular helped the flow of print in ways that were unprecedented. The governments of Great Britain and the European powers tried to control the circulation of information: they established few post offices, they taxed newspapers, they monitored what was said in the newspapers and even in the mail, and they prosecuted people who said the wrong things in print. There were attempts to do such things in America. The Stamp Tax of 1765 had included a tax on newspapers, which many Americans considered an attempt not only at direct taxation but at controlling the news. And in 1798, remember, the Federalists had jailed editors with whom they disagreed. Americans defeated both of these attempts. The First Amendment guaranteed freedom of the press, and the government of the United States (with that brief Federalist exception) did not interfere with newspapers. Just the opposite: newspapers enjoyed discounted postal rates and circulated far beyond their point of publication. A law of 1792 allowed newspapers to mail copies to each other without cost, and the editors of country weeklies cut national and international news from the New York, Baltimore, and Philadelphia papers, combined them with local advertising and legal notices, and provided their readers with cheap sources of information that were remarkably uniform throughout the North and West and in many parts of the South. The rise of a democratic and national reading public, then, was directly and knowingly subsidized by the national government.

Newspapers were the most widely distributed form of print in the new republic. In 1790, 106 newspapers were being published in the United States. In 1835, 1,258 were in publication, 90 of which were dailies. In the latter year, the number of newspapers per capita in the United States was two to three times greater than in Great Britain. Still, even in New England, only about one household in 10 subscribed to a newspaper. Yet most members of the new democratic public knew what was in them, for the papers were passed from hand to hand, read aloud in groups, and made available at taverns and public houses. Timothy Dwight, Federalist president of Yale College, hated newspapers and associated them with gambling, tavern-haunting, drinking, and democracy.

Improvements in distribution and printing technology encouraged other forms of popular literature as well. The emerging evangelical crusade (see Chapter 5) made full and innovative use of print. Sunday school tracts, temperance pamphlets, and other religious materials were printed in huge numbers in New York and distributed efficiently and cheaply through the mails— so cheaply that the American Bible Society devised a realistic plan to provide every household in America with a free Bible. Although newspapers were men's reading, the religious tracts tended to find their way into the hands of women. Women also were the principal readers of novels, a new form of reading matter that Thomas Jefferson and other authorities denounced as frivolous and aberrant. The first best-selling novel in the United States was *The Power of Sympathy,* a morally ambiguous tale of seduction and betrayal that exposed hypocrisy in male authorities who punished (generally poor and vulnerable) women for their own seductions. Such tales were seen as dangerous not only because they contained questionable subject matter but because girls and women read them silently and in private. Printed matter provided information and opinion for the men who conducted the public life of democracy. But it could also provide sustenance for the spirits and imaginations of Americans who were excluded from that public.

The increase in literacy and in printed matter accelerated both the market and democracy. In the eighteenth century, when books and newspapers were scarce, most Americans had experienced the written word only as it was read aloud by fathers, ministers, or teachers. Between 1780 and 1830 private, silent reading of new kinds of texts became common—religious tracts, inexpensive Bibles, personal letters, novels, newspapers, and magazines. No longer were adult male authorities the sole interpreters of the world for families and neighborhoods. The new print culture encouraged Americans to read, think, and interpret information for themselves.

NORTHEASTERN FARMS

In the old farming communities of the Northeast, the transformations of the early-nineteenth century sent many young people off to cities and factory towns and others to the West. Those who remained at home engaged in new forms of agriculture on a transformed rural landscape, whereas their cousins in the Northwest transformed a wilderness into cash-producing farms. In both regions, farmers turned away from the old mixed, safety-first agriculture and began to raise a single crop intended for distant markets, a decision that committed them to buying things that their forebears had grown or made. The transition to full-scale buying and selling transformed the North into a market society in the first third of the nineteenth century.

An early nineteenth-century New England farm geared toward family subsistence required only three acres of cultivated land, twelve acres of pasture and meadow, another acre for the house, outbuildings, and vegetable garden, and a thirty-acre woodlot to stoke the hearth that cooked the food and heated the house. Visitors to even the oldest towns found farmsteads, tilled fields, and pastures scattered across a heavily wooded landscape. Overcrowding had encouraged some farmers to turn woodlots into poor farmland. But New Englanders who tried to grow grain on their rocky, worn-out soil could not compete with the farmers of western New York and the Old Northwest with their fertile lands and ready access to markets. At the same time, however, the factories and cities of the Northeast provided Yankee farmers with a market for meat and other perishables. Beef became the great New England cash crop. Dairy products were not far behind, and the proximity to city markets encouraged the spread of poultry and egg farms, fruit orchards, and truck gardens. The burgeoning shoe industry bought leather from the farmers, and woolen mills created a demand for wool, and thus for great flocks of New England sheep. As a result, millions of trees were stripped from the New England landscape to make way for pastureland.

The rise of livestock specialization reduced the amount of land under cultivation. Early in the century New Englanders still tilled their few acres in the old three-year rotation: corn the first year, rye the second, fallow the third. By the 1820s and 1830s, as farmers raised more livestock and less grain, the land that remained in cultivation was farmed more intensively. Farmers saved manure and ashes for fertilizer, plowed more deeply and systematically, and tended their crops more carefully. These improved techniques, along with cash from the sale of their livestock and the availability of food at stores, encouraged Yankee farmers to allocate less and less land to the growing of food crops. In Concord,

Massachusetts—the hometown of the agrarian republic—the portion of town land in tillage dropped from 20 percent to 7 percent between 1771 and 1850.

The transition to livestock raising transformed woodlands into open pastures. As farmers leveled the forests, they sold the wood to fuel-hungry cities. It was a lucrative—though short-term—market: in 1829 a cord of wood sold for $1.50 in Maine and $7 in Boston. In the 1820s manufacturers began marketing cast-iron stoves that heated houses more cheaply and efficiently than open hearths, and canals brought cheap Pennsylvania anthracite to the Northeast. Farmers who needed pastureland could gain substantial one-time profits from the sale of cut wood. The result was massive deforestation. In 1790, in the central Massachusetts town of Petersham, forest covered 85 percent of the town lands. By 1830 the creation of pastureland through commercial woodcutting had reduced the forested area to 30 percent. (By 1850 woods covered only 10 percent of the town, the pasturelands were overgrazed and ruined, and the landscape was dotted with abandoned farms.)

With the shift to specialized market agriculture, New England farmers became customers for necessities that their forebears had produced themselves or had acquired through barter. They heated their houses with coal dug by Pennsylvania miners. They wore cotton cloth made by the factory women at Lowell. New Hampshire farm girls made straw hats for them, and the craftsmen of Lynn made their shoes. By 1830 or so, many farmers were even buying their food. The Erie Canal and the western grain belt sent flour from Rochester into eastern neighborhoods where grain was no longer grown. Many farmers found it easier to produce specialized crops for market and to buy butter, cheese, eggs, and vegetables at country stores.

The turning point came in the 1820s. The storekeepers of Northampton, Massachusetts, for instance, had been increasing their stock in trade by about 7 percent per decade since the late eighteenth century. In the 1820s they increased it 45 percent and now carried not only local farm products and sugar, salt, and coffee but bolts of New England cloth, sacks of western flour, a variety of necessities and little luxuries from the wholesale houses of New York City and Boston, as well as pattern samples from which to order silverware, dishes, wallpaper, and other household goods. Those goods were better than what could be made at home, and for the most part they were cheaper. The price of finished cloth, for instance, declined sixfold between 1815 and 1830; as a result, spinning wheels and handlooms disappeared from the farmhouses of New England. Farm families that bought the new cast-iron stoves enjoyed pies and bread baked from western white flour; the old "rye and Injun" disappeared. All of these things cost money and committed farm families to increasing their cash incomes. Standards of living rose dramatically. At the same time, northeastern farmers depended on markets in ways that their fathers and grandfathers would have considered dangerous not only to family welfare but to the welfare of the republic itself.

THE NORTHWEST

One reason the market revolution in the Northeast went as smoothly as it did was that young people with little hope of inheriting land in the old settlements moved to towns and cities or to the new farmlands of the Northwest. It was between 1815 and 1840—precisely the years in which northeastern agriculture became a cash-crop business—that migrants from the older areas transformed the Northwest Territory into a working agricultural landscape. In 1790 only ten thousand settlers lived west of the Appalachians—about one American in forty. By 1800 the number of settlers had risen to nearly a million. By 1820, two million Americans were westerners—one in four. Settlers bought land from speculators who had acquired tracts under the Northwest Ordinance in the Northwest, from English, Dutch, and American land companies in western New York, and from land dealers in the Southwest and in northern New England. They built frame houses surrounded by cleared fields, planted marketable crops, and settled into the struggle to make farms out of the wilderness and to meet mortgage payments along the way.

In the Northwest until the 1820s, most settlers were yeomen from Kentucky and Tennessee, usually a generation removed from Virginia, the Carolinas, and western Maryland. They moved along the Ohio and up the Muskingum, Miami, Scioto, Wabash, and Illinois Rivers to set up farms in the southern and central counties of Ohio, Indiana, and Illinois. When southerners moved north of the Ohio River into territory that banned slavery, they often did so saying that slavery blocked opportunities for poor whites. The Methodist preacher Peter Cartwright left Kentucky thinking, "I would get entirely clear of the evil of slavery," and "could raise my children to work where work was not thought a degradation." Similar hopes drew thousands of other southern yeomen north of the Ohio.

But even those who rejected slavery seldom rejected southern folkways. Like their kinfolk in Kentucky and Tennessee, the farmers of southern and central Ohio, Indiana, and Illinois remained tied to the river trade and to a mode of agriculture that favored free-ranging livestock over cultivated fields. The typical farmer fenced in a few acres of corn and left the rest of his land in woods to be roamed by southern hogs known as "razorbacks" and "land sharks." These animals were thin and tough (they seldom grew to over 200 pounds), and they could run long distances, leap fences, fend for themselves in the woods, and walk to distant markets. They were notoriously fierce; more settlers were injured by their own hogs than by wild animals. When it was time to gather the hogs for slaughter, many settlers played it safe and hunted them with guns.

The southern-born pioneers of the Northwest, like their cousins across the Ohio River, depended more on their families and neighbors than on distant markets. Newcomers found that they could neither rent tools from their southern neighbors nor present them with "gifts" during hard times. Southerners insisted on repaying debts in kind and on lending tools rather than renting them—thus engaging outsiders in the elaborate network of "neighboring" through which transplanted southerners made their livings. As late as the 1840s, in the bustling town of Springfield, Illinois, barter was the preferred system of exchange. "In no part of the world," said a Scotsman in southern Illinois, "is good neighborship found in greater perfection than in the western territory."

In the 1820s, with improved transportation and with hostilities between the United States and Canada at an end, northeastern migrants entered the Northwest, settling near the Great Lakes, filling the new lands of Michigan and the northern counties of the older northwestern states. Most of them were New Englanders who had spent a generation in western New York (such settlers accounted for three-fourths of the early population of Michigan). The rest came directly from New England. Arriving in the Northwest along the market's busiest arteries, they practiced an intensive, market-oriented agriculture. They penned their cattle and hogs and fattened them up, making them bigger and worth more than those farther south. They planted their land in grain and transformed the region—beginning with western New York's Genesee country in the 1820s and rolling through the Northwest—into one of the world's great wheat-producing regions. In 1820 the Northwest had exported only 12 percent of its agricultural produce. By 1840 that figure had risen to 27 percent, and it stood much higher among northern-born grain farmers.

The new settlers were notably receptive to improvements in farming techniques. Although there were plenty of southern proponents of "progress" and plenty of "backward" northerners, the line between new and old agricultural ways separated northern grain farmers from corn, hogs, and southern settlers. In breaking new land, for instance, southerners still used the old shovel plow, which dug a shallow furrow and skipped over roots. Northerners preferred newer, more expensive cast-iron plows, which cut cleanly through oak roots four inches thick. By the 1830s the efficient, expensive grain cradle had replaced the age-old sickle as the principal harvest tool in northwestern wheat fields. Instead of threshing their grain by driving cattle and horses over it, farmers bought new horse-powered and treadmill threshers and used hand-cranked fanning mills to speed the process of cleaning the grain. Within a remarkably short time, the new settlers transformed a wilderness into a modern agricultural landscape.

Most agricultural improvements were tailored to grain and dairy farming and were taken up most avidly by the northern farmers Others rejected them as expensive and "unnatural." They thought that cast-iron plows poisoned the soil and that fanning mills made a "wind contrary to nater," and thus offended God. John Chapman, an eccentric Yankee who earned the nickname "Johnny Appleseed" by planting apple tree cuttings in southern Ohio and Indiana before the settlers arrived, planted only low-yield, common trees; he regarded grafting, which farmers farther north and east were using to improve the quality of their apples, as "against nature." Southerners scoffed at the Yankee fondness for mechanical improvements, the systematic breeding of animals and plants, careful bookkeeping, and farm techniques learned from magazines and books. "I reckon," said one, "I know as much about farming as the printers do."

Conflict between intensive agriculture and older, less market-oriented ways reached comic proportions when the Illinois legislature imposed stiff penalties on farmers who allowed their small, poorly bred bulls to run loose and impregnate cows with questionable sperm, thereby depriving the owners of high-bred bulls of their breeding fees and rendering the systematic breeding of cattle impossible. When the poorer farmers refused to pen their bulls, the law was rescinded. A local historian explained that "there was a generous feeling in the hearts of the people in favor of an equality of privileges, even among bulls."

FARM FAMILIES

Households

The market revolution transformed eighteenth-century households into nineteenth-century homes. For one thing, Americans began to limit the size of their families. White women who married in 1800 had given birth to an average of 6.4 children. Those who married between 1800 and 1849 averaged 4.9 children. The decline was most pronounced in the North, particularly in commercialized areas. Rural birthrates remained at eighteenth-century levels in the southern uplands, in the poorest and most isolated communities of the North, and on the frontier. (As the New Yorker Washington Irving passed through the Northwest in the 1830s, he noted in his journal: "Illinois—famous for children and dogs—in house with nineteen children and thirty-seven dogs.") These communities practiced the old labor-intensive agriculture and relied on the labor of large families. For farmers who used newer techniques or switched to livestock or grain, large families made less sense. Moreover, large broods hampered the ability of future-minded parents to provide for their children and conflicted with new notions of privacy and domesticity that were taking shape among an emerging rural middle class.

Before 1815 farm wives had labored in the house, the barnyard, and the garden while their husbands and sons worked in the fields. With the market revolution came a sharper distinction between male work that was part of the cash economy and female work that was not. Even such traditional women's tasks as dairying, vegetable gardening, and poultry raising became men's work once they became cash-producing specialties. A Pennsylvanian who lived among businesslike New Englanders in the Northwest was appalled at such tampering with hallowed gender roles and wrote the Yankees off as "a shrewd, selfish, enterprising, cow-milking set of men."

At the same time, new kinds of women's work emerged within households. Though there were fewer children to care for, the culture began to demand forms of child-rearing that were more intensive, individualized, and mother-centered. Store-bought white flour, butter, and eggs and the new iron stoves eased the burdens of food preparation, but they also created demands for pies, cakes, and other fancy foods that earlier generations had only dreamed of. And while farm women no longer spun and wove their own cloth, the availability of manufactured cloth created the expectation that their families would dress more neatly and with greater variety than they had in the past—at the cost of far more time spent by women on sewing, washing, and ironing. Similar expectations demanded greater personal and domestic cleanliness and taste, and farm women spent time planting flower beds, cleaning and maintaining prized furniture, mirrors, rugs, and ceramics, and scrubbing floors and children. The market and housework grew hand in hand: among the first mass-produced commodities in the United States was the household broom.

Housework was tied to new notions of privacy, decency, and domestic comfort. Before 1820 farmers cared little about how their houses looked, often tossing trash and garbage out the door as food for pigs and chickens that foraged near the house. In the 1820s and 1830s, as farmers began to grow cash crops and adopt middle-class ways, they began to plant shade trees and kept their yards free of trash. They painted their houses and sometimes their fences and outbuildings, arranged their woodpiles into neat stacks, surrounded their houses with flowers and ornamental shrubs, and tried to hide their privies from view. The new sense of refinement and decorum extended into other aspects of country life. The practice of chewing (and spitting) tobacco was gradually banned in churches and meeting halls, and in 1823 the minister in Shrewsbury, Massachusetts, ordered dogs out of the meetinghouse.

Inside, prosperous farmhouses took on an air of privacy and comfort. Separate kitchens and iron stoves replaced open hearths. Many families used a set of matched dishes for individual place settings, and the availability of finished cloth permitted the regular use of table cloths, napkins, doilies, curtains, bedspreads, and quilts. Oil lamps replaced homemade candles, and the more prosperous families began to decorate their homes with wallpaper and upholstered furniture. Farm couples moved their beds away from the hearth and (along with the children's beds that had been scattered throughout the house) put them into spaces designated as bedrooms. They took the washstands and basins, which were coming into more common use, out of the kitchen and put them into the bedroom, thus making sleeping, bathing, and sex more private than they had been in the past. At the center of this new house stood the farm wife, apart from the bustling world of commerce but decorating and caring for the amenities that commerce bought, and demanding that men respect the new domestic world that commerce had made possible.

Neighborhoods

By 1830 the market revolution was transforming the rural landscape of the North. The forests had been reduced, the swamps had been drained, and most of the streams and rivers were interrupted by mill dams. Bears, panthers, and wolves had disappeared, along with the beaver and many of the fish. Now there were extensive pastures where English cattle and sheep browsed on English grasses dotted with English wildflowers like buttercups, daisies, and dandelions. Next to the pastures were neatly cultivated croplands that were regularly fertilized and seldom allowed to lie fallow. And at the center stood painted houses and outbuildings surrounded by flowers and shrubs and vegetable gardens. Many towns, particularly in New England, had planted shade trees along the country roads, completing a rural landscape of straight lines and human cultivation—a landscape that looked both settled and comfortable, and that made it easy to think of nature as a commodity to be altered and controlled.

Within that landscape, old practices and old forms of neighborliness fell into disuse. Neighbors continued to exchange goods and labor and to contract debts that might be left unpaid for years. But debts were more likely to be owed to profit-minded storekeepers and creditors, and even debts between neighbors were often paid in cash. Traditionally, storekeepers had allowed farmers to bring in produce and have it credited to a neighbor/creditor's account—a practice that made the storekeeper an agent of neighborhood bartering. In 1830 half of all the stores in rural New England still carried accounts of this sort. But storekeepers increasingly demanded cash payment or charged lower prices to those who paid cash. The farm newspapers that appeared in these years urged farmers to keep careful records of the amount of fertilizer used, labor costs, and per-acre yields, and discouraged them from relying on the old system of neighboring. Neighborly rituals like parties, husking bees, barn raisings—with their drinking and socializing—were scorned as inefficient and morally suspect wastes of time. The *Farmer's Almanac* of 1833 warned New England farmers, "If you love fun, frolic, and waste and slovenliness more than economy and profit, then make a husking."

By 1830 the efficient northern farmer concentrated on producing commodities that could be marketed outside the neighborhood and used his cash income to buy material comforts for his family and to pay debts and provide a cash inheritance for his children. Though much of the old world of household and neighborhood survived, farmers created a subsistence and maintained the independence of their households not through those spheres but through unprecedented levels of dependence on the outside world.

FACTORIES

In the fifty years following 1820, American cities grew faster than ever before or since. The old seaports—New York City in particular—grew rapidly in these years, but the fastest growth was in new cities that served commercial agriculture and in factory towns that produced for a largely rural domestic market. Even in the seaports, growth derived more from commerce with the hinterland than from international trade. Paradoxically, the market revolution in the countryside had produced the beginnings of industry and the greatest period of urban growth in U.S. history.

Factory Towns

Jeffersonians held that the United States must always remain rural. Americans, they insisted, could expand into the rich new agricultural lands of the West, trade their farm surpluses for European finished goods, and thus avoid creating cities with their dependent social classes. Some Federalists argued that Americans, in order to retain their independence, must produce their own manufactured necessities. Proponents of domestic manufactures argued that Americans could enjoy the benefits of factory production without the troublesome blight of industrial cities. They assured Americans that abundant water power—particularly the fast-running streams of the Northeast—would enable Americans to build their factories in the countryside. Such a decentralized factory system would provide employment for country women and children and thus subsidize the independence of struggling farmers. It was on those premises that the first American factories were built.

The American textile industry originated in industrial espionage. The key to the mass production of cotton and woolen textiles was a water-powered machine that spun yarn and thread. The machine had been invented and patented by Englishman Richard Arkwright in 1769. The British government, to protect its lead in industrialization, forbade the machinery or the people who worked with it to leave the country. Scores of textile workers, however, defied the law and made their way to North America. One of them was Samuel Slater, who had served an apprenticeship under Jedediah Strutt, a partner of Arkwright who had improved on the original machine. Working from memory while employed by Moses Brown, a Providence merchant, Slater built the first Arkwright spinning mill in America at Pawtucket, Rhode Island, in 1790.

Slater's first mill was a small frame building tucked among the town's houses and craftsmen's shops. Though its capacity was limited to spinning cotton yarn, it provided work for children in the mill and for women who wove yarn into cloth in their homes. Thus this first mill satisfied American requirements: it did not require the creation of a factory town, and it supplemented the household incomes of farmers and artisans. As his business grew and he advertised for widows with children, however, Slater was greeted by families headed by land-less, impoverished men. Slater's use of children from these families prompted "respectable" farmers and craftsmen to pull their children out of Slater's grow-ing complex of mills. More poor families arrived to take their places, and during the first years of the century Pawtucket grew rapidly into a disorderly mill town.

Soon Slater and other mill owners built factory villages in the countryside where they could exert better control over their operations and their workers. The practice became known as the Rhode Island or "family" system. At Slatersville, Rhode Island, at Oxford, Massachusetts, and at other locations in southern New England, mill owners built whole villages surrounded by com-pany-owned farmland that they rented to the husbands and fathers of their mill workers. The workplace was closely supervised, and drinking and other troublesome practices were forbidden in the villages. Fathers and older sons ei-ther worked on rented farms or as laborers at the mills. By the late 1820s Slater and most of the other owners were getting rid of the outworkers and buying power looms, thus transforming the villages into disciplined, self-contained factory towns that turned raw cotton into finished cloth—but at great cost to old forms of household independence. When President Andrew Jackson vis-ited Pawtucket in 1829, he remarked to Samuel Slater, "I understand you taught us how to spin, so as to rival Great Britain in her manufactures; you set all these thousands of spindles to work, which I have been delighted in viewing, and which have made so many happy, by a lucrative employment." "Yes sir," re-plied Slater. "I suppose that I gave out the psalm and they have been singing to the tune ever since."

A second act of industrial espionage was committed by a wealthy, cultivated Bostonian named Francis Cabot Lowell. Touring English factory districts in 1811, Lowell asked the plant managers questions and made secret drawings of the ma-chines he saw. He also experienced a genteel distaste for the squalor of English textile towns. Returning home, Lowell joined with wealthy friends to form the Boston Manufacturing Company—soon known as the Boston Associates. In 1813 they built their first mill in Waltham, Massachusetts, and then expanded into Lowell, Lawrence, and other new towns near Boston during the 1820s. The company built mills that differed from the early Rhode Island mills in two ways. First, they were heavily capitalized and as fully mechanized as possible; from the beginning, they turned raw cotton into finished cloth with little need for skilled workers. Second, the operatives who tended their machines were young, single women recruited from the farms of northern New England—farms that were switching to livestock raising and thus had little need for the labor of daughters. The company provided carefully supervised boarding houses for them and enforced rules of conduct both on and off the job. The young women worked steadily, never drank, seldom stayed out late, and attended church faithfully. They dressed neatly—often stylishly—and read newspapers and attended lectures. They impressed visitors, particularly those who had seen factory workers in other places, as a dignified and self-respecting workforce.

The brick mills and prim boarding houses set within landscaped towns and occupied by sober, well-behaved farm girls signified the Boston Associates' desire to build a profitable textile industry without creating a permanent working class. The women would work for a few years in a carefully controlled environment, send their wages back to their family, and return home to live as country housewives. These young farm women did in fact form an efficient, decorous workforce. But the decorum was imposed less by the owners than by the women themselves. To protect their own reputations, they punished misbehavior and shunned fellow workers whose behavior was questionable. Nor did they send their wages home or, as was popularly believed, use them to pay for their brothers' college education. Some saved their money to use as dowries that their fathers could not afford. More, however, spent their wages on themselves—particularly on clothes and books.

The owners of the factories expected that the young women's sojourn would reinforce their own paternalistic position and that of the girls' fathers. Instead, it produced a self-respecting sisterhood of independent, wage-earning women. Twice in the 1830s the women of Lowell went out on strike, proclaiming that they were not wage slaves but "the daughters of freemen." After finishing their stint in the mills, many Lowell women entered public life as reformers. Most of them married and became housewives but not on the same terms their mothers had known. One in three married Lowell men and became city dwellers. Those who returned home to rural neighborhoods remained unmarried longer than their sisters who had stayed at home and then married men about their own age who worked at something other than farming. Thus the Boston Associates kept their promise to produce cotton cloth profitably without creating a permanent working class. But they did not succeed in shuttling young women between rural and urban paternalism and back again. Wage labor, the ultimate degradation for agrarian-republican men, opened a road to independence for thousands of young women.

Cities

The market revolution hit American cities—the old seaports as well as the new marketing and manufacturing towns—with particular force. Here there was little concern for creating a classless industrial society: Vastly wealthy men of finance, a new middle class that bought and sold an ever-growing range of consumer goods, and the impoverished women and men who produced those goods lived together in communities that unabashedly recognized the reality of social class.

The richest men were seaport merchants who had survived and prospered during the world wars that ended in 1815. They carried on as importers and exporters, took control of banks and insurance companies, and made great fortunes in urban real estate. Those in Boston constituted an urbane and responsible cluster of families known as the Boston Brahmins. The elite of Philadelphia was less unified and perhaps less responsible, that of New York even less. These families continued in international commerce, profiting mainly from cotton exports and a vastly expanded range of imports, they speculated in urban real estate, and they sometimes invested in manufacturing ventures.

Below the old mercantile elite (or, in the case of the new cities of the interior, at the top of society) stood a growing middle class of wholesale and retail merchants, small manufacturers, and an army of lawyers, salesmen, auctioneers, clerks, bookkeepers, and accountants who handled the paperwork for a new market society. At the head of this new middle class were the wholesale merchants of the seaports who bought hardware, crockery, and other commodities from importers (and increasingly from American manufacturers) and then sold them in smaller lots to storekeepers from the interior. The greatest concentration of wholesale firms was on Pearl Street in New York City. Slightly below them were the large processors of farm products, including the meat packers of Cincinnati and the flour millers of Rochester, and large merchants and real estate dealers in the new inland cities. Another step down were specialized retail merchants who dealt in books, furniture, crockery, and other consumer goods. In Hartford, Connecticut, for instance, the proportion of retailers who specialized in specific commodities rose from 24 percent to 60 percent between 1792 and 1845. Alongside the merchants stood master craftsmen who had become manufacturers. With their workers busy in backrooms or household workshops, they now called themselves shoe dealers and merchant tailors. At the bottom of this new commercial world were hordes of clerks, most of them young men who hoped to rise in the world. Indeed many of them—one study puts the figure at between 25 and 38 percent—did move up in society. Both in numbers and in the nature of the work, this white-collar army formed a new class created by the market revolution—particularly by the emergence of a huge consumer market in the countryside.

In the 1820s and 1830s the commercial classes transformed the look and feel of American cities. As retailing and manufacturing became separate activities (even in firms that did both), the merchants, salesmen, and clerks now worked in quiet offices on downtown business streets. The seaport merchants built counting rooms and decorated their warehouses in the "new counting house style." Both in the seaports and the new towns of the interior, impressive brick and glass storefronts appeared on the main streets. Perhaps the most telling monuments of the self-conscious new business society were the handsome retail arcades that began going up in the 1820s. Boston's Quincy Market (1825), a two-story arcade on Philadelphia's Chestnut Street (1827), and Rochester's four-story Reynolds Arcade (1828) provided consumers with comfortable, gracious space in which to shop.

While businessmen were developing a new middle-class ethos, and while their families were flocking to the new retail stores to buy emblems of their status, the people who made the consumer goods were growing more numerous and at the same time were disappearing from view. With the exception of textiles and a few other commodities, few goods were made in mechanized factories before the 1850s. Most of the clothes and shoes, brooms, hats, books, furniture, candy, and other goods available in country stores and city shops were made by hand. City merchants and master craftsmen met the growing demand by hiring more workers. The largest handicrafts—shoemaking, tailoring, and the building trades—were divided into skilled and semiskilled segments and farmed out to subcontractors who could turn a profit only by cutting labor costs. The result was the creation of an urban working class, not only in the big seaports and factory towns but in scores of milling and manufacturing towns throughout the North and West.

The rise of New York City's ready-made clothing trade provides an example. In 1815 wealthy Americans wore tailor-made clothing; everyone else wore clothes sewn by women at home. In the 1820s the availability of cheap manufactured cloth and an expanding pool of cheap—largely female—labor, along with the creation of the southern and western markets, transformed New York City into the center of a national market in ready-made clothes. The first big market was in "Negro cottons"—graceless, hastily assembled shirts, pants, and sack dresses with which southern planters clothed their slaves. Within a few years New York manufacturers were sending dungarees and hickory shirts to western farmers and supplying shoddy, inexpensive clothing to the growing ranks of urban workers. By the 1830s many New York tailoring houses, including the storied Brooks Brothers, were offering fancier ready-made clothes to members of the new middle class.

High rents and costly real estate, together with the absence of water power, made it impossible to set up large factories in cities. But the nature of the clothing trade and the availability of cheap labor gave rise to a system of subcontracting that transformed needlework into the first "sweated" trade in America. Merchants kept a few skilled male tailors to take care of the custom trade and to cut cloth into patterned pieces for ready-made clothing. The pieces were sent out, often by way of subcontractors, to needleworkers who sewed them together in their homes. Male tailors continued to do the finishing work on men's suits. But most of the work—on cheap goods destined for the South and West—was done by women who worked long hours for piece rates that ranged from 75 cents to $1.50 per week. Along with clothing, women in garrets and tenements manufactured the items with which the middle class decorated itself and its homes: embroidery, doilies, artificial flowers, fringe, tassels, fancy-bound books, and parasols. All provided work for ill-paid legions of female workers.

Other trades followed similar patterns. For example, northeastern shoes were made in uniform sizes and sent in barrels all over the country. Like tailoring, shoemaking was divided into skilled operations and time-consuming unskilled tasks. The skilled and highly paid work of cutting and shaping the uppers was performed by men; the drudgery of sewing the pieces together went to low-paid women. In the shops of Lynn, Massachusetts, in the shoe-makers' boarding houses in Rochester and other new manufacturing cities of the interior, and in the cellars and garrets of New York City, skilled shoemakers performed the most difficult work for taskmasters who passed the work along to subcontractors who controlled poorly paid, unskilled workers. Skilled crafts-men could earn as much as $2 a day making custom boots and shoes. Men shaping uppers in boarding houses earned a little more than half of that; women binders could work a full week and earn as little as 50 cents. In this as in other trades, wage rates and gendered tasks reflected the old family division of labor, which was based on the assumption that female workers lived with an income-earning husband or father. In fact, increasing numbers of them were young women living alone or older women who had been widowed, divorced, or abandoned—often with small children.

In their offices, counting rooms, and shops, members of the new middle class entertained notions of gentility based on the distinction between manual and nonmanual work. Lowly clerks and wealthy merchants prided themselves on the fact that they worked with their heads and not their hands. They fancied that it was their entrepreneurial and managerial skills that were making the market revolution happen, whereas manual workers simply performed tasks thought up by the middle class. The old distinction between proprietorship and dependence—a distinction that had placed master craftsmen and inde-pendent tradesmen, along with farm-owning yeomen, among the respectable "middling sort"—disappeared. The men and women of an emerging working class struggled to create dignity and a sense of public worth in a society that hid them from view and defined them as "hands."

Conclusion

In 1830 the original northern states and the new states north of the Ohio River were the democratic capitalist societies that they have been ever since. The Northeast—New York City in particular—had sloughed off its old colonial sta-tus and was moving from the periphery to become part of the industrial and financial core of the world market economy. Other countries have made that transition: England was first, Japan was the most recent. Both of those coun-tries, however, de-emphasized agriculture, drew their populations into cities, and relied on the export of manufactured goods as their principal source of in-come. The American North, on the other hand, built factories and commercial farms at the same time and as parts of the same process. The market for Amer-ican manufactures was in the American countryside. (Industrial exports from the United States were insignificant until the end of the nineteenth century.)

The principal market for American food was in American towns and cities— and even on farms whose proprietors were too busy with staple crops to grow the old array of food. The result was a massive commercialization of the Northwestern, mid-Atlantic, and New England states and the beginnings of their integration into a unified northern capitalist democracy.

Source: *An Overseer Doing His Duty, Near Fredericksburg, Virginia,* 1798, by Benjamin Henry Latrobe. The Maryland Historical Society, Baltimore, Maryland.

CHAPTER 4

Cotton and Slaves: The South

THROUGHOUT THE EIGHTEENTH CENTURY, THE SOUTHERN plantation colonies had been Britain's most valuable mainland possessions. In 1790 the great planters remained among the richest and most powerful men in the new republic, although world markets for southern tobacco and rice were in a long-term decline. Their position improved in the 1790s, when international markets and technological innovation encouraged them to grow short-staple cotton. Cotton became the great southern cash crop, and the planters spread cotton culture across an expanding deep south. Northern ships carried mountains of cotton to Great Britain and returned with consumer goods, and the planters made a lot of money and bought a lot of nice things. Other southerners, however, were not as fortunate. Enslaved workers experienced longer hours and tighter discipline than in the past, they lost their families and friends to a burgeoning interstate slave trade, and they watched their masters' commitment to slavery harden into an unmovable political axiom. In addition, most white farmers were pushed to the edges of the cotton economy. They continued to practice the old-style mixed agriculture and to trade relatively little beyond their neighborhoods. In the North, country people became the great consumer market that drove regional economic development. In the South, slaves and most whites bought little, and what they bought was manufactured outside of the region.

The South experienced stupendous economic growth in the first third of the nineteenth century. But most southern investment and entrepreneurial talent went into producing cotton for export, an activity that produced wealth for the planters but strengthened the South's neocolonial dependence on Great Britain and, increasingly, on the northeastern United States. In addition, it gave the South a labor system, a leadership class, and an economic and political culture that set the region dangerously at variance with the burgeoning capitalist democracy of the North.

OLD FARMS: THE SOUTHEAST

The Chesapeake, 1790–1815

In 1790 the future of plantation slavery in the Chesapeake (the states of Virginia, Maryland, and Delaware, where the institution first took root in North America) was uncertain. The market for tobacco, their principal crop, had been precarious since before the Revolution, and it continued to decline after 1790. Tobacco also depleted the soil, and by the late eighteenth century tidewater farms and plantations were giving out.

With tobacco profits falling, many Chesapeake planters were switching to wheat, corn, and livestock. They did it on a large scale: in many parts of the region the old tobacco lands gave way to grain fields and pastureland, and by 1830 Richmond rivaled Rochester, New York, as the nation's leading flour milling center. It was a sensible move, but it left the Chesapeake with a huge investment in slaves who were less and less necessary. Grazing animals and raising wheat required less labor than tobacco. Enslaved workers planted individual tobacco plants and pruned and weeded them and picked worms off of them by hand. At harvest time they picked the leaves one at a time, then hung them to cure, packed them, and shipped them off to market. In sharp contrast, grain and livestock took care of themselves through most of the year. Planters with large numbers of slaves had to think up new uses for them. Some divided their land into small plots and rented both the plots and their slaves to white tenant farmers. Others, particularly in Maryland, recruited tenants from the growing ranks of free blacks. Still others hired out their slaves as artisans and urban laborers.

The increasing diversification of the Chesapeake economy involved assigning new chores to slave women and men. Wheat cultivation, for example, meant a switch from the hoes used for tobacco to the plow and grain cradle— both of which called for the upper-body strength of adult men. The grain economy also required carts, wagons, mills, and good roads, and thus created a need for greater numbers of slave artisans—nearly all of whom were men. Many of these were hired out to urban employers, and they lived as a semifree caste in cities and towns. In the new economy of the Chesapeake, male slaves did the plowing, mowing, sowing, ditching, and carting and performed most of the tasks requiring artisanal skills. All of this work demanded high levels of training and could be performed by someone working either by himself or in a small group with little need for supervision.

Slave women were left with the lesser tasks. Contrary to legend, few slave women in the Chesapeake worked as domestic servants in the planter's houses. A few of them were assigned to such chores as cloth manufacture, sewing, candle molding, and the preparation of salt meat. But most female slaves still did farm work—hoeing, weeding, spreading manure, cleaning stables—that was monotonous, called for little skill, and was closely supervised. This new division of labor was clearly evident during the wheat harvest. On George Washington's farm, for example, male slaves, often working beside temporary white laborers, moved in a broad line as they mowed the grain. Following them came a gang of children and women bent over and moving along on their hands and knees as they bound wheat into shocks. Thomas Jefferson, who had been shocked to see French women working in the fields, abandoned his concern for female delicacy when his own slaves were involved. At the grain harvest he instructed his overseers to organize "gangs of half men and half women."

Neither new crops nor new employments, however, erased the growing fact that Chesapeake proprietors needed less slave labor than they had in the past—or the parallel fact that their slaves reproduced at a higher rate than almost any other Americans. Nothing, it seemed, could employ the great mass of enslaved people or repay the planters' huge investment in slave labor. In this situation some Chesapeake planters (who had, after all, fought a revolution in the name of natural rights) began to manumit their slaves. The farmers of Maryland and Delaware in particular set their slaves free; by 1810, 76 percent of Delaware blacks and 23 percent of Maryland blacks were free. (In 1790 these figures had stood at 31 percent and 7 percent, respectively.) Virginia's economic and cultural commitment to the plantation was stronger, but even in the Old Dominion there was a strong movement to manumit slaves. George Washington stated that he wished "to liberate a certain species of property," and manumitted his slaves by will. (The manumissions were to take place at the death of his widow—thus, as one wag declared, surrounding Mrs. Washington with one hundred people who wanted her dead.) Robert Carter, reputedly the largest slaveholder in Virginia, also freed his slaves, as did many others. The free black population of Virginia stood at 3,000 in 1782, when the state passed a law permitting manumission. The number of free blacks rose to 12,766 in 1790, to 20,124 in 1800, and to 30,570 in 1810. These were impressive numbers, but the birthrate of Virginia slaves erased them. Between 1780 and 1810 the slave population of the state rose—despite the manumissions—from 250,000 to 400,000.

Virginia planters had strong reasons for holding on to their slaves. First, few could afford to free their slaves without compensation. Second, white Virginians feared the social consequences of black freedom. Thomas Jefferson, for instance, owned 175 slaves when he penned the phrase that "all men are created equal." He lived off their labor, sold them to pay his debts, gave them away as gifts, sold them away from their families as a punishment, and kept one of them as a mistress. Through it all he insisted that slavery was wrong. He could not imagine emancipation, however, without the colonization of freed slaves far from Virginia. A society of free blacks and whites, Jefferson insisted, would end in disaster: "Deep rooted prejudices entertained by the whites; ten thousand recollections, by the blacks, of the injuries they have sustained; new provocations; the real distinctions which nature has made . . . [will] produce convulsions which will probably never end but in the extermination of the one or the other race." Jefferson went on to a virulently racist argument for black inferiority and to the insistence that "When freed, [blacks are] to be removed beyond the reach of mixture." Near the end of an adult lifetime of condemning slavery but doing nothing to end it, Jefferson cried out that white Virginians held "a wolf by the ears": they could not hold on to slavery forever, and they could never let it go.

The Lowcountry, 1790–1820

The other region that had been a center of plantation slavery during the eighteenth century—lowcountry South Carolina and Georgia—made a massive recommitment to slave labor in the years after the Revolution. Here the principal crop was rice, which, along with other American foodstuffs, enjoyed a rise in international demand during the European wars between 1793 and 1815. The lowcountry planters, however, faced increasing competition from rice farmers in India, Java, Burma, and Europe itself. The rice coast—one of the great sources of American wealth in the eighteenth century—remained profitable, but it was losing relative position to faster-growing regions. The planters of the lowcountry, like those in Virginia, remained wealthy men. But their long-term future was uncertain.

Thousands of slaves in this region had either run away or been carried off by the British in the Revolution, and planters knew that the African slave trade was scheduled to end in 1808. They rushed to import as many African slaves as they could in the time remaining. Between 1788 and 1808, 250,00 enslaved people were brought directly from Africa to the United States—nearly all of them to Charleston and Savannah. That figure equaled the number of Africans who had been brought to North America during the whole colonial period.

In the plantation counties of coastal South Carolina and Georgia slaves made up 80 percent of the population, more than 90 percent in many parishes. Farms and slave labor forces were big, and rice cultivation demanded skilled, intensive labor—often performed by workers who stood knee-deep in water. The work and the hot, sticky climate encouraged deadly summer diseases and kept white owners and overseers out of the fields. Many of the wealthiest planters built homes in Charleston and Savannah and hired managers who organized enslaved workers according to the so-called "task system." Each morning the owner or manager assigned a specific task to each slave; when the task was done, the rest of the day belonged to the slave. Slaves who did not finish their task were punished, and when too many slaves finished early the owners assigned heavier tasks. In the eighteenth century, each slave had been expected to tend three to four acres of rice each day. In the early nineteenth, with the growth of the rice market, the assignment was raised to five acres.

The task system encouraged slaves to work hard without supervision, and slaves turned the system to their own uses. Often several slaves would work together until all their tasks were completed, and strong young slaves would sometimes help older and weaker slaves after they had finished their own tasks. Once the day's work was done, the slaves would share their hard-earned leisure out of sight of the owner. A Jamaican visitor remarked that South Carolina and Georgia planters were "very particular in employing a negro, without his consent, after his task is finished, and agreeing with him for the payment which he is to receive."

Slaves under the task system won the right to cultivate land as "private fields"—not the little garden plots common in the Chesapeake but farms of up to five acres on which they grew produce and raised livestock for market. There was a lively trade in slave-produced goods, and eventually slaves in the low country not only produced and exchanged property but passed it on to their children. The owners tolerated such activity because slaves on the task system worked hard, required minimal supervision, produced much of their own subsistence, and made money for their owners. The rice and cotton planters in South Carolina and Georgia were among the richest men in the United States.

NEW FARMS: THE COTTON BELT

While the old centers of slavery and southern power stagnated or declined, planters discovered a new and promising cash crop. British textile factories had been buying raw cotton since the mid-eighteenth century, and southern planters knew they could sell all the cotton they could grow. But long-staple cotton, the only variety that could be profitably grown, was a delicate plant that thrived only on the Sea Islands off Georgia and South Carolina. The short-staple variety was hardier, but its sticky seeds had to be removed by hand before the cotton could be milled. It took a full day for an adult slave to clean a single pound of short-staple cotton—an expenditure of labor that took the profit out of cotton. In 1790 the United States produced only 3,000 bales of cotton, nearly all of it on the long-staple plantations of the Sea Islands.

In 1793 Eli Whitney, a Connecticut Yankee who had come south to work as a tutor, set his mind to the problem of cleaning short-staple cotton. Within a few days he had made a model of a cotton "gin" (a southern contraction of "engine") that combed the seeds from the fiber with metal pins fitted into rollers. Working with Whitney's machine, a slave could clean fifty pounds of short-staple cotton in a day. Within a very few years, cotton became the great southern cash crop, and slavery and plantation agriculture had a new lease on life.

Beginning in the late 1790s planters and their slaves moved into upland South Carolina and Georgia, transforming a sparsely settled farm country into the first great short-staple cotton region. With the end of war in 1815, the Cotton Belt expanded dramatically. The defeat of native peoples and the expropriation of their land in the Southwest, the resumption of international trade, the revival of textile production in Britain and on the continent, and the emergence of factory production in the northeastern United States encouraged planters to extend the cotton lands of South Carolina and Georgia into a belt that stretched out to the Mississippi River. It happened very quickly: by 1834 the new southwestern states of Alabama, Mississippi, and Louisiana grew more than half of a vastly increased U.S. cotton crop. In 1810 the South produced 178,000 bales of ginned cotton—more than 59 times the 3,000 bales it had produced in 1790. With the opening of southwestern cotton lands, production jumped to 334,000 bales in 1820, and to 1,350,000 bales in 1840. In these years cotton made up from one-half to two-thirds of the value of all U.S. exports—a proportion that held steady until the Civil War. The South produced three-fourths of the world supply of cotton—a commodity that, more than any other, was the raw material of industrialization in Britain and Europe and, increasingly, in the northeastern United States. Cotton, in short, was a very big business.

Plantation masters—both the old southeastern nabobs and the cotton planters of newer regions—were the acknowledged economic, social, cultural, and political elite of the South. Their authority rested on economic power and their connections—often family relationships—with each other. But their power was dressed up in gentility and an aura of mastery—a visible "right to rule" that few others, North or South, could match. That power and authority was tied intimately to the ownership of slaves. When assessing a planter's standing, contemporaries seldom added up the acreage he controlled or the money that made up his family's fortune. Instead, they counted slaves. In the most common calculation, the ownership of 20 slaves made a man a gentleman-planter.

It was a good enough measure, for the planter class did indeed make itself out of slaves. Most obviously, it was the labor of enslaved persons that bought the carpets, chandeliers, fine clothes, English chivalric novels, and race horses with which planters displayed their social mastery. In the most obvious affiliation of power with slavery, the wealthiest planters surrounded themselves with black servants dressed in livery.

Southern ladies and gentlemen marked themselves off from others most clearly by the fact that they did not work. That too was a result of owning slaves. An observer of one plantation mistress noted that "She has a faithful nurse (Negro) to whose care she abandons her babes entirely, only when she has a fancy to caress them does she see them. Eight children and cannot lay to their charge the loss of a single night's rest." In short, the ownership of a slave transformed a harried housewife into a lady. A southern publicist boasted that

"The non-slaveholder knows that as soon as his saving will admit, he can become a slaveholder, and thus relieve his wife from the necessities of the kitchen and the laundry and his children from the labors of the field." Southern farmers without slaves tended to sire very large families and keep their children in the fields. The women worked outdoors as well. Southerners who owned slaves had fewer children, sent them to school, and moved their wives indoors. The skin of farm women was weathered, cracked, and darkened by the sun; plantation mistresses were less exhausted, and their skin was smoother and literally whiter. "Laborers was respected," recalled a small farmer, "but the men that owned slaves did not work and did not have there children do any work." The opposite of gentility was the South Carolina farmer who, according to a neighbor, "used to work [his daughters] in the fields like Negroes." According to northern visitors, this association of labor with slavery encouraged laziness among southern whites and robbed work of the dignity it enjoyed in other parts of the country. Most southern white farmers would have disagreed. But the association of black labor, white leisure, and white gentility was central to the plantation regime. The South would not have been the South without it.

The cotton plantations, however, were not simply country estates. They were successful agricultural businesses that returned a rate of profit equal to northeastern factories, and they were operated in a more calculating and businesslike way than the old estates on the Chesapeake and in the low country. Most obviously, cotton planters exerted a more disciplined and direct control over their enslaved workers. Masters in the old settlements had encouraged slaves to create their own livelihoods—by hiring them out, giving them time and land with which to grow their own food, and working them by the task system or under slave overseers—all of which reduced the costs of supervising and providing for slaves while allowing them pockets of autonomy within slavery.

On the cotton frontier, good land and slave labor were too valuable to be worked in casual ways, and new farms had to become profitable ventures in a short time. Enslaved men and women who had grown up with the relatively loose work routines of the lowcountry and the Chesapeake now performed the backbreaking labor of turning forests into farms. (They had to "whittle a plantation right out of the woods," recalled one slave.) Slaves worked in gangs, usually under white owners or overseers. Clearing trees, rolling logs, pulling stumps, clearing and burning brush, and building cabins, fences, and outbuildings was hard labor. The planters preferred crews of young men for these tasks, but such slaves were expensive, and everyone was put to work. A teenaged boy sold from the Chesapeake to Mississippi saw women clearing brush from new land and remarked (perhaps mistakenly) that "such work was not done by women slaves in Virginia." Another slave recalled that her mother labored with a two-horse plow "when she warn't cleanin' new ground or diggin' ditches." The labor of making new farms lasted from dawn to dusk, and enslaved men and women labored under the eyes of owners who knew that they must turn the forest into cash-producing farms or go broke.

Once established, the plantations of the Cotton Belt were among the most intensely commercialized farms in the world. Many of them grew nothing but cotton, buying food from their neighbors or from merchants who sold cornmeal and salt pork in bulk. Others grew supplementary crops and produced their own food. But nearly all of the plantation owners, from the proudest grandee to the ambitious farmer with a few slaves, organized labor in ways that maximized production and reinforced the dominance of the white men who owned the farms.

Slaves from the Chesapeake and the rice coast experienced cotton cultivation as a difficult step down. Cotton required a long growing season and a lot of attention, but it did not demand much skill. Early in the spring the land was cleared and plowed, and gangs of slaves walked the furrows dropping seeds. During the growing season black laborers constantly thinned the plants and cleared the fields of weeds—"chopping" the fields with hoes in the hot, humid Deep South summer. The cotton ripened unevenly. In a harvest season that could last long past Christmas, pickers swept through the fields selecting only the ripe bolls, then repeated the task over and over until the full crop was harvested. Cotton, in short, required constant unskilled labor. Slaves in the diversifying Chesapeake had made barrels and crates, boats, wagons, barns and storage sheds; slaves on the rice coast farther south had built complex systems of dikes and levees and had mastered the science of moving and controlling large amounts of water. In the Cotton Belt they gave up those skills and went to work with axes, hoes, and their hands.

The work was relentless. Planters in the East had found it economical to allow slaves to work at varied tasks, at irregular times, or under the tasking system. They provided slaves with only part of their food (often cornmeal and nothing else), then provided time and land with which slaves grew their own vegetables, chickens, and pigs. Planters on the cotton frontier did away with all that. Only a few Cotton Belt planters retained the task system, and these were looked upon as eccentrics by their neighbors, who worked their slaves in gangs from dawn to dusk six days a week. Cotton land was too valuable to permit slave gardens. It made more sense to keep the slaves constantly at cotton cultivation and supply them with all their food. It was a more efficient and productive way of growing cotton. It was also a way of reducing the slaves' customary privileges within slavery, and of enforcing the master's role as the giver and taker of all things. Even slaves who grew their own food did so in white-supervised fields and not in family plots. An Alabama planter put it bluntly: "Allow it once to be understood by a Negro that he is to provide for himself, and you that moment give him an undeniable claim on you for a portion of his time to make this provision; and should you from necessity, or any other cause, encroach upon his time, disappointment and discontent are seriously felt." To create "a perfect dependence," this master insisted that "my Negroes have no time whatever." The Louisiana planter Bennet H. Barrow explained that the master must make the slave "as comfortable at home as possible, affording him what is essentially necessary for his happiness—you must provide for him your self and by that means creat[e] in him a habit of perfect dependence on you."

On the whole, the exploitation of slave labor after 1820 became both more rigorous and more humane. Planters imposed a new and more total control over their slaves, but they clothed it within a larger attempt to make North American slavery into a system that was both paternalistic and humane—and, of course, to make themselves into gentlemen. Food and clothing seems to have improved, and individual cabins for slave families became standard. State laws often forbade the more brutal forms of discipline, and they uniformly demanded that slaves be given Sunday off. Material standards seem to have risen. One rough indicator is physical height. On the eve of the Civil War, southern slaves averaged about an inch shorter than northern whites. But they were fully three inches taller than newly imported Africans, two inches taller than slaves on the Caribbean island of Trinidad, and an inch taller than British Marines. Slaves suffered greater infant mortality than whites, but those who survived infancy lived out "normal" life spans. Brazil, Cuba, and other slave societies had to import Africans to make up for the deaths of slaves, but the slave population of the southern states increased threefold—from 657,000 to 1,981,000—between 1790 and 1830. With the import of new Africans banned after 1808 (and with runaways outnumbering new Africans who were smuggled into the country), the increase was due entirely to the fact that—alone among slave societies of the Western Hemisphere—the American slave population was healthy enough to reproduce itself.

Humane treatment, we have seen, came at a price. At the same time that they granted slaves protection from the worst kinds of brutality, Cotton Belt states enacted slave codes that defined slaves as persons without rights. The Louisiana code of 1824, for instance, stated that "[The slave] is incapable of making any kind of contract . . . They can transmit nothing by succession . . . The slave is incapable of exercising any public office, or private trust . . . He cannot be a party in any civil action. . . . Slaves cannot marry without the consent of their masters, and their marriages do not produce any of the civil effects which result from such contract." It was an exact negative image of the rights enjoyed by the white men who owned the plantations, controlled the slaves, and wrote the laws.

THE SOUTHERN YEOMANRY

Some southern boosters advertised cotton as a "democratic" crop that could be cultivated at a profit by almost any southern farmer. But that is not how it worked out. Cotton, like other plantation crops, rewarded economies of scale: planters with big farms and many slaves operated more efficiently and more profitably than farmers with fewer resources. The wealthier planter families bought up good cotton land with ready access to markets and turned it into large plantations. They also bought up the majority of slaves. Only 30 to 35 percent of southern white families owned at least one slave in 1830, and that percentage dropped as time passed. On the eve of the Civil War, only one white family in four would own a slave. Among the minority of southerners who were slaveowners, half owned fewer than five. Fewer than 5 percent of white southerners owned 20 or more slaves—the roughly agreed-upon number that separated planters from farmers. Cotton, it turned out, was not democratic: among southern whites it produced not only an unequal distribution of wealth but a dual economy: plantations at the commercial center and a marginally commercial yeomanry on the fringes.

As land prices and local taxes rose in the plantation counties, many of the poorer whites moved out. Large numbers of them, we have seen, moved into non-slave territory north of the Ohio River. Most, however, stayed in the South—away from the plantations in neighborhoods with few slaves and limited commercial activities: the eastern slopes of the Appalachians from the Chesapeake through Georgia, the western slopes of the mountains in Kentucky and Tennessee, the pine-covered hill country of northern Mississippi and Alabama, and in swampy, hilly, heavily wooded lands throughout the southern states. Within the lowland plantation counties, large numbers of slaveless farmers remained on forested, poor, and isolated pockets of land. All of these areas were unsuitable for plantation crops. Here the farmers built a yeoman society that retained many of the characteristics of the eighteenth-century countryside, North and South. But while northern farmers commercialized in the nineteenth century, their southern cousins continued in a household- and neighborhood-centered agriculture until the Civil War and beyond.

Indeed many southern farmers stayed outside the market almost entirely. The mountaineers of the southern Appalachians sent a trickle of livestock and timber out of their neighborhoods, but the mountains remained largely outside the market until the coming of big-business coal mines in the late nineteenth century. Moreover, farmers in large parts of the upcountry South preferred raising livestock to growing cotton or tobacco. They planted cornfields and let their pigs run loose in the woods and on unfenced private land. In late summer and fall they rounded up the animals and sold them to drovers who herded them cross-country and sold them to flatland merchants and planters. Thus these hill-country yeomen lived off a market with which they had little firsthand experience. It was a way of life that sustained some of the most fiercely independent neighborhoods in the country.

A larger group of southern yeomen practiced mixed farming for household subsistence and neighborhood exchange, with the surplus sent to market. Most of them owned their own land. Indeed the settlement of new lands in the old backcountry and the southwestern states reversed the eighteenth-century drift toward white tenancy. Few of these farmers kept slaves. In the counties of upland Georgia, for instance, between seven in ten and nine in ten households were without slaves. These farmers practiced a "subsistence plus" agriculture that was complicated by the nature of southern cash crops. Northern yeomen before 1815 had grown grain and livestock with which they fed their families and traded with neighbors. Whatever was left over they sent to market. But cotton, like tobacco and other southern cash crops, was not a food. It could be turned into clothing and often was: farm women in the South spun and wove small cotton crops into clothes for their families. (This at a time when cards, spinning wheels, and looms were disappearing from northern farmhouses.) Most middling and poor southern farmers played it safe: they put their improved land into corn and sweet potatoes and set pigs and cattle loose to browse the remaining land. The more substantial and ambitious of them cultivated a few acres of cotton. They grew more cotton as transportation made markets more accessible, but few southern yeomen became wholly dependent on the market. With the income from a few bales of cotton they could pay their debts and taxes and buy coffee, tea, sugar, tobacco, cloth, and shoes. But they continued to enter and leave the market at will and to retain the ability to subsist within their neighborhoods. In the yeoman neighborhoods of the southern states, the economic and social practices of the eighteenth century were alive and well.

The way of life in most southern farm neighborhoods discouraged businesslike farming and individual ambition. Because few farms were self-sufficient, farmers routinely traded labor and goods with each other. In the plantation counties, such cooperation tended to reinforce the power of planters who put some of their resources at the disposal of their poorer neighbors. In the upcountry, cooperation reinforced neighborliness. As one upland Georgian remarked, "Borrowing . . . was neighboring." Debts contracted within the network of kin and neighbors were generally paid in kind or in labor, and creditors often allowed their neighbors' debts to go unpaid for years.

Among southern neighborly restraints on entrepreneurialism, none was more distinctive than the region's attitude toward fences. Northerners never tired of comparing their neatly fenced farms with the dilapidated or absent fences of the South. In the capitalist North, well-maintained fences were a sign of ambitious, hardworking farmers. The poor fences of the South, they said, were a sign of laziness. Actually, the scarcity of fences in most southern neighborhoods was the result of local custom and state law. Georgia, for instance, required farmers to fence their planted fields but not the rest of their land. In country neighborhoods where families fished and hunted for food, and where livestock roamed freely, fences conflicted with a local economy that required neighborhood use of privately owned land. In this sense, the northerners were right: the lack of fences in the South reflected neighborhood constraints on the private use of private property, and thus on individual acquisitiveness and ambition. Such constraints, however, were necessary to the subsistence of families and neighborhoods as they were organized in the upland South.

Southern farmers marketed their cotton and food surpluses at country stores, and again the patterns of the eighteenth and early nineteenth centuries persisted. Northern stores, particularly in the more commercializing regions, were stocking their shelves with a wider and wider variety of imported and domestic goods to serve farm families that no longer produced for themselves and had money in their pockets. Southern yeomen, on the other hand, bought very little. A relatively prosperous backwoods farmer in South Carolina recalled that "My farm gave me and my whole family a good living on the produce of it, and left me, one year after another, one hundred and fifty silver dollars, *for I never spent more than ten dollars a year,* which was for salt, nails and the like. Nothing to wear, eat or drink was purchased, as my farm provided all." Families such as these continued to live without carpets or curtains, to eat homegrown food from wooden or pewter plates, and to wear everyday cloth spun and woven by the women of the family—though many who could afford it wore clothing fashioned from machine-made cloth on Sunday. And like the rest of their transactions, yeomen seldom bought items or settled transactions in cash. The store of Leach Carrigan and Samuel Carrigan in low-country South Carolina, for instance, traded 85 percent of its merchandise for cotton. Whereas the northern countryside and the lowland plantation districts functioned as businesses, the old barter economy—and the forms of family independence and neighborly cooperation on which it rested—persisted in the southern upcountry.

Unlike the plantations, the farm neighborhoods of the South were places in which white people worked. Most farmers relied solely on family labor. They sired many children and put them to work at an early age. Farm wives often labored in the fields, particularly at peak times. Even those who were spared from field work took up heavy burdens. A southern yeoman remembered that his mother worked "in the house sutch as cooking carding spinning and weaving and washing. Thare [were] 14 in the family," and "she did not have any servant to help her." George Washington Lewis, who grew up on his father's southern farm, recalled a boyhood filled with hard labor. He "chopped, plowed, hoed, carded, reaped, mowed and bound sheaves, in fact all kinds of work necessary on a farm and lots of it. Split rails, built fences, log roled and danced with the girls at quiltings." We may be happy to know that this boy found time for fun, but we must note—as northern critics did not—that he spent most of his waking hours at hard physical labor.

SLAVES

The Slave Trade and the Slaves

The slow decline of the seaboard South and the expansion of the cotton frontier fostered a huge interstate trade in slaves. Slaves in the Chesapeake had lived for generations in the same neighborhoods—old communities filled with kinfolk, ancestral graveyards, family gardens, and familiarity with each other and with local whites out of which they had made a complex and distinctively African American way of life within the boundaries of slavery. Slaves along the South Carolina–Georgia rice coast, laboring in large, isolated groups under minimal white supervision, had made their own African American ways. In the first thirty years of the nineteenth century hundreds of thousands of these people were torn from their communities and sold on to the cotton frontier. It began a period of cultural destruction and reconstruction equaled only by the process of enslavement itself.

The international slave trade ended in 1808, but even before that date the principal source of slaves for the emerging Cotton Belt was the old seaboard states. As early as the 1790s, the Chesapeake states of Virginia, Delaware, and Maryland were net exporters of slaves. Those states sent 40,000 to 50,000 thousand slaves south and west in that decade. The number rose to 120,000 in the 1810s. The slave families and slave communities of the Chesapeake lost one in twelve of their members in the 1790s, one in ten between 1800 and 1810, and one in five between 1810 and 1820. In the 1820s South Carolina and Kentucky joined the slave exporting states (this despite the fact that South Carolina sent many thousands out of the lowcountry and into its new upcountry Cotton Belt), and 150,000 slaves left their homes and crossed state lines. The trade in slaves reordered the human geography of the South. In 1790 planters in Virginia and Maryland had owned 56 percent of all American slaves; by 1860 they owned only 15 percent.

Some enslaved migrants—estimates run as high as 30 percent—left their old neighborhoods in the company of masters (or masters' sons) and familiar fellow slaves. These made new plantations and new lives in the Southwest surrounded by some of the people they had known at home. But most were sold and resold as individuals in an organized interstate slave market. Soon after the Revolution men known as "Georgia Traders" appeared in the Upper South, buying slaves on speculation and selling them farther south. By 1820 the slave trade had become an organized business with sophisticated financing, with accurate knowledge of slave prices in various southern markets, with a well-traveled shipping route between Norfolk and New Orleans, and with systems of slave pens and safe houses along the roads of the interior. The domestic slave trade was the biggest and most "modern" business in the South—with the single exception of the plantation itself. The centrality of that trade advertised the nature of southern economic development: while northerners exchanged wheat, upholstered furniture, books, and shoes with each other, Southerners exchanged slaves.

Most slaves moved into the Cotton Belt with other slaves who were strangers and under the temporary ownership of traders who knew them only as merchandise. Those who were transported by ship experienced some of the horrors of the old Middle Passage from Africa—cramped quarters, minimal food, discipline at the hands of nervous white crewmen, and the odd murder or casual rape. Those who walked from the old plantations to the Southwest had their own share of terrors. The journey could take as long as seven weeks, and traders organized it with military precision. An old slave remembered the order of march: "them speculators would put the chillens in a wagon usually pulled by oxen and the older folks was chained or tied together sos dey could not run off." The slave Charles Ball remembered the same thing in poignant detail: he went south in an unwilling parade of about fifty, in which the women

> were tied together with a rope, about the size of a bed cord, which was tied like a halter round the neck of each; but the men . . . were very differently caparisoned. A strong iron collar was closely fitted by means of a padlock round each of our necks. A chain of iron about a hundred feet long was passed through the hasp of each padlock, except at the two ends, where the hasps of the padlocks passed through a link of the chain. In addition to this, we were handcuffed in pairs. . . .
>
> The poor man to whom I was ironed, wept like an infant when the blacksmith, with his heavy hammer, fastened the ends of the bolts that kept the staples from slipping from our arms.

A white observer came upon a line of slaves on the road and pronounced it "a procession of men, women, and children resembling that of a funeral." Traders and slaves camped along the roads or spent nights crammed into public houses and slave pens. Beatings, rapes, and other abuses along the road entered black folk memory and stayed there. One often repeated (and apparently true) story told of a small boy taken from his mother's arms and left with a tavern keeper to pay a bar bill.

The Slave Trade and the Slave Family

The slave trade and the movement into the Cotton Belt hurt the slave communities of the eastern states and hampered the making of new ones in the West. Slaves would repair their personal and cultural lives within slavery. But before 1830 there was far more destruction than renewal. We can view that intimately by looking into the most vital of slave institutions: the slave family.

In law, in the census, and in the minds of planters, slaves were members of a plantation household over which the owner exercised absolute authority not only as owner but also as paternal protector and lawgiver. Yet both slaveholders and slaves knew that slaves could not be treated like farm animals or little children. Wise slaveholders learned that the success of a plantation depended less on terror and draconian discipline (though whippings—and worse—were common) than on the accommodations by which slaves traded labor and obedience for some measure of privilege and autonomy within the bonds of slavery. After achieving privileges, the slaves called them their own: holidays, garden plots, friendships and social gatherings both on and off the plantation, hunting and fishing rights, the right to trade slave-made goods, and—most vitally—the right to live in families of their own. Together, these privileges provided some of the ground on which slaves in the old plantation states had made their own lives within slavery. The domestic slave trade and the movement onto the cotton frontier cut that ground from beneath their feet. Slaves learned painfully that they were not members of families or communities— either the masters' or their own. They were property, and they could be bought and sold.

The most precious privilege on Chesapeake plantations was the right to make and maintain families. As early as the Revolutionary era, most Chesapeake slaves lived in units consisting of mother, father, and small children. On Charles Carroll's Maryland farms in 1773, for example, 325 of the 400 slaves lived in such families. At Thomas Jefferson's Monticello, most slave marriages were for life, and small children almost always lived with both parents. The most common exceptions to this practice were fathers who had married away from their own plantations and who visited "broad wives" and children during their off hours. Owners encouraged stable marriages because they made farms more peaceful and productive and because they flattered the owners' own religious and paternalistic sensibilities. For their part, slaves demanded families as part of the price of their labor.

Yet slave families had always been vulnerable. Many slaveholders assumed that they had the right to coerce sex from female slaves. Some (including Thomas Jefferson) kept slaves as mistresses. The planters tended, however, to keep these liaisons within bounds. Although the slave community seldom punished sex before marriage, it took adultery seriously. Slaveholders knew that violations of married slave women could be enormously disruptive and strongly discouraged them. Slave sales also threatened marriages and family and community relations. But most sales before 1800 or so took place within neighborhoods; they changed and often damaged slave families without destroying them. The most serious threat was the death or bankruptcy of the slaveholders —events that led to the liquidation of estates and the division of property among heirs or creditors. Yet even these events, compared with what came later, tended to keep slaves in the same extended neighborhood.

That changed with the growth of the Cotton Belt and the interstate slave trade. Masters in the seaboard states claimed (often truthfully) that they tried to keep slave families together, and that they sold slaves to traders only out of dire necessity or as a means of getting rid of troublesome individuals. The latter category could be used as a threat. One slave remembered that "Slaves usually got scared when it became clear that Negro-Trader [John] White was in the community. The owners used White's name as a threat to scare the slaves when they had violated some rule." "If a man did anything out of the way," recalled another slave, "he was in more danger of being sold than being whipped." Thomas Jefferson, reputedly the kindest of masters, punished a troublesome slave by selling him in 1803, hoping that he would be sent into "so distant an exile . . . as to cut him off completely from ever being heard of [again]."

Chesapeake planters and slaves knew, however, that the slave trade was more than a means of settling debts or punishing rebellious individuals. It had become an important source of income. Myths of slave "breeding farms" in the Chesapeake are just that—myths. Slaves in the exporting states continued to live in families that produced and nurtured their own children. But the children could expect to be sold on to long-distance markets when they came of age. The systematic selling of teenaged and young adult slaves (those who commanded the highest prices on the market) became a standard way in which Chesapeake gentlemen maintained their status. John Randolph of Roanoke, one of the great planter-politicians of Virginia, routinely translated younger members of his "plantation family" into cash. In 1823 he traveled to New York to see the great match race between the northern horse Eclipse and the southern horse Sir Henry. In a moment of pride and exuberance he shouted from the grandstand that he would bet "a year's crop of negroes" on the southern champion.

Professional slave traders made no effort to hide their willingness to break slave families and communities. Neither did the southwestern planters who bought slaves from the older states. One pioneer planter insisted that "it is better to buy *none in families,* but *to select only choice, first rate, young hands from 14 to 25 years of age,* (buying no children or aged negroes)." Seaboard planters, trying to convince themselves and anyone who would listen that they were responsible paternalists, made a sharp division between the plantation "family" and the well-known horrors of the domestic slave trade, but the slaves knew better. A Virginia slave woman had this to say of the planter who had sold her daughters: "He was a mean dirty slave trader."

Beginning almost as soon as they were transplanted and continuing through the last days of slavery, Cotton Belt slaves began the old process of negotiation with their masters, and they began to rebuild lives within slavery. The masters set harsher working conditions and longer hours than slaves had known in their old homes. Slaves could not hope to reinstitute the task system, the family gardens and little farms, the varied tasks, or the uneven hours of labor that they had known on the coast. Yet despite masters' lack of encouragement, gardens—some of them large and profitable—quickly appeared in the new slave quarters. And enslaved workers found that they could hold masters to agreed-upon standards of time and work. Masters who demanded longer than customary hours or labor on Sunday found the work going slower. In the 1840s a Mississippi planter noted that slaves had adapted to the long hours, close supervision, and pace of work under the gang system but would perform the new customary workload and nothing more. "All of them know what their duty is upon a plantation, and that they are generally willing to do, and nothing more." When asked to work harder or longer "they will not submit to it, but become turbulent and impatient of control, and all the whips in Christendom cannot drive them to perform more than they think they ought to do, or have been in the long habit of doing . . . " One enslaved worker remembered that "We could talk and do anything we wanted to, ust so we picked the cotton; we used to have lots of fun."

They soon had families as well. Although cotton planters preferred young men for the labor of clearing the land, they soon began importing nearly equal numbers of women, encouraging marriage, and providing cabins for slave families. Families made for greater peace and quiet on the plantations, and they were a good long-term investment in the production of new slaves. The slaves grasped the opportunity. As early as the 1820s, 51 percent of rural Louisiana slaves lived in families composed of two parents and their children. That figure was much smaller than it had been on the old farms, but in view of what the slaves had been through it was surprisingly large.

Slaveholders who encouraged slave marriages—perhaps even solemnizing them with a religious ceremony—knew that marriage implied a form of self-ownership that conflicted with the slaves' status as property. Some conducted ceremonies in which couples "married" by jumping over a broomstick; others had the preacher omit the phrases "let no man put asunder" and "till death do you part" from the ceremony. Slaves knew that such ceremonies had no legal force. A Virginia slave remarked, "We slaves knowed that them words wasn't bindin'. Don't mean nothin' lessen you say, 'What God has jined, caint no man pull asunder.' But dey never would say dat. Jus' say 'Now you married.'" A black South Carolina preacher routinely ended the ceremony with "Till death or buckra [whites] part you."

Slaves built their sense of family and kinship around such uncertainties. Because separation from father or mother was common, children spread their affection among their adult relatives, treating grandparents, aunts, and uncles almost as though they were parents. In fact, slaves often referred to all their adult relatives as "parents." They also called nonrelatives "brother," "sister," "aunt," and "uncle," thus extending a sense of kinship to the slave community at large. Slaves chose as surnames for themselves the names of former owners, Anglicized versions of African names, or names that simply sounded good. They rarely chose the name of their current owner, however. Families tended to use the same given names over and over, naming boys after their father or grandfather—perhaps to preserve the memory of fathers who might be taken away. They seldom named girls after their mother, however. Unlike Southern whites, slaves never married a first cousin—even though many members of their community were close relatives. The origins and functions of some of these customs are unknown. We know only that slaves practiced them consistently, often without the knowledge of the slaveholders.

Slave Religion

Until the mid-eighteenth century, neither enslaved Africans nor their masters showed much interest in christianizing the slaves. That changed with the rise of evangelical Christianity in the South. Blacks participated in the revivals of the southern Great Awakening, and the number of Christian slaves increased steadily in the second half of the eighteenth century. In the slave communities of the Upper South, as well as the burgeoning free and semifree urban black populations of both the North and South, the evangelical revivals of the late eighteenth and early nineteenth centuries appealed powerfully to African Americans who sensed that the bonds of slavery were loosening. By 1820 most blacks in the Chesapeake considered themselves Christians. They would take their religion with them when they were sold farther south.

Between 1780 and 1820 Chesapeake slaves embraced Christianity and began to turn it into a religion of their own. Slaves attended camp meetings, listened to itinerant preachers, and joined the Baptist and Methodist congregations of the southern revival. The revivalists, in turn, welcomed slaves and free blacks to their meetings and sometimes recruited them as preachers. Evangelical preaching, singing, and spiritual exercises were much more attractive than the cold, high-toned lectures of the Anglicans. So were the humility and suffering of evangelical whites, most of whom were poor men and outsiders. Finally, the slaves gloried in the evangelicals' assault on the slaveholders' culture and in the antislavery sentiments of many white evangelicals (see Chapter 5). The result was a huge increase in the number of African American Christians. Methodists, who counted converts more carefully than some others, claimed 20,000 black members in 1800—one in three American Methodists.

The integrated congregations, however, did not last. There were exceptions, but most congregations were in fact internally segregated, with blacks sitting in the back of the church or upstairs in the gallery, and with only whites serving in positions of authority. Blacks, with both positive and negative encouragement from whites, organized independent churches in Baltimore, Wilmington, Richmond, Norfolk, and the scattered villages that had risen to serve the Chesapeake's new mixed economy. Even Charleston boasted an independent Methodist conference made up of 4,000 slaves and free blacks in 1815. By 1820 roughly 700 independent black churches operated in the United States. There had been none at all 30 years earlier. And on the plantations, slaves met informally—sometimes with the masters' permission, sometimes without it—to preach and pray.

It is difficult to define either the extent or the emotional meaning of slave Christianity before 1830. We know that by that date most slaves in the Upper South were Christians and that they were turning evangelical Protestantism into an African American religion. We know also that thousands of these new Christians were sold into the cotton states. But the fullest religious accounts (the narratives of escaped slaves and the remembrances of former bondsmen and women in particular) center on slave belief and practice in the 1840s and 1850s. We can sketch slave Christianity as of 1830 only in outline.

Slaves understood and used the message of Christianity in different ways than did southern whites. The biblical notion that slavery could be punishment for sin, and the white southern notion that God intended blacks to be slaves, never took root among enslaved Christians. Hannah Scott, a slave in Arkansas, remarked on what she heard a white preacher say: "But all he say is 'bedience to de white folks, and we hears 'nough of dat without him telling us." One slave asked a white preacher, "Is us slaves gonna be free in heaven?" The preacher had no answer. As one maid boldly told her mistress, "God never made us to be slaves for white people."

Another way in which slave religion differed from what was preached to them by whites was in the practice of conjuring, folk magic, root medicine, and other occult knowledge—most of it passed down from West Africa. Such practices provided help in areas in which Christianity was useless. They could cure illnesses, make people fall in love, ensure a good day's fishing, or bring harm to one's enemies. Sometimes African magic was in competition with plantation Christianity. Just as often, however, slaves combined the two. For instance, slaves sometimes determined the guilt or innocence of a person accused of stealing by hanging a Bible by a thread, then watching the way it turned. The form was West African; the Bible was not. The slave root doctor George White boasted that he could "cure most anything," but added that "you got to talk wid God an' ask him to help out." "Maum Addie," a slave in coastal South Carolina, dealt with the malevolent African spirits called plat-eyes with a combination of African potions, the Christian God, and a stout stick: "So I totes mah powder en sulphur en I carries mah stick in mah han en puts mah truss in Gawd."

Although Christianity could not cure sick babies or identify thieves, it gave slaves something more important: a sense of themselves as a historical people with a role to play in God's cosmic drama. In slave Christianity, Moses the liberator (and not the slaveholders' Abraham) stood beside Jesus. Indeed the slaves' appropriation of the book of Exodus denied the smug assumption of the whites that they were God's chosen people who had escaped the bondage of despotic Europe to enter the promised land of America. To the slaves, America was Egypt, they were the chosen people, and the slaveholders were Pharaoh. Thomas Wentworth Higginson, a Boston abolitionist who went south during the Civil War to lead a Union regiment of freed South Carolina slaves, wrote that his men knew the Old Testament books of Moses and the New Testament book of Revelation. "All that lies between," he said, "even the life of Jesus, they hardly cared to read or to hear." He found their minds "a vast bewildered chaos of Jewish history and biography; and most of the events of the past, down to the period of the American Revolution, they instinctively attribute to Moses." The slaves' religious songs, which became known as spirituals, told of God's people, their travails, and their ultimate deliverance. In songs and sermons the figures of Jesus and Moses were often blurred, and it was not always clear whether deliverance—accompanied by divine retribution—would take place in this world or the next. But deliverance always meant an end to slavery, with the possibility that it might bring a reversal of relations between slaves and masters. "The idea of a revolution in the conditions of the whites and blacks," said the escaped slave Charles Ball, "is the corner-stone of the religion of the latter."

Religion and Revolt

Compared with slaves in Cuba, Jamaica, Brazil, and other New World plantation societies, North American slaves seldom went into organized, armed revolt. The environment of the United States was unfriendly to such events.
American plantations were relatively small and dispersed, and the southern
white population was large, vigilant, and very well armed. Whites also enjoyed—until the cataclysm of the Civil War—internal political stability. There
were thus few situations in which slaves could hope to win their freedom by violent means. Thousands of slaves demonstrated their hatred of the system by
running away. Others fought masters or overseers, sabotaged equipment and
animals, stole from planters, and found other ways to oppose slavery. But most
knew that open revolt was suicide.

Christianity convinced slaves that history was headed toward an apocalypse
that would result in divine justice and their own deliverance. It thus contained
the possibility of revolt. But slave preachers seldom indulged in prophecy and
almost never told their congregations to become actively engaged in God's divine plan, for they knew that open resistance was hopeless. Slave Christians believed that God hated slavery and would end it, but that their role was to have
faith in God, to take care of one another, to preserve their identity as a people,
and to await deliverance. Only occasionally did slaves take retribution and deliverance into their own hands, and each time they were armed with some mix
of republican equalitarianism and evangelical Christianity.

Masters who talked of liberty, natural rights, and equality before God sometimes worried that slaves might imagine that such language could apply to
themselves. The Age of Democratic Revolution took a huge step in that direction in 1789, when the French Revolution—fought in the name of "Liberty,
Equality, and Fraternity"—went beyond American notions of restored English
liberties and into the heady regions of universal natural rights. Among the first
repercussions outside of France was a revolution on the Caribbean island of
Hispaniola in the French colony of Santo Domingo. That island's half-million
slaves fought out a complicated political and military revolt that began with the
events in Paris in 1789 and resulted—after the defeats of Spanish, English, and
French armies—with the creation of the independent black republic of Haiti on
the western one-third of the island. Slave societies throughout the hemisphere
heard tales of terror from refugee French planters and stories of hope from the
slaves they brought with them (12,000 of these entered South Carolina and
Louisiana alone). In 1800 a conservative Virginia white man complained that
"Liberty and Equality has been infused into the minds of the negroes." A South
Carolina congressman agreed that "this newfangled French philosophy of
liberty and equality" was stirring up the slaves. Even Thomas Jefferson, who
applauded the spread of French republicanism, conceded that "the West Indies

appears to have given considerable impulse to the minds of the slaves . . . in the United States."

Slaves from the 1790s onward whispered of natural rights and imagined themselves as part of the Democratic Revolution. This covert republic of the slaves sometimes came into the open, most ominously in Richmond in 1800, where a slave blacksmith named Gabriel hatched a conspiracy to overthrow Virginia's slave regime. Gabriel had been hired out to Richmond employers for most of his adult life; he was shaped less by plantation slavery than by the democratic, loosely interracial underworld of urban artisans. In the late 1790s the repressive acts of the Federalist national government and the angry responses of the Jeffersonian opposition (see Chapter 1), along with the news from Haiti, drove the democratic sensibilities of that world to new heights. Gabriel's plans took shape within that heated ideological environment.

Gabriel, working with his brother and other hired-out slave artisans, planned his revolt with military precision. Working at religious meetings, barbecues, and the grog shops of Richmond, they recruited soldiers among slave artisans, adding plantation slaves only at the last moment. Gabriel planned to march an army of 1,000 men on Richmond in three columns. The outside columns would set diversionary fires in the warehouse district and prevent the militia from entering the town. The center would seize Capitol Square, including the treasury, the arsenal, and Governor James Monroe.

Although his army would be made up of slaves, and although his victory would end slavery in Virginia, Gabriel hoped to make a republican revolution, not a slave revolt. His chosen enemies were the Richmond "merchants" who had controlled his labor. Later, a coconspirator divulged the plan: The rebels would hold Governor James Monroe hostage and split the state treasury among themselves, and "if the white people agreed to their freedom they would then hoist a white flag, and [Gabriel] would dine and drink with the merchants of the city on the day when it would be agreed to." Gabriel expected what he called "the poor white people" and "the most redoubtable republicans" to join him. He in fact had the shadowy support of two Frenchmen, and rumors indicated that other whites were involved—though never at levels that matched the delusions of the conspirators. Gabriel planned to kill anyone who opposed him, but he would spare Quakers, Methodists, and Frenchmen, for they were "friendly to liberty." Unlike those of earlier slave insurgents, Gabriel's dreams did not center on violent retribution or a return to or reconstruction of West Africa. He was an American revolutionary, and he dreamed of a truly democratic republic for Virginia. His army would march into Richmond under the banner "Death or Liberty."

Gabriel and his coconspirators recruited at least 150 soldiers who agreed to gather near Richmond on August 30, 1800. The leaders expected to be joined by 500 to 600 more rebels as they marched upon the town. On the appointed day, however, it rained heavily. Rebels could not reach the meeting point, and amid white terror and black betrayals Gabriel and his henchmen were hunted down, tried, and sentenced to death. In all, the state hanged 27 supposed conspirators, while others were sold and transported out of Virginia. The condemned carried their radical republican dreams to their graves. A white Virginian marveled that the rebels on the gallows displayed a "sense of their [natural] rights, [and] a contempt of danger." When asked to explain the revolt, one condemned man replied in terms that could only have disturbed the white republicans of Virginia: "I have nothing more to offer than what General Washington would have had to offer, had he been taken by the British and put to trial by them. I have adventured my life in endeavoring to obtain the liberty of my countrymen, and am a willing sacrifice in their cause."

Denmark Vesey, a free black of Charleston, South Carolina, hatched the most ambitious conspiracy. Vesey was a leading member of an African Methodist congregation that had seceded from the white Methodists and been independent from 1817 to 1821. At its height, the church had 6,000 members, most of them slaves. Vesey and some of the other members read widely in political tracts, including the antislavery arguments in the Missouri debates (see Chapter 6) and in the Bible. They talked about their delivery out of Egypt, with all white men, women, and children being cut off. They identified Charleston as Jericho and planned its destruction in 1822. A few dozen Charleston blacks would take the state armory, then arm rural slaves who would rise up to help them. They would kill the whites, take control of the city, and then commandeer ships in the harbor and make their getaway—presumably to black-controlled Haiti. Word of the conspiracy spread secretly into the countryside, largely through the efforts of Gullah Jack, who was both a Methodist and an African conjurer. Jack recruited African-born slaves as soldiers, provided them with charms as protection against whites, and used his spiritual powers to terrify others into keeping silent.

In the end, the Vesey plot was betrayed by slaves. As one coerced confession followed another, white authorities hanged Vesey, Gullah Jack, and 34 other accused conspirators—22 of them in one day. But frightened whites knew that most of the conspirators (estimates ranged from 600 to 9,000) remained at large and unidentified.

In August 1831, in a revolt in Southampton County, Virginia, some 60 slaves shot and hacked to death 55 white men, women, and children. Their leader was Nat Turner, a Baptist lay preacher. Turner was neither a conjurer like Gullah Jack (indeed, he violently opposed plantation conjurers) nor a republican revolutionary like Denmark Vesey or the Richmond slave Gabriel. He was, he told his captors, a Christian prophet and an instrument of God's wrath. As a child, he had prayed and fasted often, and the spirit—the same spirit that had spoken to the prophets of the Bible—had spoken directly to him. When he was a young man, he had run away to escape a cruel overseer. But when God said that He had not chosen him merely to have him run away, Nat had returned. He justified his return by quoting one of the slaveowners' favorite verses of scripture: "He who knoweth his master's will and doeth it not, shall be beaten with many stripes." But Turner made it clear that his Master was God, not a slaveowner.

Around 1830, Turner received visions of the final battle in Revelation, recast as a war between white and black spirits. He saw Christ crucified against the night sky, and the next morning he saw Christ's blood in a cornfield. Convinced by a solar eclipse in February 1831 that the time had come, Turner began telling other slaves about his visions, recruited his force, and launched his bloody and hopeless revolt.

The revolts of Gabriel, Turner, and Vesey, along with scores of more limited conspiracies, deeply troubled southern whites. Slaveholders were committed to a paternalism that was increasingly tied to the South's attempt to make slavery both domestic and Christian. For their part, slaves recognized that they could receive decent treatment and pockets of autonomy in return for outward docility. Gabriel, Vesey, and Turner opened wide cracks in that mutual charade. During the Turner revolt, slaves whose masters had been murdered joined the rebels without a second thought. A plantation mistress who survived by hiding in a closet listened to the murders of her husband and children, then heard her house servants arguing over possession of her clothes. A Charleston grandee named Elias Horry, upon finding that his coachman was among the Vesey conspirators, asked him, "What were your intentions?" The formerly docile slave replied that he had intended "to kill you, rip open your belly, and throw your guts in your face."

THE PLANTATION AND SOUTHERN GROWTH

On the eve of the Civil War James H. Hammond, a slaveholding senator from South Carolina, asked, "What would happen if no cotton was furnished for three years. . . . England would topple headlong and carry the whole civilized world with her save the south. No, you dare not make war on cotton. No power on earth dares to make war on cotton. Cotton is king." Hammond was arguing, as Jefferson had argued in 1807, that farmers at the fringes of the world market economy could coerce the commercial-industrial center. He was wrong. The commitment to cotton and slavery had isolated the South politically. It had also deepened the South's dependence on the world's financial and industrial centers. The North underwent a qualitative market revolution that transformed the Northeast from a part of the old colonial periphery (the suppliers of food and raw materials) into a part of the core (the suppliers of manufactured goods and financing) of the world market economy. In contrast, southerners continued to export plantation staples in exchange for imported goods. In the process, the South worked itself deeper and deeper into dependence—now as much on the American Northeast as on the old colonial rulers in London.

The cotton plantation was, of course, productive and remunerative. The best estimates put the annual rate of return on the larger plantations at 10 percent—higher than factories, banks, and other more "modern" enterprises. But planters—both because land and slaves were the great sources of social esteem in the South and because the plantations paid off—tended to invest their profits in luxury goods and in more slaves and land. The result was a lack of diversification and an increasing concentration of resources in the hands of the planter class. There was significant economic growth in the South, but it happened on the largest farms, and most southern whites remained marginal to the market economy.

The commercialization of the northern family farm created a rural demand for credit, banking facilities, farm tools, clothing, and other consumer goods and services, spurring a revolution in commerce, finance, and industry. The South, on the other hand, remained a poor market for manufactured goods. Most white farmers continued to rely on the production of their households and neighbors. They bought finished goods from the outside, but at a rate that was far lower than their northern counterparts. The slaves wore cheap cloth made in the Northeast and bought by their masters, and their trade in slave-made goods, while it was crucial to subsistence and a valued form of "independence" within slavery, resulted in only low-level (often furtive) entry into the market. For their part, the larger planters furnished themselves and their homes with finery from Europe. In the North the exchange of farm produce for finished goods was creating self-sustaining economic growth. But the South continued export its plantation staples and to build only those factories, commercial institutions, and cities that served the plantation. A market revolution produced commercial agriculture, urbanization, a specialized labor force, and technological innovation in the North. In the South it simply produced more cotton and more slavery.

Not that the South neglected technological change and agricultural improvement. Southerners developed Eli Whitney's hand-operated, table-top cotton gin into big machines capable of performing complex milling operations. They improved steamboat design as well, creating flat-bottomed boats that could travel far up shallow rivers. They also developed—among others—a machine with a huge wooden screw powered by horses or mules to press ginned cotton into tight bales for shipping. There were, however, few such innovations, and they had to do with the processing and shipping of cotton. And despite the experiments of a few gentleman-planters, there were almost no improvements in the *cultivation* of cotton. The truth is that cotton was a labor-intensive crop that discouraged innovation. Moreover, plantation slaves often resisted their enslavement by sabotaging expensive tools and draft animals, scattering manure in haphazard ways, and passively resisting innovations that would have added to their drudgery. So the cotton fields continued to be cultivated by enslaved people working with clumsy, mule-drawn plows that barely scratched the soil, by women wielding heavy hoes, and by gangs who harvested the crop by hand.

Southern state governments spent little on internal improvements. A Virginia canal linked the flour mills at Richmond with inland grain fields, and another would connect Chesapeake Bay with the National Road, thus finally realizing— too late—Washington's and Jefferson's dreams of a thoroughfare between the Chesapeake and the Ohio Valley. But Cotton Belt planters built their farms on alluvial land with ready access to the South's magnificent system of navigable rivers. They had little interest in expensive, state-supported internal improvements that their own neighborhoods did not need. Upcountry whites, particularly in the Upper South, sometimes campaigned for roads and canals, but they seldom got such measures through planter-dominated legislatures.

Nor did the South build cities, much less a regional *system* of cities. The old northern seaports grew dramatically in the early nineteenth century, and they extended their sway over systems of satellite cities. New York, which became America's great city in these years, exercised not only commercial but cultural power over the old capital at Albany, as well as new Erie Canal cities such as Utica, Syracuse, Rochester, and Buffalo. Between 1800 and 1840 the urban proportion of New York state's population rose from 12.7 percent to 19.4 percent— despite the settlement of huge tracts of new agricultural land. In Massachusetts the urban population rose from 15.4 percent to 37.9 percent in these years. By 1840 every northeastern and mid-Atlantic state with the exception of Maine and Vermont had at least 10 percent of its people living in cities. No southern state urbanized at that level. Virginia, at 6.9 percent, had the largest urban population of any of the future Confederate states.

Commercial and manufacturing cities sprouted up throughout the interior of the North. The few southern cities were located on the periphery of the region and served as transportation depots for plantation crops. River cities like Louisville, Memphis, and St. Louis were little more than stopping places for steamboats. The great seaports of New Orleans, Charleston, and Baltimore had in the past shipped plantation staples directly to British and European markets. But as the nineteenth century progressed, they sent more and more of their goods by coasting vessel to New York City, where it was transshipped to foreign ports. In turn, Europe's manufactured goods were funneled into New York, then sold off to the southern (and northern) countryside. The commercial metropolis of the southern United States was less and less London and more and more New York. What had *not* changed was the colonial status of the South.

Lith. of P.S. Duval & Co. Phila.

Source: Library of Congress, Prints and Photographs Division (reproduction number LC USZ62-119893).

CHAPTER 5

———✦———

Family, Race, Religion

THE EXPANSION OF MARKET SOCIETY UNSETTLED THE OLD republic. Fathers no longer passed their land and their ways of life on to their sons, and with that, fathers no longer wielded power or had all the answers. Young people grew up knowing that they would live in unfamiliar neighborhoods and make their livings in unfamiliar ways, and they listened less intently to elders who held family land and fading memories of the Revolution. The philosopher Ralph Waldo Emerson, who reached adulthood in Massachusetts in the 1830s, later mused that he had had the misfortune to be young when age was respected, and to have grown old when youth counted for everything. Arriving in America at about the time Emerson came of age, the French visitor Alexis de Tocqueville observed that paternal power was largely absent in American families. "All that remains of it," he said, "are a few vestiges in the first years of childhood. . . . But as soon as the young American approaches manhood, the ties of filial obedience are relaxed day by day; master of his thoughts, he is soon master of his conduct. . . . At the close of boyhood the man appears and begins to trace out his own path."

The patriarchal household—the fundamental building block of Jefferson's republic—was deeply shaken, and the young stepped (or just as often stumbled) out of the corporate republic and into the individualistic and democratic world of the nineteenth century. They made new selves out of disparate ingredients: old and new religious and family forms, the reformulation of citizenship and public life, and the discovery of the primal value of white skin.

CHURCH AND FAMILY: THE NORTH

Northerners experienced change more abruptly and completely than did southerners. They responded to the collapse of authority—in their families, in their communities, and in society at large—in a variety of ways. Some became unattached, unashamed individualists. This was not necessarily an admirable thing. The word individualist entered the American vocabulary in the 1820s. It was borrowed from the French, who used it to describe people who cared only about themselves. Some became drunkards. (The first third of the nineteenth century witnessed the highest levels of alcohol consumption in American history.) But these were far outnumbered by the mass of northerners who found comfort, explanations, and ultimate sources of authority in religion. The largest and most enduring cultural accompaniment to the rise of democracy and the market was a national revival of religion.

The Decline of the Established Churches

The Founding Fathers had been largely indifferent to organized religion, though a few were pious men. Some, like George Washington, attended church out of a sense of obligation. Many of the better educated, including Thomas Jefferson, subscribed to deism, the belief that God had created the universe and set it in motion but did not intervene in its affairs. Many simply did not bother themselves with thoughts about religion. When asked why the Constitution mentioned neither God nor religion, Alexander Hamilton is reported to have smiled and answered, "We forgot."

Many Americans shared Hamilton's forgetfulness. In state after state, postrevolutionary constitutions withdrew government support from religion, and the First Amendment to the U.S. Constitution clearly prescribed the national separation of church and state. Reduced to their own sources of support, the established churches did not grow with the new republic. The Episcopal Church, which until the Revolution had been the established Church of England in the southern colonies, went into decline. In Virginia, only 40 of the 107 Episcopal parishes supported ministers in the early nineteenth century. Nor did the Episcopal Church travel west with southern settlers. Of the 408 Episcopal congregations in the South in 1850, fully 315 were in the old seaboard states.

In New England, the old churches fared little better. The Connecticut Congregationalist Ezra Stiles reported in 1780 that 60 parishes in Vermont and an equal number in New Hampshire were without a minister. In Massachusetts, according to Stiles's reports, 80 parishes lacked a minister. In all, about one-third of New England's Congregational pulpits were vacant in 1780, and the situation was worse to the north and west. In Vermont between 1763 and 1820, the founding of churches followed the incorporation of new towns by an average of 15 years, an indication that frontier settlement in that state proceeded almost entirely without the benefit of organized religion. In 1780 nearly all of the 750 Congregational churches in the United States were in New England. In the next 40 years, although the nation's population rose from 4 to 10 million, the number of Congregational churches rose by only 350. Ordinary women and men were leaving the churches that had dominated the religious life of colonial America, sometimes ridiculing the learned clergy as they departed. To Ezra Stiles and other conservatives, it seemed that the republic was plunging into atheism.

It was not. Even as Stiles fretted and wrung his hands, the United States was on the verge of the greatest revival of religion in its history. The revivals of the first third of the nineteenth century transformed countless individuals and families, and by the 1820s nearly all visitors from Europe noted the religiosity of Americans. The revival was national, and it crossed denominational lines. The people of the United States, however, did not experience it as citizens of an undifferentiated nation but as northerners and southerners, blacks and whites, women and men, rich and poor, farmers and city people. By 1830 Americans held very different views of the Christian individual, the Christian family, and the ideal Christian society. The pages that follow describe emerging notions of self, family, and society among the northern middle class, the plain people of the North, and the white people of the South.

Church and Family: A New Middle Class

"The most valuable class in any community," declared the poet-journalist Walt Whitman in 1858, "is the middle class . . ." At that time, the term middle class (and the social group that it described) was no more than thirty or forty years old. The market revolution since 1815 had created new towns and cities and transformed the old ones, and it had turned the rural North into a landscape of family-owned commercial farms. Those who claimed the title "middle class" were largely the new kinds of proprietors who rose up within the market revolution—city and country merchants, master craftsmen who had turned themselves into manufacturers, and the mass of market-oriented farmers.

A disproportionate number of them were New Englanders. New England was the first center of factory production, and southern New England farms were thoroughly commercialized by 1830. Yankee migrants dominated the commercial heartland of western New York and the northern counties of the Northwestern states. Even in the seaport cities (New York's Pearl Street wholesale houses are a prime example) businessmen from New England were often at the center of economic innovation. This Yankee middle class invented cultural forms that became the core of an emerging business civilization. They upheld the autonomous and morally accountable individual against the claims of traditional neighborhoods and traditional families. They devised an intensely private, mother-centered domestic life. Most of all, they adhered to a reformed Yankee Protestantism whose moral imperatives became the foundation of American middle-class culture.

The evangelists who preached this new message—Albert Barnes of Philadelphia, Lyman Beecher of Boston and Cincinnati, Edward Kirk of Albany, Gardiner Spring of New York, the famed itinerant Charles Grandison Finney, and many, many others—were heirs to what was left of Yankee Calvinism. As children, they had learned the old Puritan truths about providence, predestination, and original sin. The earthly social order (the fixed relations of power and submission between men and women, rich and poor, children and parents, and so on) was necessary because humankind was innately sinful and prone to selfishness and disorder. Christians must obey the rules governing their station in life; attempts to rearrange the social order were both sinful and doomed to failure. Yet while they reaffirmed those conservative Puritan beliefs, they routinely ignored them in their daily lives. The benefits of market society were clearly the result of human effort. So was the progress of religious revivals. Just as clearly, they added up to "improvement" and "progress." And as middle-class Christians increasingly made what they knew was material and moral improvement, the doctrines of human inability and natural depravity, along with faith in divine providence, became troubled.

It was to such religious troubles that Charles Finney and evangelists of his ilk preached what became the organizing principle of northern middle-class evangelicalism: "God," Finney insisted, "has made man a moral free agent." Neither the social order nor the ills of this world nor the spiritual state of individuals were fixed or divinely ordained. People would make themselves and the world better by choosing right over wrong, though they would choose right only after prayer and a conversion experience in which they submitted their rebellious wills to the will of God. It was a religion that valued individual holiness over a permanent and sacred social order. It made the spiritual nature of individuals a matter of prayer, submission, and choice. Thus it gave Christians the means—through evangelism and the spread of revivals—to bring on the thousand-year reign of Christianity that would precede the Second Coming of Christ. As Charles Finney told an audience in Rochester, New York, "If [Christians] were united all over the world the Millennium might be brought about in three months."

Yankee evangelists had been moving toward Finney's formulation since the turn of the century. Like Finney, they borrowed revival techniques from the Methodists (week-long meetings, meetings in which women prayed in public, an "anxious bench" for the most likely converts) but toned them down for their own more "respectable" and affluent audience. Although they used democratic methods and preached a message of individualism and free agency, middle-class evangelicals retained the Puritans' Old Testament sense of cosmic history: they enlisted personal holiness and spiritual democracy in a fight to the finish between the forces of good and the forces of evil in this world. In acting out the imperatives of the new evangelicalism, they created what quickly became known as the "Evangelical United Front." By the late 1820s the American Bible Society, the American Tract Society, the American Sunday School Union, the American Board of Commissioners for Foreign Missions, the American Temperance Society, and many smaller organizations—all head-quartered in New York City—were bombarding the republic with Bibles, tracts, and calls for religious and humanitarian reform.

This aggressive and public missionary crusade was coupled, paradoxically, with an intensely private and emotionally loaded family life. Reformist evan-gelicals made crucial distinctions between the home and the world—distinc-tions that grew from the disintegration of the old patriarchal household econ-omy. Men in cities and towns now went off to work, leaving wives and children to spend the day at home. Even commercializing farmers made a clear distinc-tion between (male) work that was oriented toward markets and (female) work that was tied to the maintenance of the household. The new middle-class evan-gelicalism encouraged this division of domestic labor. The public world of pol-itics and economic exchange, said the preachers, was the proper sphere of men. Women, on the other hand, were to exercise new kinds of moral influence within households. As an evangelical in Utica, New York, put it, "Each has a distinct sphere of duty—the husband to go out into the world—the wife to su-perintend the household." "Man profits from connection with the world," he went on, "but women never; their constituents [sic] of mind are different. The one is raised and exalted by mingled association. The purity of the other is maintained in silence and seclusion."

This new domestic order was a clear break with the patriarchal family. True, middle-class evangelicals reserved formal power to fathers. But they granted unprecedented domestic authority to mothers, and the result was a feminiza-tion of family life. In the old yeoman-artisan republic, the fathers who owned property, headed households, and governed family labor were lawgivers and disciplinarians, assigned the task of governing women, children, and other underlings who were mired in passion and unable to govern themselves. Middle-class evangelicals raised new spiritual possibilities for women and children. Mothers replaced fathers as the principal child-rearers, and they en-listed the doctrines of free agency and individual moral responsibility in that task. Middle-class mothers raised their children with love and reason, not fear. They sought to develop the children's conscience and their capacity to love, to teach them to make good moral choices, and to prepare themselves for conver-sion and a lifetime of Christian service. Thus mothers assumed responsibility for making children who would be carriers of the new middle-class culture, and fathers, ministers, and other authorities recognized the importance of that job. Edward Kirk, a minister in Albany, insisted that "the hopes of human society are to be found in the character, in the views, and in the conduct of mothers."

The new ethos of moral free agency was mirrored in the Sunday schools. When Sunday schools first appeared in the 1790s, their purpose was to teach working-class children to read and write by having them copy long passages from the Bible. Their most heavily publicized accomplishments were feats of memory. In 1823 Jane Wilson, a 13-year-old in Rochester, memorized 1,650 verses of scripture. Pawtucket, Rhode Island, claimed a mill girl who could recite the entire New Testament. Beginning in the 1820s, the emphasis shifted from promoting feats of memory to preparing children's souls for conversion. Middle-class children were now included in the schools, corporal punishment was forbidden, and Sunday school teachers tried to develop the moral sensibilities of their charges. They had the children read a few Bible verses each week and then led them in a discussion of the moral lessons conveyed by the text. The proudest achievements of the new schools were children who made good moral choices. Thus Sunday schools became training grounds in free agency and moral accountability—a transformation that made sense only in a world where children could be trusted to make moral choices, and where they would make better selves and a better world by making the right choices.

Church and Family: The Northern Plain Folk

From the 1820s onward, northern middle-class evangelicals proposed their religious and domestic values as a national culture for the United States. But even in their own region they were surrounded and often outnumbered by Americans who rejected their cultural leadership. The plain people of the North were a varied lot: settlers in the lower Northwest who remained culturally southern, hill-country New Englanders, New Yorkers, and Pennsylvanians who had experienced little of what their middle-class cousins called "progress," refugees from the countryside who had taken up urban wage labor. What they shared was a cultural conservatism—often grounded in the traditional, father-centered family—that rejected reformist religion out of hand.

Religious transformation had begun earlier and had progressed further among the northern plain folk than it had among their more prosperous neighbors. The collapse of the established churches, the social dislocations of the postrevolutionary years, and the increasingly antiauthoritarian, democratic sensibilities of ordinary Americans provided fertile ground for the growth of new democratic sects. The first third of the nineteenth century was the era of camp-meeting revivalism, years in which Methodists and Baptists grew from small, half-organized sects into the great popular denominations they have been ever since. They were also years in which fiercely independent dropouts from older churches were putting together a loosely organized movement that would become the Disciples of Christ. At the same time, ragged, half-educated preachers were spreading the Universalist and Freewill Baptist messages in up-country New England, whereas in western New York young Joseph Smith was receiving the visions that would lead to Mormonism.

The result was, first of all, a vast increase in the variety of choices on the American religious landscape. But within that welter of new churches stood a roughly uniform democratic style shared by the fastest-growing sects. First, they renounced the need for an educated, formally authorized clergy. Religion was now a matter of the heart and not the head. Crisis conversion (understood in most churches as personal transformation that resulted from direct experience of the Holy Spirit) was a necessary credential for preachers; a college degree was not. The new preachers substituted emotionalism and storytelling for Episcopal ritual and Congregational theological lectures. Stories attracted listeners, and they were harder for the learned clergy to refute. The new churches also held up the Bible as the one source of religious knowledge, thus undercutting all theological discourse and placing every literate Christian on a level with the best-educated minister. These tendencies often ended in Restorationism—the belief that all theological and institutional changes since the end of biblical times were man-made mistakes, and that religious organizations must restore themselves to the purity and simplicity of the church of the Apostles. In sum, this loose democratic creed rejected learning and tradition and raised up the priesthood of all believers.

Baptists and Methodists were by far the most successful at preaching to the new populist audience. The United States had only 50 Methodist churches in 1783; by 1820 it had 2,700. Over those same years the number of Baptist churches rose from 400 to 2,700. Together, in 1820, these two denominations outnumbered Episcopalians and Congregationalists by 3 to 1, almost a reversal of their relative standings 40 years earlier. Baptists based much of their appeal in localism and congregational democracy. Methodist success, on the other hand, entailed skillful national organization. Bishop Francis Asbury, the head of the church in its fastest-growing years, built an episcopal bureaucracy that seeded churches throughout the republic and sent circuit-riding preachers to places that had none. These early Methodist missions were grounded in self-sacrifice to the point of martyrdom. Asbury demanded much of his itinerant preachers, and until 1810 he strongly suggested that they remain celibate. "To marry," he said, "is to locate." Asbury also knew that married circuit riders would leave many widows and orphans behind, for hundreds of them worked themselves to death. Of the men who served as Methodist itinerants before 1819, at least 60 percent died before the age of 40.

From seaport cities to frontier settlements, few Americans escaped the sound of Methodist preaching in the early nineteenth century. The Methodist preachers were common men who spoke plainly, listened carefully to others, and carried hymnbooks with simple tunes that anyone could sing. They also, particularly in the early years, shared traditional folk beliefs with their humble flocks. Some of the early circuit riders relied heavily on dreams; some could predict the future; others visited heaven and hell and returned with full descriptions. In the end, however, it was the hopefulness and simplicity of the Methodist message that attracted ordinary Americans. The Methodists rejected the old terrors of Calvinist determinism and taught that although salvation comes only through God, men and women can decide to open themselves to divine grace and thus play a decisive role in their own salvation. They also taught that a godly life is a gradual, lifetime growth in grace—thus allowing for repentance for minor, and sometimes even major, lapses of faith and behavior. It was by granting responsibility (one might say sovereignty) to the individual believer that the Methodists established their democratic credentials and drew hundreds of thousands of Americans into their fold.

The doctrines of churches favored by the northern plain folk varied as much as the people themselves. They ranged from the "free grace" doctrines of the Methodists to the iron-bound Calvinism of most Baptists, from the fine-tuned hierarchy of the Mormons to the near-anarchy of the Disciples of Christ. They included the most popular faiths (Baptists and Methodists came to contain two-thirds of America's professing Protestants, North and South) to such smaller sects as Hicksite Quakers, Adventists, and Freewill Baptists. Yet for all their diversity, these churches had important things in common. Most shared an evangelical emphasis on individual experience over churchly authority. Most favored democratic, local control of religious life and distrusted outside organization and religious professionalism—not only the declining colonial establishments but the emerging missionary network created by middle-class evangelicals. They rejected middle-class optimism and reformism, reaffirming God's providence and humankind's duty to lead godly lives within an imperfect and sinful world.

The most pervasive strain in the religious life of common folk was a belief in providence—the conviction that human history was part of God's vast and unknowable plan, and that all events were willed or allowed by God. Middle-class evangelicals spoke of providence, too, but they seemed to assume that God's plan was manifest in the progress of market society and middle-class religion. Humbler evangelicals held to the older notion that providence was immediate, mysterious, and unknowable. They believed that the events of everyday life were parts of a vast blueprint that existed only in the mind of God—and not in the vain aspirations of women and men. When making plans, they added the caveat, "The Lord willing," and they learned to accept misfortune with fortitude. They responded to epidemics, bad crop years, aches and pains, illness, and early death by praying for the strength to endure, asking God to "sanctify" their suffering by making it an opportunity for them to grow in faith. As a minister told the Scots Covenanters of Cambridge, New York, "It is through tribulation that all the saints enter into the kingdom of God." "The tempest sometimes ceases," he went on, "the sky is clear, and the prospect is desirable, but by the by the gathering clouds threaten a new storm; here we must watch, and labor, and fight, expecting rest with Christ in glory, not on the way to it."

Baptists, Methodists, Disciples of Christ, and the smaller popular sects evangelized largely among persons who had been bypassed or hurt by the market revolution. Many had been reduced to dependent, wage-earning status. Others had become market farmers or urban storekeepers or master workmen; few had become rich. Their churches taught them to reject the world and its material enjoyments.

Often their rhetoric turned to criticism of market society, its institutions, and its centers of power. The Quaker schismatic Elias Hicks, a Long Island farmer who fought the worldliness and pride of wealthy Quakers, listed these among the mistakes of the early nineteenth century: the Erie Canal, fancy food and other luxuries, banks and the credit system, the city of Philadelphia, and the study of chemistry. The Vermont Baptist William Miller expressed his hatred for banks, insurance companies, stock-jobbing, chartered monopolies, individual greed, and the city of New York. In short, what the evangelical middle class identified as the march of progress, poorer and more conservative evangelicals often condemned as a descent into worldliness that would almost certainly provoke God's wrath.

Along with doubts about social and economic change and the middle-class churches that embraced it, members of the popular sects often held to the patriarchal family form in which they had been raised, and with which both the market revolution and middle-class domesticity seemed at war. For hundreds of thousands of northern Protestants, the erosion of domestic patriarchy was a profound cultural loss and not, as it was for many in the middle class, an avenue to personal liberation. Their cultural conservatism was apparent in their efforts to sustain the father-centered family of the old rural North, or to revive it in new forms.

The weakening of the patriarchal family and the attempt to shore it up were central to the life and work of one of the most unique and successful of the new religious leaders of the period: the Mormon Prophet Joseph Smith. Smith's father was a landless Vermont Baptist who moved his wife and nine children to seven rented farms within twenty years. Around 1820, when young Joseph was approaching manhood, the family was struggling to make mortgage payments on a small farm outside Palmyra, New York. That farm—Joseph referred to it as "my father's house"—was a desperate token of the Smith family's commitment to yeoman independence and an endangered rural patriarchy. Despite the labors of Joseph and his brothers, a merchant cheated the Smith family out of the farm. With that, both generations of the Smiths faced lifetimes as propertyless workers. To make matters worse, Joseph's mother and some of his siblings began to attend an evangelical Presbyterian church in Palmyra—apparently against the father's wishes.

Before the loss of the farm, Joseph had received two visions warning him away from existing churches and telling him to wait for further instructions. In 1827 the Angel Moroni appeared to him and led him to golden plates that translated into The Book of Mormon. It told of a light-skinned people, descendants of the Hebrews, who had sailed to North America long before Columbus. They had had an epic, violent history, a covenanted relationship with God, and had been visited and evangelized by Jesus following His crucifixion and resurrection.

Joseph Smith later declared that his discovery of The Book of Mormon had "brought salvation to my father's house" by unifying the family. It eventually unified thousands of others under a patriarchal faith based on restored theocratic government, male dominance, and a democracy among fathers. The good priests and secular leaders of The Book of Mormon are farmers who labor alongside their neighbors; the villains are self-seeking merchants, lawyers, and bad priests. The account alternates between periods when the people obey God's laws and periods when they do not—each period accompanied by the blessings or punishments of a watchful, wrathful God. Smith carried that model of brotherly cooperation and patriarchal authority into the Church of Jesus Christ of Latter-day Saints that he founded in 1830. The new church was ruled not by professional clergy but by an elaborate lay hierarchy of adult males. On top sat the father of Joseph Smith, rescued from destitution and shame, who was appointed Patriarch of the Church. Below him were Joseph Smith and his brother Hyrum, who were called First and Second Elders. The hierarchy descended through a succession of male authorities that finally reached the fathers of households. Smith claimed that this hierarchy restored the ancient priesthoods that had disappeared over the eighteen centuries of greed and error that he labeled the "Great Apostasy" of the Christian churches. But Americans who knew the history of the market revolution and the Smith family's travails within it might have noted similarities between the restored ancient order and a poor man's visionary retrieval of the social order of the eighteenth-century North.

Joseph Smith was unusual. But middle-class missionaries knew that the greatest challenge to their success was the entrenched patriarchy of the northern lower orders. "Like us," said a missionary to New York's poor, "they *might* exercise parental authority, while they felt all the yearnings of parental love. Like us, they *might* be benefited by parental correction, whilst they clung in filial submission, at the parent's feet. But among *them*, parental authority is only the consciousness of exertion of *Power*; and filial affection is but the dread and hatred of its coercion." Assuming that these deformed patriarchs were beyond help, the reformers often targeted women and children (as they had Joseph Smith's mother and sisters), making their home visits when husbands and fathers were away. A Universalist minister told women in the factory town of Pawtucket, Rhode Island, how to handle such visits: "Refuse to listen to his harangues, but in the presence of father, husband or protector . . . which the common principles of female delicacy demand of you." For the most part, northern plain people rejected middle-class missionaries and continued to build their families and raise their children in customary, father-dominated ways.

CHURCH AND FAMILY: THE SOUTH

The Making of the Bible Belt

In the first third of the nineteenth century evangelical Protestantism transformed the South into what it has been ever since: the Bible Belt. That transformation began when poor and middling whites found spiritual alternatives to the culture of the gentry—to their formalistic Episcopalianism, their love of luxury and display, and their enjoyment of money and power. Early southern Baptists and Methodists demanded a violent conversion experience followed by a life of piety and a rejection of what they called "the world." To no small degree, "the world" was the economic, cultural, and political world controlled by the planters. James McGready, who preached in rural North Carolina in the 1790s, openly condemned the gentry: "The world is in all their thoughts day and night. All their talk is of corn and tobacco, of land and stock. The price of merchandise and negroes are inexhaustible themes of conversation. But for them, the name of Jesus has no charms; it is rarely mentioned unless to be profaned." This was dangerous talk, as McGready learned when young rakes rode their horses through one of his outdoor meetings, tipped over the benches, set the altar on fire, and threatened to kill McGready himself.

Southern Baptists, Methodists, and Presbyterians spread their message in the early nineteenth century through the camp meeting, and this too was subversive of southern social distinctions. Though its origins stretched back into the eighteenth century, the first full-blown camp meeting took place at Cane Ridge, Kentucky, in 1801. Here the annual "Holy Feast," a three-day communion service of Scotch–Irish Presbyterians, was transformed into an outdoor, interdenominational revival at which hundreds experienced conversion under Presbyterian, Methodist, and Baptist preaching. Estimates of the crowd at Cane Ridge ranged from 10,000 to 20,000 persons, and by all accounts the enthusiasm was nearly unprecedented. Some converts fainted; others succumbed to uncontrolled bodily jerkings, while a few barked like dogs—all of them visibly taken by the Holy Spirit. Such exercises fell upon women and men, whites and blacks, rich and poor, momentarily blurring social hierarchy in moments of profound and very public religious ecstasy. A witness to a later camp meeting recounted that "to see a bold and courageous Kentuckian (undaunted by the horrors of war) turn pale and tremble at the reproof of a weak woman, a little boy, or a poor African; to see him sink down in deep remorse, roll and toss, and gnash his teeth, till black in the face, entreat the prayers of those he came to devour . . . who can say the change was not supernatural?" (Southern white men, even when under religious conviction, sometimes resisted this loss of mastery and self-control. One preacher remembered a "fine, strong, good-looking young man" who felt himself giving in to camp-meeting preaching. He "found no relief until he drew a large pistole out of his pocket, with which he intended to defend himself if any one should offer to speak to him on the subject of religion.")

The early southern evangelicals irritated and angered the elite and white men generally, for they seemed to question not only worldliness but the white male dominance that held the southern world together. The conversion of wives and children (not to mention slaves) could trouble southern families; the conversion of white men could "unman" them and render them "womanish." In the North, some strains of evangelicalism led to a radical freedom that questioned worldly power and social hierarchy in all its forms. But the governors of southern farms and southern families found that they had little to worry about in their own region. The Baptists, Methodists, and Presbyterians of the South, though they never stopped railing against greed and pride, found that they could not conquer the South without learning to live comfortably with a system of fixed hierarchy and God-given social roles—with slavery and father-dominated families in particular.

Slavery became a major case in point. For a brief period after the Revolution, evangelicals included slavery on their list of worldly sins. Methodists and Baptists preached to slaves as well as to whites, and Bishop Francis Asbury, the principal architect of American Methodism, admired John Wesley's statement that slavery was against "all the laws of Justice, Mercy, and Truth." In 1780 a conference of Methodist preachers ordered circuit riders to free their slaves and advised all Methodists to do the same. In 1784 the Methodists declared that they would excommunicate members who failed to free their slaves within two years. Many lay Methodists took the order seriously. On the Delmarva Peninsula (Delaware and the eastern shore of Maryland and Virginia), for instance, Methodist converts freed thousands of slaves in the late eighteenth century. Other evangelicals shared their views. As early as 1787, southern Presbyterians prayed for "final abolition," and two years later Baptists condemned slavery as "a violent deprivation of the rights of nature and inconsistent with a republican government."

The period of greatest evangelical growth, however, came during the years in which the South committed irrevocably to plantation slavery. As increasing numbers of both slaves and slaveowners came within the evangelical fold, the southern churches had to rethink their position on human bondage. The Methodists never carried out their threat to excommunicate slaveholders, confessing in 1816 that southerners were so committed to slavery that "little can be done to abolish the practice so contrary to moral justice." Similarly, the Baptists and Presbyterians never translated their antislavery rhetoric into action. By 1820, evangelicals were coming to terms with slavery. Instead of demanding freedom for slaves they suggested, as the Methodist James O'Kelly put it, that slaveowners remember that slaves were "dear brethren in Christ" who should not be treated cruelly and who should be allowed to attend religious services. After 1830, with large numbers of the planter elite converted to the evangelical fold, this would evolve into a full-scale effort to Christianize the institution of slavery.

Gender, Power, and the Evangelicals

Southern men, yeomen as well as planters, distrusted the early evangelicals for more than their views on slavery. The preachers seemed even more grievously mistaken about white manhood and the integrity of white families. Southerners were localistic and culturally conservative. Farm and plantation labor and the routines of daily life were conducted within households, and prospects for most whites remained rooted in inherited land and family help. Whereas the new northern middle class nourished a cosmopolitan culture, an individualism, and a domestic sentimentalism that subverted traditional authority, southerners distrusted outsiders and defended rural neighborhoods grounded in the sovereignty of fathers over their property and families, and in the power, judgment, skills, and physical prowess of those fathers.

To many, patriarchy and evangelicalism seemed incompatible. Most southern whites regarded themselves less as individuals than as representatives of families. Southern boys often received the family names of heroes as first names: Jefferson Davis, or Thomas Jefferson (later, General "Stonewall") Jackson. More often, however, they took the name of a related family—Peyton Randolph, Preston Brooks, Langdon Cheves—and carried them as proud and often burdensome badges of who they were. Children learned early on that their first duty was to their family's reputation. When young Benjamin Tillman of South Carolina was away at school, his sister wrote "Don't relax in your efforts to gain a good education. . . . I want you to be an ornament to your family." Two years later, another sister wrote, "Do, Bud, study hard and make good use of your time. . . . I want you to do something for the Tillman name."

In the white South, reputation and the defense of family honor were everything. Boys and girls were taught to act as though everyone were watching them, ready to note any hint of inadequacy. A boy with a reputation for cowardice, for ineptness at riding or fighting, or for failure to control his emotions or hold his liquor, was an embarrassment to his family. Membership in the South's democracy of white men depended less on wealth than on the maintenance of personal and family integrity. An "unsullied reputation," insisted Albert Gallatin Brown of Mississippi, placed a man "on a social level with all his fellows." As John Horry Dent, an Alabama slaveholder and bad amateur poet put it,

> Honor and shame from all conditions rise;
> Act well your part and their [sic] the honor lies.

Among southern white men, wealth generally counted for less than maintaining one's personal and family honor and thus winning membership in the democracy of honorable males.

The code of honor, while it forged ties of equality and respect among white men, made rigid distinctions between men and women and whites and blacks. Women and girls who misbehaved—with transgressions ranging from simple gossip to poor housekeeping to adultery—damaged not only their own reputation but also the honor of fathers, brothers, or husbands who could not control them. Such a charge could mean social death in a rural society made up of honor-bound extended families.

The early evangelicals seemed to threaten southern patriarchy. They preached individual salvation to women, children, and slaves—sometimes sending newly pious dependents home to harangue ungodly heads of households, and often hinting that the "family" of believers could replace blood ties. Their churches sometimes intervened in family disputes or disciplined family members in ways that subverted patriarchal control. Perhaps worse, many of the preachers failed to act out the standards of southern manhood in their own lives. James McGready and other camp-meeting preachers often faced hecklers and rowdies. When attacked, they either ran off or quietly took their beatings. White men often met the turn-the-other-cheek meekness of the preachers (not to mention the celibacy of the Methodists) with suspicion and contempt. They felt the same about the hugging, kissing, crying, and bodily "exercises" acted out in evangelical meetings.

As they had with slavery, southern evangelicals came to terms with the notions of manhood and the father-centered families of the South. The preachers learned to assert traditional forms of manhood. Their fathers and often they themselves, they said, had fought the British and Indians heroically. They also revealed that they had themselves often been great drinkers, gamblers, fighters, and fornicators before submitting to God, and they also began fighting back when attacked. Peter Cartwright, who conquered much of Kentucky and southern Illinois for Methodism, told numerous stories of how he outwitted and often outfought rowdies who attacked his meetings. On many occasions he walked out of the pulpit to confront hecklers and punched more than a few of them. Another Methodist overheard a man blaspheming and threw him into a fire and held him down with his foot. The preachers also made it clear that they would pose no threat to the authority of fathers. They discouraged the excesses of female and juvenile piety. At the same time, church disciplinary cases involving adultery, wife-beating, private drunkenness, and other offenses committed within families became more and more rare.

More fundamentally, evangelicals upheld the southern world of fixed hierarchy and God-given social roles, and the churches that grew out of southern revivals reinforced localistic neighborhoods and the patriarchal family. Some southern communities began when a whole congregation moved on to new land; others were settled by the chain migration of brothers and cousins, and subsequent revivals spread through family networks. Rural isolation limited most households to their own company during the week, but on Sundays church meetings united the neighborhood's cluster of extended families into a community of believers. In most neighborhoods, social connections seldom extended beyond that. The word "church" referred ultimately to the worldwide community of Christians, and the war between the "church" and the "world" referred to a cosmic history that would end in millennial fire. But in the day-to-day understandings of southern evangelicals, the church was the local congregation and the world was local sins and local sinners—many of whom were related to members of the church. Although they patrolled their own congregations, however, southern evangelicals seldom thought about changing the world.

Southern evangelicalism rested on the sovereignty of God, a conviction of human imperfection, and an acceptance of disappointment and pain as part of God's grand and unknowable design. It also assumed that patriarchal social relations were crucial to Christian living within an imperfect and often brutal world. Southerners revered the patriarch and slaveholder Abraham more than any other figure in the Bible, and John C. Calhoun would proclaim "Hebrew Theocracy" the best government ever experienced by humankind. The father must—like Abraham—govern and protect his household, the mother must assist the father, and the women, children, and slaves must faithfully act out the duties of their stations. Eternal salvation was possible for everyone, but the saved lived out their godliness by striving to be a good mother, a good father, a good slave. By the same token, a Christian never questioned his or her God-given social role.

RACE

The post-Revolutionary emancipation of slaves in the North, coupled with the hardening of slavery farther south, encouraged Americans to rethink the racial order as well as the religious and domestic order of their society. White Americans had long assumed that Africans belonged at the bottom of society. But they had assumed that others belonged there as well. In a colonial world in which many whites were indentured servants, tenants, apprentices, and workers who lived in their employers' homes, where increasing numbers of blacks were formally free and many others were hired out as semifree, few Americans made rigid distinctions concerning the "natural" independence of whites and the "natural" dependence of blacks. (All Americans, after all, were colonial subjects of the British king.) The language of colonial social division separated gentlemen from the "middling sort," and relegated the propertyless and dependent to the "lower orders" or the "lower sort." Whites and blacks worked beside each other on farms, on merchant ships, and in the city streets; they lived on the same blocks; they patronized the same bars and entertainments. Although the better-off whites were far from color blind, they wrote off poverty, disorder, drunkenness, and rioting as the work not of blacks but of an undifferentiated substratum of "Negroes, sailors, servants, and boys."

Modern racism—the notion that blacks were a separate and hopelessly inferior order of humankind—emerged from developments in the early nineteenth century: national independence and the crucial new distinction between Americans who were citizens and those who were not, the recommitment to slavery in the South, the making of what would be called "free labor" in the North. Whites who faced lifetimes of wage labor and dependence struggled to make dignity and self-respect out of that situation. At the same time, freed slaves entered the bottom of a newly defined "free labor" society and tried to do the same. With plenty of help from the wealthy and powerful, whites succeeded in making democracy out of the rubble of the old patriarchal republic. In the process, they defined nonwhites as constitutionally incapable of self-discipline, personal independence, and political participation.

Free Blacks

There had been sizeable pockets of slavery in the northern colonies. But revolutionary idealism, coupled with the growing belief that slavery was inefficient, led one northern state after another to abolish it. Vermont, where there were almost no slaves, outlawed slavery in its revolutionary constitution. By 1804 every northern state had taken some action, usually by passing laws that called for gradual emancipation. The first of such laws, and the model for others, was passed in Pennsylvania in 1780. This law freed slaves born after 1780 when they reached their twenty-eighth birthday. Slaves born before 1780 would remain slaves, and slave children would remain slaves through their prime working years. Some northern slaveowners, in violation of the laws, sold young slaves into the South as their freedom dates approached. Still, the emancipation laws worked: by 1830 only a handful of aging blacks remained slaves in the North.

Gradual emancipation did not stop at the Mason-Dixon line. We have seen already that thousands of Delaware and Maryland slaveholders voluntarily freed their slaves in the decades following the Revolution. A smaller but significant proportion of Virginians did the same. Indeed Virginia seriously considered abolishing slavery outright. In 1832 a Virginia constitutional convention argued the question of immediate emancipation by state law. With the western counties supporting abolition (but insisting that freed blacks be transported from the state) and some of the eastern, slaveholding counties threatening to secede from the state if abolition won, the legislature rejected emancipation by a vote of 73 to 58. They then voted to consider emancipation at a later date by a vote of 67 to 60. (In the Deep South, where slavery was a big and growing business, whites did not talk about emancipation. They assumed that slavery was permanent, and that the only proper status for blacks was bondage and submission to whites.)

From Virginia on north, the rising population of free blacks gravitated to the cities and towns. Most of those who had been slaves in cities stayed there. They were joined by thousands of free blacks who decided to abandon a countryside that had little use for blacks who were not slaves. In many cities—Philadelphia and New York City in particular—they met a stream of free blacks and fugitive slaves from the Upper South, where the bonds of slavery were growing tighter, and where free blacks feared re-enslavement. Thus despite the flood of white immigrants from Europe and the American countryside, African Americans constituted a sizeable minority in the rapidly expanding cities. New York City's black population, 10.5 percent in 1800, was still 8.8 percent in 1820; Philadelphia, the haven of thousands of southern refugees, was 10.3 percent African American in 1800 and 11.9 percent in 1820.

Blacks in the seaport cities tended to take stable, low-paying jobs. A few became successful (occasionally wealthy) entrepreneurs, whereas some others practiced skilled trades. Many of the others took jobs as waiters or porters in hotels, as merchant seamen, as barbers, and as butlers, maids, cooks, washerwomen, and coachmen for wealthy families. Others worked as dockworkers and laborers. Still others became dealers in used clothing, or draymen with their own carts and horses, or food vendors in the streets and in basement shops. (In New York, oysters were a black monopoly.) As never before, free black faces and voices became part of the landscape and soundscape of cities and towns—hawking buttermilk, hot corn, and oysters, talking and laughing in the streets, jostling their way through city crowds. More than a few whites were disturbed. The New York journalist Mordecai Noah, like many other elite whites, had expected freed slaves to be grateful and deferential to their former masters, but "instead of thankfulness for their redemption, they have become impudent and offensive beyond all precedent."

While free blacks made themselves visible and audible in the streets, African Americans with money established businesses and institutions of their own. At one end were black-owned gambling houses, saloons, brothels, oyster cellars, and dance halls that often served a mixed clientele. At the other end were institutions built by self-consciously "respectable" free blacks to assert their dignity and "uplift" their once-dependent people. Most prominent among these were churches. which sprang up wherever African Americans lived. In Philadelphia, black preachers Richard Allen and Absalom Jones rebelled against segregated seating in St. George's Methodist Church and, in 1794, founded two separate black congregations; by 1800, about 40 percent of Philadelphia's blacks belonged to one of those two churches. The African Methodist Episcopal Church grew from Allen's church, and established itself as a national denomination in 1816. Schools and relief societies, usually associated with churches grew quickly. Black Masonic lodges attracted hundreds of members. Many of the churches and social organizations took names that proudly called up the blacks' African origins. In Philadelphia, for instance, there were African Methodists, Abyssinian Baptists, the Daughters of Ethiopia, the African Dorcas Society—to name only a few. Not only their names and activities but their presence as black-owned buildings filled with respectable former slaves caught the attention of their white and black neighbors. It was from this matrix of black businesses and institutions that black abolitionists—David Walker in Boston, Fredrick Douglass in New Bedford and Rochester, the itinerant Sojourner Truth, and many others—would emerge to demand abolition of slavery and equal rights for black citizens.

Whereas thousands of former slaves enjoyed a new independence and indulged in new aspirations, many whites felt themselves slipping into powerlessness and dependence. The Revolution established the Americans as a people who had won their freedom through force of arms. An emerging public culture placed great emphasis on personal independence—independence that was based in the ownership of productive property. In postrevolutionary America, the most important social and political distinction was not between black and white or even between rich and poor. It was between the heads of independent households and the women, slaves, servants, apprentices, and others who were their dependents. At the same time, however, wage labor increased, reducing the number of northern whites who were, by traditional measures, independent. The North abandoned indentured servitude, apprenticeship, year-long labor contracts, and the provision of room and board by employers and replaced them with the modern contract of hourly wage labor. Increasing thousands of white apprentices, journeymen, and laborers could no longer expect to become proprietors. Dependent sons on small farms faced the same ambushed expectations. After 1815 an unprecedented proportion of Americans faced lifetimes as hireling workers. They also faced the loss of citizenship and public respect that accompanied economic dependence. They fought that threat in a number of ways: their skills and labor, they said, constituted a kind of property; their manhood conferred judgment and strength and thus independence. These were assertions of worth, competence, and independence that had little to do with proprietorship or the ownership of property. In ways that were sometimes subtle but just as often brutal, they often made those assertions at the expense of African Americans. Along with the value of their labor and their manhood, threatened white men discovered the decisive worth of their white skins.

Whites in the early nineteenth century began refusing to work alongside blacks, and some of the earliest and most decisive racist assaults came when whites asserted their control over some occupations and relegated blacks to others. They chased blacks out of skilled jobs by pressuring employers to discriminate, and often by outright violence. As a result, African Americans were almost completely eliminated from the skilled trades, and many unskilled and semiskilled blacks lost their jobs on the docks, in warehouses, and in the merchant marine. By 1834 a Philadelphian reported that "colored persons, when engaged in their usual occupations, were repeatedly assailed and maltreated, usually on the [waterfront]. Parties of white men have insisted that no blacks shall be employed in certain departments of labor." And as their old jobs disappeared, blacks were systematically excluded from the new jobs that were opening up in factories. By the 1830s black workers in Philadelphia were noting "the difficulty of getting places for our sons as apprentices . . . owing to the prejudices with which we have to contend."

Even whites who remained in positions of personal dependence (servants, waiters, and other jobs that were coming to be defined as "black" work) refused the signs and language of servility. White servants refused to wear livery, which became the uniform of black servants of the rich. Whites also refused to be called servants. As early as 1807, when an English visitor asked a New England servant for her master, the woman replied that she had no master. "I am Mr.—'s *help*," she said. "I'd have you know, *man*, that I am no *sarvant*; none but *negars* are *sarvants*." The Englishwoman Frances Trollope, who spent the late 1820s in the United States, explained: "It is more than petty treason to the republic to call a free citizen a *servant*."

There was trouble off the job as well. As early as the 1790s, whites had disrupted African American church meetings, and they frequently attacked black celebrations of northern emancipation and Haitian independence. Black neighborhoods and institutions came under increasing attack. In the late 1820s and early 1830s every northern city experienced antiblack rioting. In 1829 white mobs destroyed black homes and businesses in Cincinnati. Hundreds of blacks fled that city for Canada; many others sought refuge in slaveholding Kentucky. Another major race riot would break out in Philadelphia in 1834 between working-class whites and blacks at a street carnival. Although blacks seem to have won the first round, the whites refused to accept defeat. Over the next few nights, they wrecked a black-owned tavern, broke into black households to terrorize families and steal their property, attacked whites who lived with, socialized with, or operated businesses catering to blacks, wrecked the African Presbyterian Church, and destroyed a black church on Wharton Street by sawing through its timbers and pulling it down.

Like these Philadelphians, mobs often targeted whites who socialized or co-operated with blacks. Integrated taverns, dance halls, brothels, and boarding houses were burned in city after city. And white respectables who helped blacks became special targets. Free blacks who built churches, schools, and other institutions of respectability often had the assistance of whites (usually middle-class evangelicals) in their attempts to "uplift" the survivors of slavery. Black leaders and a small number of white reformers dreamed of an America in which godly behavior—and not skin color—would win entrance into the American community of respect. By the early 1830s they formed antislavery societies that called not only for immediate and universal emancipation but for equal rights as well. These became the targets of some of the most vicious mobs. In July 1834, for instance, a New York City mob sacked the house of the white abolitionist merchant Lewis Tappan, moved on to the Rev. Charles Finney's Chatham Street Chapel (Finney was the leading middle-class evangelical in the North), where abolitionists were said to be meeting, and finished the evening by attacking a British (and thus supposedly aristocratic) actor at the Bowery theater. The manager saved his theater by waving two American flags and ordering an American actor to perform popular minstrel routines for the mob. Democracy and working-class aspirations, it seemed, were in league with racism.

Above all, white populists pronounced blacks unfit to be citizens of the republic. Federalists and other upper-class whites had often supported various forms of black suffrage; less privileged whites opposed it. The insistence that blacks were incapable of citizenship reinforced an equally natural white male political capacity. The exclusion of blacks (by democrats whose own political competence was often doubted by wealthier and better-educated whites) protected the republic while extending citizenship to all white men. The most vicious racist assaults were often carried out beneath symbols of the revolutionary republic. Antiblack mobs in Baltimore, Cincinnati, and Toledo called themselves Minute Men and Sons of Liberty. Philadelphia blacks who gathered to hear the Declaration of Independence read on the Fourth of July were attacked for "defiling the government." The antiabolitionist mob that sacked Lewis Tappan's house destroyed his furniture, but they rescued a portrait of George Washington and carried it as a banner during their later attacks on Finneyite evangelicals and English actors.

The more respectable and powerful whites had long been worried about the mixed-race underclass of the cities and towns. Now, as the disorder that they expected of the lower orders took the form of race riots, the authorities responded. But rather than protect the jobs, churches, schools, businesses, friends, and political rights of African Americans from criminal attack, they determined to stop the trouble by removing black people—from employment, from public festivities, from their already-limited citizenship, and, ultimately, from the United States.

In the earliest years of independence blacks had participated in the nation's public festive life. African Americans were present (along with the poorer whites) at the fringes of militia musters, parades, and other public celebrations. In New England, "Negro Election Day" began in the mid-eighteenth century and flourished through the early nineteenth. Here free blacks, with white audiences and some white participation, elected a black governor and other officials, who then presided over a public party that could last four or five days. In New York and New Jersey, blacks adopted the Dutch spring festival of Pinkster (Whitsuntide) and danced and drank and elected a black "King"— again, with lower-class whites looking on and often joining in. An offended elite New Yorker reported that Pinkster drew "the blacks and a certain class of whites, together with children of all countries and colors . . . a motley group of thousands . . . presenting to the eye of a moral observer, a kind of chaos of sin and folly, of misery and fun." We might guess that it was more than the drinking and dancing that offended him; it was the spectacle of mixed-race celebrations.

When such celebrations turned violent, men of power acted to stop them. The City of Albany banned Pinkster festivities in 1811, and other localities followed suit. New England legislatures moved election day from the spring to the colder months, thus discouraging Negro Election Day and other disorderly activities. Authorities who attempted to make militia training days more efficient and less socially troublesome instituted a number of reforms in the late 1820s. As a part of that, blacks were banned from militia musters. In part, these were tied to attempts to quiet down the old public life of colonial days and substitute more decorous and respectable forms. But they contained the assumption that decorum and respectability could occur only in the absence of black participation.

Wealthier and better-educated whites shared their compatriots' belief that the United States would never be a racially integrated democracy. By far the largest organization that addressed itself to problems of slavery and race in these years was the American Colonization Society, which envisioned sending freed blacks (but not slaves) "back" to Africa. The society held its first meeting at the end of 1816—in the chamber of the House of Representatives, with Bushrod Washington, stepson of George Washington, as president. Early members included Henry Clay, John Taylor of Caroline, Andrew Jackson, and other political and social leaders of the West, the middle states, and the Upper South. The Colonizationists did not see slavery as the problem. Like white rioters, they saw the problem as black freedom. African Americans, they said, would continue to suffer from white prejudice and their own deficiencies as long as they stayed in the United States. They would exercise freedom and learn Christian and republican ways only if exported to Liberia, on the west coast of Africa. A few free blacks took them up on the offer. But most adamantly refused, insisting that colonization was not an offer of freedom but an attempt to round up native-born citizens who were not white and make them disappear. Colonizationists frequently denounced white violence against free blacks. Just as often, however, they blamed the "degradation" of blacks as the root of the problem. Colonization remained the principal racial doctrine of white respectables—in a chronological line running from Henry Clay to Abraham Lincoln—north of the Lower South until the end of slavery.

CITIZENSHIP

The transition from republic to democracy—and the relation of that transition to the decline of rural patriarchy—took on formal, institutional shape in a redefinition of republican citizenship. The revolutionary constitutions of most states retained colonial freehold (property) qualifications for voting. In the yeoman societies of the late eighteenth century, freehold qualifications granted the vote to between one-half and three-quarters of adult white men. Many of the disfranchised were dependent sons who expected to inherit citizenship along with land. Some states dropped the freehold clause and gave the vote to all adult men who paid taxes, but with little effect on the voting population. Both the freehold and taxpaying qualifications tended to grant political rights to adult men who headed households, thus reinforcing classical republican notions that granted full citizenship to independent fathers and not to their dependents. Statesmen often defended the qualifications in those terms. Arthur St. Clair, the territorial governor of Ohio, argued for retention of the Northwest Ordinance's 50-acre freehold qualification for voting in territorial elections in set-piece republican language: "I do not count independence and wealth always together," he said, "but I pronounce poverty and dependence inseparable." When Nathaniel Macon, a respected old revolutionary from North Carolina, saw that his state would abolish property qualifications in 1802, he suggested that the suffrage be limited to married men. Like St. Clair's proposition, it was an attempt to maintain the old distinction between citizen-householders and disfranchised dependents.

Between 1790 and 1820 republican notions of citizenship grounded in fatherhood and proprietorship gave way to a democratic insistence on equal rights for all white men. There were a number of reasons for that development. First, the proportion of adult white men who could not meet property qualifications multiplied at an alarming rate. In the new towns and cities artisans and laborers and even many merchants and professionals did not own real estate. And in the West, new farms were often valued at below property qualifications. This became particularly troublesome after the War of 1812, when a large proportion of veterans could not vote. In Shenandoah County, Virginia, for instance, 700 of 1,000 men at a militia muster claimed that they were disfranchised; in Loudoun County, the comparable figure was 1,000 of

1,200. In 1829 the "Non-Freeholders of the City of Richmond" petitioned for the right to vote, arguing that the ownership of property did not make a man "wiser and better." "Virtue" and "intelligence," they insisted, were "not among the products of the soil." Even the aging Thomas Jefferson had come to believe, by 1824, that property restrictions violated "the principle of equal political rights."

Under the impetus of growing disfranchisement (and of Republican legislatures and state conventions eager to increase their constituencies), state after state extended the vote to include all adult white men. In 1790 only Vermont granted the vote to all free men. Kentucky entered the Union in 1792 without property or taxpaying qualifications; Tennessee followed with a freehold qualification, but only for newcomers who had resided in their counties for less than six months. The federal government dropped the 50-acre freehold qualification in the territories in 1812; of the eight territories that became states between 1796 and 1821 none kept a property qualification, only three maintained a taxpaying qualification, and five explicitly granted the vote to all white men. In the same years, one eastern state after another widened the franchise. By 1840 only Rhode Island retained a propertied electorate—primarily because Yankee farmers in that state wanted to retain power in a society made up more and more of urban, immigrant wage earners. (When Rhode Island finally reformed the franchise in 1843, the new law included a freehold requirement that applied only to the foreign-born and explicitly withheld the franchise from blacks.) With that exception, the white men of every state held the vote.

Early nineteenth century suffrage reform gave political rights to propertyless men and thus took a long step away from the Founders' republic and toward mass democracy. At the same time, however, reformers explicitly limited the democratic franchise to those who were white and male. New Jersey's revolutionary constitution, for instance, had granted the vote to "persons" who met a freehold qualification. This loophole enfranchised property-holding widows, many of whom exercised their rights. A law of 1807 abolished property restrictions and gave the vote to all white men; the same law closed the loophole that had allowed propertied women to vote. The question of woman suffrage would not be raised again until women raised it in 1848; it would not be settled until well into the twentieth century.

New restrictions also applied to African Americans. The revolutionary constitutions of Massachusetts, New Hampshire, Vermont, and Maine—northeastern states with tiny black minorities—granted the vote to free blacks. New York and North Carolina laws gave the vote to "all men" who met the qualifications, and propertied African Americans (a tiny but symbolically crucial minority) in many states routinely exercised the vote. Postrevolutionary laws that extended voting rights to all white men often specifically excluded or severely restricted votes for blacks. Free blacks lost the suffrage in New York, New Jersey, Pennsylvania, Connecticut, Maryland, Tennessee, and North

Carolina—all states in which they had previously voted. By 1840 fully 93 percent of blacks in the North lived in states that either banned or severely restricted their right to vote. And the restrictions were explicitly about race. A delegate to the New York constitutional convention of 1821, noting the movement of freed slaves into New York City, argued against allowing them to vote: "The whole host of Africans that now deluge our city (already too impertinent to be borne), would be placed upon an equal with the citizens." At the Tennessee convention that eliminated property and residence requirements for whites while it stripped the vote from free blacks in 1834, delegate G. W. L. Marr declared that "We the People" meant "we the free white people of the United States and the free white people only." The convention declared blacks "outside the social compact." A year later, the old republican Nathaniel Macon told a North Carolina convention that in 1776 free blacks had been "no part of the then political family."

Thus the "universal" suffrage of which many Americans boasted was far from universal. New laws dissolved the old republican connections between political rights and property, and thus saved the citizenship of thousands who were becoming propertyless tenants and wage earners. The same laws that gave the vote to all white men, however, explicitly barred other Americans from political participation. Faced with the disintegration of Jefferson's republic of proprietor-patriarchs, the wielders of power had chosen to blur the emerging distinctions of social class while they hardened the boundaries of sex and race. In 1790 citizenship had belonged to men who were fathers and farm owners. Forty years later, the citizenry was made up of those who were (the phrase came into use at this time) "free, white, and twenty-one." Much more explicitly and completely than had been the case at the founding, America in 1830 was a white man's republic.

CHAPTER 6

———»·o·«———

Democrats and National Republicans

JEFFERSON'S REPUBLICANS, LIKE THEIR FEDERALIST PREDECES-
SORS, argued and governed against a backdrop of world war. Questions of national sovereignty, neutral rights, Atlantic trade, international republicanism,
and British, French, and Spanish intrigue decisively shaped the American political environment. So did the presence of independent Indian peoples in the
West. That changed with the peace of 1815. Europe entered a long period of
peace and white hegemony east of the Mississippi was secure; neither Indians
nor the powers of Europe threatened the United States. Now politicians worried less about international affairs and more about westward expansion and
an exhilarating and uneven national market revolution. They also worried
about a deepening chasm between a North that had committed to economic
diversity and market integration and a South that remained tied to plantation
slavery and the export economy. The dominant Democratic-Republicans
splintered over these questions. In the 1820s politicians revived Jefferson's old
party of southern and northern agrarians into a national coalition committed
to minimal government, states rights, and the avoidance of trouble between
the sections. Their opponents supported an economic nationalism that would,
they promised, minimize sectional divisions. The result was the election of
Andrew Jackson in 1828 and a two-party system that persisted until the eve of
the Civil War.

THE AMERICAN SYSTEM

President James Madison delivered his annual message to the Fourteenth Congress in December 1815. He asked for legislation to create a new national bank, a tariff to protect American manufacturers, and congressional support for those canals and roads "which can best be executed under national authority." Congress agreed. Made up overwhelmingly of Jeffersonian Republicans and led by the young southern and western nationalists who had favored the war, this Congress reversed many of the positions taken by Jefferson's old party. It chartered a national bank, enacted a protective tariff, and debated a national system of roads and canals at federal expense. Most prewar Republicans had viewed such programs as heresy. But by 1815 the Republican majority in Congress had come to accept them as orthodox and necessary. Secretary of the Treasury Albert Gallatin explained: "The War has renewed and reinstated the national feelings which the Revolution had given and which were daily lessened. The people have now more general objects of attachment with which their pride and political opinions are connected. They are more American."

Even as they convinced themselves that they had won the war, Republicans were painfully aware of the weaknesses that the war had displayed. Put simply, the United States had been unable to coordinate a national fiscal and military effort: bad roads, local jealousies, and a bankrupt treasury had nearly lost the war. In addition, the war and the years leading up to it convinced many Republicans—including Jefferson and Madison—that the export economy rendered the United States dangerously dependent on a Europe (and especially a Great Britain) that was not dependable. Finally, many of the younger Republicans in Congress were interested less in ideological purity than in bringing commerce into new regions. The nation, they said, must abandon Jefferson's export-oriented agrarianism and encourage prosperity and national independence through subsidies to commerce, manufactures, and internal improvements.

National Republicans

The man most closely associated with this shift in republicanism was Henry Clay of Kentucky. Retaining his power in the postwar Congress, Clay headed the drive for protective tariffs, the bank, and internal improvements. He would call his program the "American System," arguing that it would foster national economic growth and a salutary harmony between geographical sections, thus a happy and prosperous republic.

In 1816 Congress chartered a Second Bank of the United States, headquartered in Philadelphia and empowered to establish branches wherever it saw fit. The government agreed to deposit its funds in the bank, to accept the bank's notes as payment for government land, taxes, and other transactions, and to buy one-fifth of the bank's stock. The Bank of the United States was more powerful than the one that had been rejected (by one vote) by a Republican Congress in 1811. The fiscal horrors of the War of 1812, however, had convinced most representatives that it would be a good idea to move toward a national currency and centralized control of money and credit. The alternative was to allow state banks—which had increased in number from 88 to 208 between 1813 and 1815—to issue the unregulated and grossly inflated notes that had weakened the war effort and promised to throw the anticipated postwar boom into chaos.

With no discussion of the constitutionality of what it was doing, Congress chartered the Bank of the United States as the sole banking institution empowered to do business throughout the country. Notes issued by the bank would be the first semblance of a national currency (they would soon constitute from one-tenth to one-third of the value of notes in circulation). Moreover, the bank could regulate the currency by demanding that state bank notes used in transactions with the federal government be redeemable in gold. In 1816 the bank set up shop in Philadelphia's Carpenter's Hall, and in 1824 moved around the corner to a Greek revival edifice modeled after the Parthenon—a marble embodiment of the republican conservatism that directors of the Bank of the United States promised as their fiscal stance. From that vantage point they would fight (with a few huge lapses) a running battle with state banks and local interests in an effort to impose fiscal discipline and centralized control over an exploding market economy.

The same Congress drew up the nation's first overtly protective tariff in 1816. Shut off from British imports during the war, the Americans had built their first factories—almost entirely in southern New England and the mid-Atlantic. The British planned to flood the postwar market with cheap goods and kill American manufactures, and a majority in Congress determined to stop them. Shepherded through the House by Clay and his fellow nationalist John C. Calhoun of South Carolina, the Tariff of 1816 raised import duties an average of 25 percent, extending protection to the nation's infant industries at the expense of foreign trade and American consumers. Again, wartime difficulties and wartime nationalism had paved the way: since Americans could not depend on imported manufactures, Congress saw the encouragement of domestic manufactures as a patriotic necessity and a spur to commerce between the sections. The tariff was well supported by the Northeast and the West, with enough southern support to ensure its passage by Congress. Tariffs would rise and fall between 1816 and the Civil War, but the principle of protectionism would persist.

Many of the Founders had seen a national transportation system as essential to the prosperity and safety of the union. George Washington had urged roads and canals linking the Atlantic states with the interior—both to provide western farmers with the civilizing benefits of commerce and to secure their loyalty to the United States. Thomas Jefferson, though he worried less about frontier barbarism, shared Washington's views, and like his fellow Virginian he favored improvements that would channel western commerce through Chesapeake Bay. He and Washington both insisted that the most sensible route would link the Potomac River with the Ohio. In 1802 President Jefferson signed a bill that began construction of the Cumberland Road (often called the National Road) from Cumberland, Maryland, to the Ohio River at Wheeling. In 1811 Secretary of the Treasury Albert Gallatin issued a report outlining a vast system of canals and roads that would tie the country together.

These early dreams and projects were meant to serve the postcolonial economy: they would deliver farm produce to the coast and then to international markets; the coastal towns would receive imported goods and ship them back into the countryside. As early as 1770, George Washington had dreamed of making the Potomac River a busy "Channel of Commerce between Great Britain" and the farmers of the interior. Others dreamed of other routes and rivers, but nearly all proponents of transportation into the West (with the partial exception of Gallatin) shared the great assumption of Washington's early vision: the export economy would remain dominant; the United States would be an independent, unified, and prosperous economic colony of the Old World.

Henry Clay's American system grew into a new vision: a national transportation network that would make the United States economically independent of Europe and geographically interdependent within itself. The Bank of the United States would supply fiscal stability and a uniform, trustworthy currency. The tariff would encourage northeasterners to build factories and citizens in other parts of the country to buy what American manufacturers made, and agriculturalists would enjoy expanded internal markets: the West would sell food to the cities and to the plantation South, and the South would supply the burgeoning textile industry with cotton. The system would not deny international trade, but it would make the United States an economically integrated and independent nation.

The need for internal improvements was widely acknowledged in 1816. The British wartime blockade had hampered coastal shipping and made Americans dependent on the wretched roads of the interior. Many members of the Fourteenth Congress, after spending days of bruising travel on their way to Washington, were determined to give the United States an efficient transportation network. Some urged completion of the National Road linking the Chesapeake with the trans-Appalachian West. Some talked of an inland canal system to link the northern and southern coastal states. Others wanted a federally subsidized turnpike from Maine to Georgia.

Bills to provide federal subsidies for internal improvements, however, had a hard time winning approval in the postwar Congress. Internal improvements were subject to local ambitions: canals and roads that helped one place hurt another. Some areas—southern New England and eastern Pennsylvania are examples—had already built good roads and did not want to subsidize the competition. There were also objections based in old Republican ideals. Roads and canals were big public works projects with scores of contractors and subcontractors—all dependent on government subsidies, with the potential for becoming a system of corruption that was both necessary and impossible to stop. Finally, federally sponsored improvements, however beneficial, were constitutionally doubtful. In the Constitutional Convention, Benjamin Franklin had proposed that the power to build roads and cut canals within the states be written into the Constitution, and his proposal had been voted down. National support for internal improvements could be justified only by the "necessary and proper" and "general welfare" clauses. The Republicans could charter a Second Bank of the United States because Hamilton's bank had established the precedent. Roads and canals—extensive local projects at national expense—would stretch those clauses much further, worrying many Republicans that future legislatures would justify whatever struck them as necessary and proper at any given time. When Congress agreed to complete the National Road—the one federal internal improvement already under way—President Madison and his Republican successor James Monroe vetoed the bills, refusing to support further internal improvements without a constitutional amendment. In 1822 Monroe even vetoed a bill authorizing repairs on the National Road, stating once again that the Constitution did not empower the federal government to build roads within the states. As a result, the financing and construction of roads and canals fell to the states—overwhelmingly the *northern* states. Henry Clay watched his vision of transportation as a nationalizing force turn into southern inaction and northern regionalization, a dangerous trend that continued throughout his long political life.

Commerce and the Law

The courts of the early republic rivaled Congress in playing a nationalizing and commercializing role. The Revolution replaced British courts with national and state legal systems based in English common law—systems that made legal action accessible to most white males. Thus many of the disputes generated in the transition to market society ended up in court. The courts removed social conflicts from the public arena and brought them into peaceful courtrooms. There they dealt with the conflicts in language that only lawyers understood and resolved them in ways that tended to promote the entrepreneurial use of private property, the sanctity of contracts, and the right to do business shielded from neighborhood restraints and democratic politics.

John Marshall, who presided over the Supreme Court from 1801 to 1835, took the lead. From the beginning he saw the Court as a conservative hedge against the excesses of provincialism and democratically elected legislatures.

His early decisions protected the independence of the courts and their right to review legislation. From 1816 onward, his decisions encouraged business and strengthened the national government at the expense of the states.

Marshall's most important decisions protected the sanctity of contracts and corporate charters against state legislatures. For example, in *Dartmouth College v. Woodward* (1816), Dartmouth defended a royal charter granted in the 1760s against changes introduced by a Republican legislature that wanted to transform Dartmouth from a privileged bastion of Federalism into a state college. Daniel Webster, who was a Dartmouth alumnus, the school's highly paid lawyer, and one of the few avowed Federalists left in Congress, finished his argument before the Supreme Court on a histrionic note: "It is, sir, as I have said, a small college. And yet there are those who love it—." Reputedly moved to tears, Marshall ruled that Dartmouth's original corporate charter could not be altered by legislation. Though in this case the Supreme Court was protecting Dartmouth's independence and its chartered privileges, Marshall and Webster knew that the decision also protected the hundreds of turnpike and canal companies, manufacturing corporations, and other ventures that held privileges under corporate charters granted by state governments. Once the charters had been granted, the states could neither regulate the corporations nor cancel their privileges. Thus corporate charters acquired the legal status of contracts, beyond the reach of democratic politics.

Two weeks after deciding the *Dartmouth* case, Marshall handed down the majority decision in *McCulloch v. Maryland*. The Maryland legislature, nurturing old Jeffersonian doubts about the constitutionality of the Bank of the United States, had attempted to tax the Bank's Baltimore branch—which in fact was a corrupt and ruinous institution (see later subsection entitled *The Panic of 1819*). The Bank had challenged the legislature's right to do so, and the court decided in favor of the Bank. Marshall stated, first, that the Constitution granted the federal government "implied powers" that included chartering the Bank, and he denied Maryland's right to tax the Bank or any other federal agency: "The power to tax," he said, "involves the power to destroy." It was Marshall's most explicit blow against Jeffersonian strict construction. Americans, he said, "did not design to make their government dependent on the states." And yet there were many, particularly in Marshall's native South, who remained certain that that was precisely what the Founders had intended.

In *Gibbons v. Ogden* (1824) the Marshall Court broke a state-granted steamship monopoly in New York harbor. The monopoly, Marshall argued, interfered with federal jurisdiction over interstate commerce. Like the *Dartmouth* case and *McCulloch v. Maryland*, this decision empowered the national government in relation to the states. And like them, it encouraged private entrepreneurs. As surely as congressmen who supported the American System, John Marshall's Supreme Court assumed a natural and beneficial link between federal power and market society.

Meanwhile, the state courts were working quieter but equally profound transformations of American law. In the early republic, state courts had often viewed property not only as a private possession but as part of a neighborhood. Thus when a miller built a dam that flooded upriver farms or impaired the fishery, the courts might make him take those interests into account, often in ways that reduced the business uses of his property. By 1830 New England courts routinely granted the owners of industrial mill sites unrestricted water rights, even when the exercise of those rights inflicted damage on their neighbors. As early as 1805, the New York Supreme Court in *Palmer v. Mulligan* had asserted that the right to develop property for business purposes was inherent in the ownership of property. In the courts of northern and western states, what was coming to be called "progress" demanded legal protection for the business uses of private property, even when such uses conflicted with old common law restraints.

BAD FEELINGS

The years beginning with 1816 were dubbed the "Era of Good Feelings": a period without party competition. The Federalists, disgraced by their opposition to the war and by the Hartford Convention, retreated to their last bastion in New England; they would never again be a national force. The Old Republicans of Virginia and North Carolina manned the ramparts of states rights and constitutional fundamentalism, but they mustered few votes. With the extremes outnumbered and on the defensive, Republican majorities from the West, the mid-Atlantic, and the inland South took steps toward building an integrated commercial network through federal intervention in the economy.

Two events in 1819 turned the good feelings to bad. First, the angry debate that surrounded Missouri's admission as a slave state revealed the centrality and vulnerability of slavery within the Union. Second, a severe financial collapse led many Americans to wonder whether the marriage of government and market expansion was a good idea. Some of the doubts were populist and democratic, some were proslavery, some were both. By 1820 the National Republicans faced a growing opposition determined to reconstruct the limited-government, states'-rights coalition that had elected Thomas Jefferson. By 1828 they had formed the Democratic Party, with Andrew Jackson at its head.

The Panic of 1819

In 1819 "the onward spirit of the age" suffered a major setback: the Panic of 1819 and the depression that followed it. The origins of the panic were international and numerous: European agriculture was recovering from the Napoleonic Wars, thereby reducing the demand for American foodstuffs; war and revolution in Latin America had cut off the supply of precious metals (the base of the international money supply) from the mines of Mexico and Peru; debt-ridden European governments hoarded the available specie; and American bankers and businessmen met the situation by expanding credit (particularly in the booming cotton South) and issuing bank notes that were mere dreams of real money. Coming in the first years of the market revolution, this speculative boom was encouraged by American bankers who had little experience with corporate charters, promissory notes, bills of exchange, or stocks and bonds.

One of the reasons Congress had chartered the Second Bank of the United States in 1816 was to impose order on the postwar boom. But the Bank itself, under the presidency of the genial Republican politician William Jones, became a large part of the problem: the western branch offices in Cincinnati and Lexington became embroiled in the speculative boom, and insiders at the Baltimore branch hatched criminal schemes to enrich themselves. With matters spinning out of control, Jones resigned early in 1819. The new president, Langdon Cheves of South Carolina, curtailed credit and demanded that state bank notes received by the Bank of the United States be redeemed in specie (precious metals). By doing so, Cheves rescued the Bank from the paper economy created by state-chartered banks but at huge expense: when the state banks were forced to redeem their notes in specie, they demanded payment from their own borrowers, and the national money and credit system collapsed.

The depression that followed the Panic of 1819 was the first failure of the market economy. There had been local ups and downs since the 1780s, but this collapse was nationwide. Employers who could not meet their debts went out of business, and hundreds of thousands of wage workers lost their jobs. In Philadelphia, unemployment reached 75 percent; 1,800 workers in that city were imprisoned for debt. A tent city of the unemployed sprang up on the outskirts of Baltimore. Other cities and towns were hit as hard, and the situation was no better in the countryside. A single session of the county court at Nashville handled over 500 suits for debt. Thomas Jefferson reported that farms in his Virginia neighborhood were selling for what had earlier been a year's rent. Jefferson knew these problems firsthand: he had cosigned bank loans for an old friend, was caught up "by a catastrophe I had never contemplated," and spent his remaining years trying to avoid bankruptcy.

Faced with a disastrous downturn that none could control and few understood, many Americans turned their resentment on the banks, particularly on the Bank of the United States. It was the first collapse of the nationally integrated credit system. When state banks defaulted, the national bank inherited the paper on thousands of farms and on much of the commercial real estate in western towns. Thomas Hart Benton, senator from the new state of Missouri, exclaimed "All the flourishing cities of the West are mortgaged to this money power." John Jacob Astor of New York, reputedly the richest man in America, admitted that "there has been too much Speculation and too much assumption of Power on the Part of the Bank Directors which has caused the institution to become unpopular." William Gouge, who would become the Jacksonian Democrats' favorite economist, put it more bluntly: when the Bank demanded that state bank notes be redeemed in specie, he said, "the Bank was saved and the people were ruined." By the end of 1819 the Bank of the United States had won the name that it would carry to its death in the 1830s: the Monster. Particularly in the South and West, the collapse produced a visceral and lasting popular suspicion—not of commerce but of the privileged gambler-insiders who shaped the national market from offices in Philadelphia and Washington.

Missouri

The national government played a central—and sometimes troubled—role in the settlement of the West. The federal government destroyed the Indians east of the Mississippi, sold off millions of acres of land at low prices, and negotiated the purchase of Florida (which included the Gulf Coast east of Louisiana) and of treaties that pacified the Canadian–U.S. border. With that, the southern Cotton Belt and the northwestern grain belt came into being. Congress organized the territories and brought in new states—free states north of the Ohio River as specified by the Northwest Ordinance of 1786, slave states in the Southwest. Before long, Americans began to move outside the original territory of the United States and into the southern portions of Jefferson's Louisiana Purchase. Louisiana itself, strategically crucial and already the site of sugar plantations and the town of New Orleans, entered the Union in 1812. Settlers were also filtering into northern Louisiana and the Arkansas and Missouri territories.

Early in 1819 Missouri applied for admission to the Union as the first new state to be carved out of the Louisiana Purchase—with a constitution that allowed slavery. New York Congressman James Tallmadge, Jr., quickly proposed two amendments to the Missouri statehood bill. The first would bar additional slaves from being brought into Missouri (16 percent of Missouri's territorial population were slaves). The second would emancipate Missouri slaves born after admission when they reached their twenty-fifth birthday. Put simply, the Tallmadge Amendments would admit Missouri only if Missouri agreed to become a free state.

The congressional debates on the Missouri question had little to do with humanitarian objections to slavery and everything to do with political power. Rufus King of New York, an old Federalist who led the northerners in the Senate, insisted that he opposed the admission of any new slave state "solely in its bearing and effects upon great political interests, and upon the just and equal rights of the freemen of the nation." Northerners had long chafed at the added representation in Congress and in the electoral college that the Constitution's three-fifths rule (which counted each slave as 60 percent of a person for pur-poses of apportionment) granted to the slave states. The rule had, in fact, added significantly to southern power: in 1790 the South, with 40 percent of the white population, controlled 47 percent of the votes in Congress—enough to decide close votes both in Congress and in presidential elections. Federalists pointed out that of the twelve additional electoral votes the three-fifths rule gave to the South, ten had gone to Thomas Jefferson in 1800 and had given him the elec-tion. Without the bogus votes provided by slavery, they argued, Virginia's stranglehold on the presidency would have been broken with Washington's departure in 1796.

In 1819 the North held a majority in the House of Representatives. The South, thanks to the recent admissions of Alabama and southern-oriented Illinois, con-trolled a bare majority in the Senate. Voting on the Tallmadge Amendments was starkly sectional: northern congressmen voted 86 to 10 for the first amendment, 80 to 14 for the second; southerners rejected both, 66 to 1 and 64 to 2. In the Sen-ate, a unanimous South defeated the Tallmadge Amendments with the help of the two Illinois senators and three northerners. Deadlocked between a Senate in favor of admitting Missouri as a slave state and a House dead set against it, Con-gress broke off one of the angriest sessions in its history and went home.

The new Congress that convened in the winter of 1819–1820 passed the leg-islative package that became known as the Missouri Compromise. Massachu-setts offered its northern counties as the new free state of Maine, thus neutral-izing fears that the South would gain votes in the Senate with the admission of Missouri. Senator Jesse Thomas of Illinois then proposed the so-called Thomas Proviso: if the North would admit Missouri as a slave state, the South would agree to outlaw slavery in territories north of a line extending from the south-ern border of Missouri to Spanish (within a year, Mexican) territory. That line would open Arkansas Territory (present-day Arkansas and Oklahoma) to slav-ery and would close to slavery the remainder of the Louisiana Territory, land that subsequently became all or part of nine states.

Congress admitted Maine with little debate. But the admission of Missouri, even under the terms of the Thomas Proviso, met northern opposition. A joint Senate–House committee finally decided to separate the two bills. With half of the southern representatives and nearly all of the northerners supporting it, the Thomas Proviso passed. Congress then took up the admission of Missouri. With the votes of a solid South and fourteen compromise-minded northerners, Missouri entered the Union as a slave state. President Monroe applauded the "patriotic devotion" of the northern representatives "who preferr'd the sacrifice of themselves at home to" endangering the Union. His words were prophetic: nearly all of the fourteen were voted out of office when they faced angry northern voters in the next election.

The Missouri crisis brought the South's commitment to slavery and the North's resentment of southern political power into collision, revealing an uncompromisable gulf between slave and free states. The votes on the Missouri question had divided Congress, for the first time, into northern and southern blocs. Southern Republicans claimed that it was Federalists who had raised the issue of slavery, hoping to resurrect themselves as the majority Northern party. Indeed the northern Federalist minority did favor banning slavery in Missouri. But a band of northern Republicans also insisted that it was "the right and duty of Congress" to stop the expansion "of the intolerable evil and the crying enormity of slavery." Some southerners responded with the first congressional defenses of the moral rightness and social necessity of slavery. Nathaniel Macon, an Old Republican of North Carolina, denounced what some northerners used as a trump card: "A clause in the Declaration of Independence has been read, declaring that 'all men are created equal'; follow that sentiment and does it not lead to universal emancipation?" To state this was enough to refute it: emancipation was unthinkable, and Jefferson was wrong.

Whereas northerners vowed to relinquish no more territory to slavery, southerners talked openly of disunion and civil war. A Georgia politician announced that the Missouri debates had lit a fire that "seas of blood can only extinguish." John Quincy Adams saw the debates as an omen: northerners would unanimously oppose the extension of slavery whenever the question came to a vote. Adams confided to his diary: "Here was a new party ready formed, . . . terrible to the whole Union, but portentiously terrible to the South—threatening in its progress the emancipation of all their slaves, threatening in its immediate effect that Southern domination which has swayed the Union for the last twenty years. . . ." Viewing the crisis from Monticello, the aging Thomas Jefferson was distraught: "A geographical line, coinciding with a marked principle, moral and political, once conceived and held up to the angry passions of men, will never be obliterated; every new irritation will mark it deeper and deeper . . . This momentous question, like a fire-bell in the night, awakened and filled me with terror. I considered it at once the knell of the Union."

REPUBLICAN REVIVAL

The crises of 1819–1820 prompted demands for a return to Jeffersonian principles. President James Monroe's happily proclaimed "Era of Good Feelings" was, according to many worried Republicans, a disaster. Without opposition, Jefferson's dominant Republican Party had lost its way. The nationalist Congress of 1816 had enacted much of the Federalist program under the name of Republicanism; the result, said the old Republicans, was an aggressive government that overstepped its constitutional bounds and helped bring on the Panic of 1819. At the same time, the collapse of Republican Party discipline in Congress had allowed the Missouri question to degenerate into a sectional free-for-all, dividing the legislature (and potentially the nation) into angry northern and southern blocs. By 1820 many Republicans, alternately fearing consolidation and disunion, were calling for a Jeffersonian revival that would limit government power and guarantee slavery within the Union.

The busiest and the most astute of those Republicans was Martin Van Buren, leader of New York's Bucktail Republican faction, who took his seat in the Senate in 1821. An immensely talented man with no influential family connections (his father was a Hudson Valley tavern keeper) and little formal education, Van Buren had built his political career out of a commitment to Jeffersonian principles, personal charm, and party discipline. Arriving in Washington in the aftermath of the Missouri debates and the Panic of 1819, he hoped to apply his political expertise to what he perceived as a dangerous turning point in national politics.

Van Buren's New York experience, along with his reading of national politics, told him that disciplined political parties were necessary democratic tools. The Founders—including Jefferson—had denounced parties, claiming that republics rested on civic virtue, not competition. Van Buren, on the other hand, claimed that the Era of Good Feelings had turned public attention away from politics, allowing privileged insiders—many of them unreconstructed Federalists—to create an active, burgeoning national state and to allow the explosive question of slavery into congressional debate. Van Buren insisted that competition and party divisions were inevitable and good, but that they must be made to serve the republic. The answer was to invite true republicans into the old Jeffersonian coalition, and to allow the Federalists and their sympathizers to organize an opposition. "We must always have party distinctions," he said, "and the old ones are the best. . . . If the old ones are suppressed, geographical differences founded on local instincts or what is worse, prejudices between free & slave holding states will inevitably take their place." Working with like-minded politicians, Van Buren reconstructed the coalition of northern and southern agrarians that had elected Thomas Jefferson. The result was the Democratic Party and, ultimately, a national two-party system that persisted until the eve of the Civil War.

With the approach of the 1824 presidential election, Van Buren and his friends supported William H. Crawford, Monroe's secretary of war and a staunch states-rights Republican from Georgia. The Van Burenites controlled the Republican congressional caucus, the body that traditionally chose the party's presidential candidates. The public distrusted the caucus as undemocratic, for it represented the only party in government and thus could dictate the choice of a president. But Van Buren continued to regard it as a necessary tool of party discipline. With most congressmen fearing their constituents, only a minority showed up for the caucus vote. They dutifully nominated Crawford.

With Republican Party unity broken, the list of sectional candidates grew. John Quincy Adams was the son of a Federalist president, successful secretary of state under Monroe, and one of the northeastern Federalist converts to Republicanism who, according to people like Van Buren and Crawford, had blunted the republican thrust of Jefferson's old party. He entered the contest as New England's favorite son. Henry Clay of Kentucky, a nationalist who claimed the American System as his own, and who was respected as the "Great Compromiser" who had crafted the deals that ended the Missouri crisis, was the western candidate. John C. Calhoun of South Carolina announced his candidacy, but when he lost the endorsement of large and crucial Pennsylvania, he dropped out of the swarm of presidential hopefuls and put himself forward as the sole candidate for vice president.

The wild card was Andrew Jackson of Tennessee. In 1824 Jackson was known only as a military hero—scourge of the southwestern Indians and victor over the British at New Orleans. He was also a frontier nabob with a reputation for violence: he had killed a rival in a duel (it began in an argument over a horse race), had engaged in a shootout in a Nashville tavern, and had reputedly stolen his wife from her estranged husband. According to Jackson's detractors, such impetuosity marked his public life as well. As commander of U.S. military forces in the South in 1818, Jackson had been ordered to chase marauding Seminole warriors into Spanish Florida—long a sanctuary for Indian raiders and runaway Georgia slaves. Jackson had done that and more. He invaded West Florida, summarily executed Seminoles, raised the American flag over Spanish Pensacola and a second Spanish fort, and hanged two British subjects who had been supplying the Seminoles. Secretary of State John Quincy Adams had belatedly approved Jackson's unauthorized foray, knowing that the show of American force would encourage the Spanish to sell Florida to the United States. Secretary of War Crawford, on the other hand, was appalled at General Jackson's raid. As an "economy" measure, Crawford had reduced the number of major generals in the U.S. Army from two to one, thus eliminating Jackson's job. After being appointed governor of newly acquired Florida in 1821, Jackson retired from public life later that year. In 1824 eastern politicians knew Jackson only as a "military chieftain" and "the Napoleon of the woods"— a frontier hothead and, possibly, a robber-bridegroom.

Jackson may have been all of those things. But what the easterners did not take into account in the election of 1824 was his immense national popularity. In the sixteen states that chose presidential electors by popular vote (six states still left the choice to their legislatures), Jackson polled 152,901 votes to Adams's 114,023 and Clay's 47,217. Crawford, who suffered a crippling stroke during the campaign, won 46,979 votes. Jackson's support was more nearly national than that of any of his opponents. Adams carried only his native New England and a portion of New York. Clay won only in Ohio, Missouri, and his home state of Kentucky. The stricken Crawford's support centered in the Southeast and the portions of New York that Van Buren was able to deliver. Jackson carried 84 percent of the votes of his own Southwest, and won victories in Pennsylvania, New Jersey, North Carolina, Indiana, and Illinois, while running a close second in several other states.

Jackson assumed that he had won the election: he had received 42 percent of the popular vote to his nearest rival's 33 percent (again, in the sixteen states in which there was a popular vote), and his support was far more national than that of any other candidate. His 99 electoral votes, however, were 32 shy of the plurality demanded by the Constitution. And so, acting under the Twelfth Amendment, the House of Representatives selected a president from among the top three candidates. As the candidate with the fewest electoral votes, Henry Clay was eliminated. But he remained Speaker of the House, and he had enough support to throw the election to either Jackson or Adams. Rumors circulated (originally spread by an obscure Pennsylvania congressman) that Clay had offered to swing his support to Jackson in exchange for appointment as secretary of state—an office that Jefferson, Madison, and Monroe (and, prospectively, John Quincy Adams) had all used as a springboard to the presidency. When Jackson turned him down, according to Jacksonian legend, Clay went to Adams and offered the same deal. Adams, according to Jackson's story, accepted what became known as the "Corrupt Bargain" in January 1825. A month later, the House of Representatives voted: Clay's supporters (including the Kentucky delegation, which had been instructed by the state legislature to vote for Jackson), joined by several old Federalists, switched to Adams, giving him a one-vote victory. Soon after becoming president, Adams appointed Henry Clay as his secretary of state.

Whether there was in fact a "Corrupt Bargain" between Adams and Clay will probably never be known. Opponents of the story pointed out that Clay did not need a bargain to support his fellow nationalist John Quincy Adams over either the unqualified Jackson or the crusty (and crippled) states-rights Republican William Crawford. Just as surely, Clay was Adams's natural choice as secretary of state and presidential successor. But whatever the actual chain of events, Adams and Clay had acted out popular suspicions of a bargain for the presidency, and that was an act of great political stupidity.

Reaction to the alleged "Corrupt Bargain" dominated the Adams administration and spurred a populist rhetoric of intrigue and betrayal that nourished a rising democratic movement. Before the vote took place in the House of Representatives, Andrew Jackson remarked, "Rumors say that deep intrigue is on foot," and predicted that there would be "bargain & sale" of the presidency. After the election, Jackson declared that the "gamester" Henry Clay had subverted the democratic will to his own purposes, and that "the rights of the people have been bartered for promises of office." "So you see," Jackson said, "The Judas of the West has closed the contract and will receive the thirty pieces of silver. His end will be the same." Others in Washington were equally appalled. Robert Y. Hayne of South Carolina denounced the "monstrous union between Clay & Adams," while Louis McLane of Delaware declared the coalition of Clay and Adams utterly "unnatural & preposterous." The charge of corruption would follow Clay for the rest of his political life and destroy his dreams of becoming president. Adams himself admitted that he would take office under a cloud: the election had not gone off "in a manner satisfactory to pride or just desire; not by the unequivocal suffrages of a majority of the people; with perhaps two-thirds of the whole people adverse to the actual result."

Andrew Jackson regarded the intrigues that robbed him of the presidency in 1825 as the culmination of a long train of corruption that the nation had suffered over the last ten years. Although in the campaign he had made only vague policy statements, he had firm ideas of what had gone wrong with the republic. In 1821, after having been "betrayed" by members of Monroe's cabinet over his raid into Florida, Jackson had retired to his plantation near Nashville, had pondered the state of the nation, and had filled page after page with what he called "memorandoms." (This was the kind of semiliterate gaffe that appalled his educated eastern opponents and pleased nearly everyone else.) A frontier planter with a deep distrust of banks, Jackson claimed that the Panic of 1819 was caused by self-serving miscreants in the Bank of the United States. He insisted that the national debt was another source of corruption; it must be paid off and never allowed to recur. The federal government under James Monroe was filled with swindlers, and in the name of a vague nationalism they were taking power for themselves and scheming against the liberties of the people. The politicians had been bought off, said Jackson, and had attempted—through "King Caucus"—to select a president by backstairs deals rather than by popular election. Finally, in 1825, they had stolen the presidency outright.

Like hundreds of thousands of other Americans, Jackson sensed that something had gone wrong with the republic—that selfishness and intrigue had corrupted Jefferson's old party and the government that it controlled. In the language of revolutionary republicanism, which Jackson had learned as a boy in the Carolina backwoods and would speak throughout his life, a corrupt power once again threatened to snuff out liberty. In his "memorandoms," Jackson set against the designs of that power the classic republican safeguard: a virtuous citizenry. But unlike most of his revolutionary forebears, he believed that government should be subject to the will of popular majorities. An aroused public, he said, was the republic's best hope: "My fervent prayers are that our republican government may be perpetual, and the people alone by their virtue, and independent exercise of their free suffrage can make it perpetual."

More completely than any of his rivals, Jackson captured the rhetoric of the revolutionary republic. And, with his fixation on secrecy, corruption, and intrigues, he transformed both that rhetoric and his own biography into popular melodrama. Finally, with a political alchemy that his opponents never understood, Jackson submerged old notions of republican citizenship into a firm faith in majoritarian democracy: individuals might become selfish and corrupt, he believed, but a democratic majority was, by its very nature, opposed to corruption and governmental excess. Thus the republic was safe only when governed by the will of the majority. The "Corrupt Bargain" of 1825 had made that clear: either the people or political schemers would rule.

While Jackson fumed, Martin Van Buren and others trying to resurrect the purity of Jefferson's old party organized. Early on, they decided to throw their support to Jackson in 1828: he was a states-rights, limited government Republican like themselves, and he was by far the strongest candidate. Jackson smoldered and plotted revenge. At the same time, his supporters organized Congress and opposed Adams at every turn. The presidency of John Quincy Adams became little more than a prologue to the election of 1828.

The Presidency of John Quincy Adams

John Quincy Adams was abundantly prepared to be president of the United States. The son of a Federalist president, he had been an extraordinarily successful secretary of state under Monroe, guiding American diplomacy in the postwar world. In the Rush–Bagot Treaty of 1817 and the British–American Convention of 1818 Adams helped pacify the Great Lakes, restore American fishing rights off of Canada, and draw the United States–Canadian boundary west to the Rocky Mountains—actions that transformed the Canadian–American frontier from a battleground into the peaceful border that it has been ever since. He pacified the southern border as well. In 1819, following Jackson's raid into Florida, the Adams–Onis Treaty procured Florida for the United States and defined the United States–Spanish border west of the Mississippi in ways that gave the Americans claims to the Pacific Coast in the Northwest.

Trickier problems had arisen when Spanish colonies in the Americas declared themselves independent republics. Spain could not prevent this, and the powers of Europe, victorious over Napoleon and determined to roll back international republicanism, talked openly of helping the Spanish or of annexing South American territory for themselves. Both the Americans and the British opposed such a move, and the British proposed a joint statement outlawing the interference of any outside power (including themselves) in Latin America. Adams had thought it better for the United States to make its own policy than to "come in as cock-boat in the wake of the British man-of-war." In 1823 he wrote what became the Monroe Doctrine. Propounded at the same time that the United States recognized the new Latin American republics, it declared American opposition to any European attempt at colonization in the New World without (as the British had wanted) denying the right of the United States to annex new territory. Though the international community knew that the British navy, and not the Monroe Doctrine, kept the European powers out of the Americas, Adams had announced that the Western Hemisphere would be made up of independent republics, and that the United States was determined to be the preeminent power among them.

As president, Adams tried to translate his fervent nationalism into domestic policy. But while the brilliant, genteel Adams had dealt smoothly with European diplomats, as president of a democratic republic he went out of his way to isolate himself and offend popular democracy. ("I well know," he said soon after assuming the presidency, "that I never was and never shall be what is commonly termed a popular man.") In his first annual message to Congress, Adams outlined an ambitious program of internal improvements under the auspices of the federal government. He also wanted a national university in Washington, for the education of a nonsectional elite. He recommended creation of a naval academy and a national astronomical observatory ("lighthouses of the skies," he called them). He wanted a uniform standard of weights and measures, and he wanted to imitate European governments' "profound, laborious, and expensive researches into the figure of the earth and the comparative length of the pendulum vibrating seconds in various latitudes from the equator to the pole." While his congressional audience tried to figure that out, Adams concluded: "The spirit of improvement is abroad upon the earth, . . . While foreign nations less blessed with . . . freedom . . . than ourselves are advancing with gigantic strides in the career of public improvement, were we to slumber in indolence or fold up our arms and proclaim to the world that we are palsied by the will of our constituents, would it not . . . doom ourselves to perpetual inferiority?"

Congressmen could not believe their ears. Here was a president who had received only one third of the popular vote and who had entered office accused of intrigues against the democratic will. And yet at the first opportunity he was telling Congress to pass an ambitious program and not to be "palsied" by the will of the electorate. Even members of Congress who favored Adams's program (and there were many of them) were afraid to vote for it.

Adding to his reputation as an enemy of democracy whenever opportunity presented itself, Adams heaped popular suspicions not only on himself but on his program. Hostile politicians and journalists never tired of joking about Adams's "lighthouses to the skies." More lasting, however, was the connection they drew between federal public works projects and high taxes, intrusive government, the denial of democratic majorities, and expanded opportunities for corruption, secret deals, and special favors. Congress never acted on most of the president's proposals. The National Road was extended from Wheeling to Zanesville, Ohio, and there were some subsidies to other internal improvements as well. But there were no observatories, no national university, no experiments with pendulums, and the Naval Academy was voted down. (The Naval Academy at Annapolis was finally established in 1845.)

President Adams was equally unsuccessful in his dealings with other countries and other peoples. His First Annual Message mentioned that a congress had been called in Panama to discuss questions common to the republics of the Western Hemisphere—both the newly independent nations of South and Central America and the United States. Adams told Congress that he and Secretary

Clay had accepted the invitation. The outcry was immediate. Many southerners wanted nothing to do with a conference of new nations that had banished slavery, that might use the conference to discuss that issue, and that would appoint delegates who were former slaves. In addition, Adams's acceptance of the invitation was a perceived violation of the treaty-making power of the Senate and a potential "entangling alliance" with other nations. From his plantation in Tennessee, Andrew Jackson branded the Panama Congress an "attempt to destroy the constitutional checks of our government, and to reduce it to a despotism. . . . to register the *edicts* of the President." John Randolph of Roanoke, who had now brought his eccentricities to the Senate, screamed that the Panama Mission was a "Kentucky cuckoo's egg," nurtured by the unholy alliance between Adams and Clay—"the puritan and the black-leg." (An infuriated Clay challenged Randolph to a duel over this speech, and the secretary of state and the senator met on the field of honor. Clay's shot passed harmlessly through Randolph's flowing coat, and Randolph fired a gentlemanly shot into the air.) Senator Martin Van Buren, looking for ways to undermine Adams, organized congressional opposition to the Panama Mission. The Senate delayed the appointment of ministers, Congress delayed the appropriations, and the American representative (there had been two, but one had died in the meantime) arrived only at the end of the Panama Congress. Strict construction, the defense of southern interests, and Van Buren's organization of Congress had won a major battle with President Adams.

Adams's attention then turned to the Caribbean. In 1818 the British had banned American ships from their island colonies. The Americans had responded by banning British ships from those islands from American ports. After a period of diplomatic wrangling it was clear that Britain would not rescind its ban. President Adams asked Congress to stop American trade with British colonies, both in the Caribbean and North America, in order to coerce the British. Seeing another opportunity to embarrass Adams, Martin Van Buren killed the bill in the Senate, and Adams had no alternative but to reinstate the old 1818 restrictions in March 1827—one of the great public failures of his diplomatic career. *"You may rest assured,"* said Van Buren at this point, *"that the re-election of Mr. Adams is out of the question."*

Perhaps Adams's greatest failure—diplomatically, politically, and morally—had to do with Indian lands in Georgia. When Adams entered office, a final crisis between frontier whites and the native peoples of the eastern woodlands was under way. By the 1820s few Native Americans were left east of the Appalachians. The Iroquois of New York were penned into tiny reservations, and the tribes of the Old Northwest were broken and scattered. But in the Old Southwest 60,000 Cherokees, Creeks, Choctaws, Chickasaws, and Seminoles remained on their ancestral lands, with tenure guaranteed by federal treaties that (at least implicitly) recognized them as sovereign peoples. Congress had appropriated funds for schools, tools, seeds, and training to help these "Civilized Tribes" make the transition to farming. Most government officials assumed (this had been standard doctrine under the Jeffersonians) that the tribes would eventually trade their old lands and use their farming skills on new land west of the Mississippi.

Southwestern whites resented federal Indian policy as an affront to both white democracy and states' rights. The poorer farmers coveted the Indians' land, and states-rights southerners denied that the federal government had the authority to make treaties or to recognize sovereign peoples within their states. Resistance centered in Georgia. In 1802 that state had ceded its western portions to the national government, on condition that the United States extinguish Indian titles to those lands. The United States accepted the land and did not act on the titles in question until President Monroe's representatives concluded the Treaty of Indian Springs early in 1825, in which the Creeks sold their lands in Georgia and most of their property in Alabama. The treaty was fraudulent: the United States negotiators were close to the government of Georgia, and the principal Creek negotiator, Chief William McIntosh, had no authority to represent the Creeks—who promptly assassinated him and denied the validity of the treaty. Although the federal Indian agent screamed that the Treaty of Indian Springs was a fraud, the Senate ratified it on the day before Adams's inauguration, and the new president signed it. But as information accumulated, Adams had second thoughts. He told Governor George Troup of Georgia to postpone his plans to survey the ceded land, received a delegation of Creek chiefs in Washington, and sent the army to Georgia to keep the peace. Under the new Treaty of Washington, the Creeks retained significant parts of their Georgia land. Governor Troup rejected the treaty and sent surveyors on to Creek lands, telling President Adams, who was contemplating the use of force, that "From the first decisive act of hostility, you will be considered and treated as a public enemy . . . and what is more, the unblushing allies of the savages whose cause you have adopted." Adams backed down and passed the question on to Congress, which did nothing, and Georgia got its way. A defeated and humiliated President Adams confided to his diary: "We have talked of benevolence and humanity . . . but none of this benevolence is felt where the right of the Indian comes into collision with the interest of the white man." What he did not record was that a president of the United States had allowed himself to be bullied by the governor of a state.

The Election of 1828

As early as 1825, it was clear that the election of 1828 would pit Adams against Andrew Jackson. To the consternation of his chief supporters, Adams did nothing to prepare for what promised to be a stiff contest. He refused to build a party apparatus and did not remove even his noisiest enemies from appointive office. By default, his cabinet secretaries made appointments in their own departments. At the State Department, Henry Clay appointed able men who supported the administration. ("Nobody," he said, "can say that *I* neglect my friends.") But John McLean, the postmaster general, was a Jackson supporter who used appointments and the power of his office to favor the opposition. President Adams, who acknowledged McLean as an able administrator, refused to fire him. He would not, he insisted, let the presidency become "an electioneering machine." The opposition was much more active. Van Buren and like-minded Republicans (with their candidate Crawford hopelessly incapacitated) switched their allegiance to Jackson. They wanted Jackson elected, however, not only as a popular hero but as head of a disciplined and committed Democratic Party that would continue the states-rights, limited-government positions of the old Jeffersonian Republicans.

The new Democratic Party linked popular democracy with the defense of southern slavery. Van Buren began preparations for 1828 with a visit to John C. Calhoun of South Carolina. Calhoun was moving along the road from postwar nationalism to states-rights conservatism; he also wanted to stay on as vice president and thus keep his presidential hopes alive. After convincing Calhoun to support Jackson and endorse limited government, Van Buren wrote to Thomas Ritchie, editor of the *Richmond Enquirer* and leader of Virginia's Republicans—the man who could deliver Crawford's southern supporters to Jackson. In his letter, Van Buren proposed to revive the alliance of "the planters of the South and the plain Republicans of the North" that had elected Jefferson. Reminding Ritchie of how one-party government had allowed the Missouri question to get out of hand, Van Buren insisted that "if the old [party loyalties] are suppressed, prejudices between free and slave holding states will inevitably take their place." Thus a new Democratic Party, committed to an agrarian program of states' rights and minimal government and dependent on the votes of both slaveholding and nonslaveholding states (beginning, much like Jefferson's old party, with Van Buren's New York and Ritchie's Virginia), would ensure democracy, the protection of slavery, and the preservation of the Union. The alternative, Van Buren firmly believed, was an expensive and invasive national state (Adams's "lighthouses to the skies"), the isolation of the slaveholding South, and thus mortal danger to the republic.

The new Jacksonian Democratic Party needed publicists as well as political leaders, and Van Buren's growing coalition put together an impressive network of party newspapers. Party leaders financed Duff Green's *United States Telegraph* in Washington, D.C. They also brought Thomas Ritchie's *Richmond Enquirer* and the *Albany Argus*, mouthpiece for the Van Buren party in New York, into the Jackson camp, along with Isaac Hill's *New Hampshire Patriot*, James Gordon Bennett's *New York Enquirer*, Nathaniel Greene's *Boston Statesman*, and the *Argus of Western America*, edited by Amos Kendall and Francis Preston Blair in Kentucky. These editors put the new skills of popular entertainment and manipulation at the disposal of the Democratic Party. The growing importance of political newspapers was recognized by Jackson himself: following his election, he rewarded fifty-nine journalists with government positions.

The presidential campaign of 1828 was an exercise in slander rather than a debate on public issues. Adhering to custom, neither Adams nor Jackson campaigned directly. But their henchmen viciously personalized the campaign. Jacksonians hammered away at the "Corrupt Bargain" of 1825 and at the dishonesty and weakness that Adams had supposedly displayed in that affair. The Adams forces attacked Jackson's character. They reminded voters of his duels and tavern brawls and circulated a "coffin handbill" describing Jackson's execution of militiamen during the Creek War. One of Henry Clay's newspaper friends circulated the rumor that Jackson was a bastard and that his mother was a prostitute. But the most egregious slander of the campaign centered on Andrew Jackson's marriage. In 1790 Jackson had married Rachel Donelson, probably aware that she was estranged but not formally divorced from a man named Robards. Branding the marriage an "abduction," the Adams team screamed that Jackson had "torn from a husband the wife of his bosom," and had lived with her in a state of "open and notorious lewdness." They branded Rachel Jackson (now a deeply pious plantation housewife) an "American Jezebel," a "profligate woman," and a "convicted adulteress" whose ungoverned passions made her unfit to be first lady of a "Christian nation."

The Adams strategy backfired. Many voters agreed that only a man who strictly obeyed the law was fit to be president, and that Jackson's "passionate" and "lawless" nature disqualified him. Many others, however, criticized Adams for permitting Jackson's private life to become a public issue. Some claimed that Adams's rigid legalism left no room for privacy or for local notions of justice. Whatever the legality of their marriage, Andrew and Rachel Jackson had lived as models of marital fidelity and romantic love for nearly forty years; their neighbors had long ago forgiven whatever transgressions they may have committed. Thus on the one hand, Jackson's supporters accused the Adams campaign of a gross violation of privacy and honor. On the other, they defended Jackson's marriage—and his duels, brawls, executions, and unauthorized military ventures—as a triumph of what was right and just over what was narrowly legal. The attempt to brand Jackson as a lawless man, in fact, enhanced his image as a melodramatic hero who battled shrewd, unscrupulous, legalistic enemies by drawing on his natural nobility, sense of justice, and force of will.

The campaign caught the public imagination. Voter turnout was double what it had been in 1824, totaling 56.3 percent. Jackson won the election with 56 percent of the popular vote (a landslide that would not be matched until the twentieth century) and with a margin of 178 to 83 in electoral votes. Adams carried New England, Delaware, and most of Maryland and took 16 of New York's 36 electoral votes. Jackson carried every other state. It was a clear triumph of democracy over genteel statesmanship, of limited government over expansive nationalism, and of the South and the West over New England. Just as clearly, it was a victory of popular melodrama over old forms of cultural gentility.

Newspapers estimated that from 15,000 to 20,000 citizens (Duff Green's *Telegraph* claimed 30,000) came to Washington to witness Jackson's inauguration on March 4, 1829. They were "like the inundation of the northern barbarians into Rome," remarked Senator Daniel Webster; many had traveled as much as 500 miles, and "they really seem to think that the country is rescued from some dreadful danger." As members of the Washington establishment watched uneasily, the crowd filled the open spaces and the streets near the east portico of the Capitol Building, where Jackson was to deliver his inaugural address.

Jackson arrived at the Capitol in deep mourning. In December his wife Rachel had gone to Nashville to shop and had stopped to rest in a newspaper office. There, for the first time, she read the accusations that had been made against her. She fainted on the spot. Though she had been in poor health, no one would ever convince Jackson that her death in January had not been caused by his political enemies. As he arrived to assume the presidency, he wore a black suit and black tie, a black armband, and a black hat band that trailed down his neck in what was called a weeper.

Jackson's inaugural address was vague. He promised "proper respect" for states' rights and a "spirit of equity, caution, and compromise" on the question of the tariff, which was beginning to cause sectional controversy. He promised to reform the civil service by replacing "unfaithful or incompetent" officers, and he vowed to retire the national debt through "a strict and faithful economy." Beyond that, he said very little, though he took every opportunity to flatter the popular majority. He had been elected "by the choice of a free people" (and not, as he did not have to say, by King Caucus or Corrupt Bargains), and he pledged "the zealous dedication of my humble abilities to their service and their good." He finished—as he often finished an important statement— by reminding Americans that a benign providence looked over them. He then looked up to a roar of applause.

The new president traveled slowly from the Capitol to the White House, with the throng following and growing noisier along the way. The crowd followed him into the White House, where orange punch and other refreshments had been laid out. Soon Jackson's well-wishers were ranging through the mansion, muddying the carpets, tipping things over, breaking dishes, and standing in dirty boots on upholstered chairs. Jackson had to retreat to avoid being crushed. The White House staff lured much of the crowd outside by moving the punch bowls and liquor to the lawn. A wealthy Washington matron who had admired the well-behaved crowd at the inaugural address exclaimed, "What a scene did we witness! The Majesty of the People had disappeared, and a rabble, a mob, of boys, negros, women, children, scrambling, fighting, romping. What a pity, what a pity." Another guest pronounced the occasion a "Saturnalia . . . of mud and filth." A Democratic newspaper reported more favorably:

"General Jackson is their own President . . . he was greeted by them with an enthusiasm which bespoke him the Hero of a popular triumph."

Conclusion

From 1828 onward, American politics operated within a national system of two parties. National Republicans (they would soon call themselves Whigs) supported the nationalism of the American System. Democrats argued for the limited, inexpensive government that since Jefferson's day had been a bulwark of both republicanism and slavery. Thus the party system provided answers to the questions of slavery and economic development that had brought it into being. Democrats successfully fought off the American System in the 1830s and 1840s: they dismantled the Bank of the United States, refused federal support for roads and canals, and revised the tariff in ways that mollified the export-oriented South. The result, however, was not a return to the Jeffersonian arcadia that many Democrats had envisioned but an inadvertent experiment in laissez-faire capitalism. The stupendous growth of the American economy after 1830 became a question of state and local action, with the result that the North and South continued to develop in their own ways—ways that were on an increasingly visible collision course. On the specific questions of slavery and sectionalism, the party system did what Van Buren had hoped it would do: Because the Whig and (especially) Democratic parties needed both southern and northern support, they were careful to focus national political debate on economic development, avoiding any discussion of sectional questions. It worked that way until the party system disintegrated on the eve of the Civil War.

Afterword

TOCQUEVILLE'S DEMOCRACY

IN 1830 THE FRENCHMAN ALEXIS DE TOCQUEVILLE CAME TO America and wrote about what he saw. He was not alone. After 1815 scores of British and European writers visited the United States. They wanted to see the one great republic that had survived the Age of the Democratic Revolution. Many of the visitors were contemptuous of democracy, and these wrote books that described America as vulgar, unpleasant, and doomed to failure. Others were democrats who wrote more admiringly about the United States. Tocqueville's *Democracy in America* went beyond mere condemnation or praise, and it has outlasted all the others. An aristocrat with liberal sensibilities, Tocqueville believed that democracy was the key to the emerging modern world. Despite their recent victories, he knew that the age of aristocrats and kings was coming to an end, and he wrote about Americans to tell Europeans about their own democratic future.

Tocqueville asserted that the great truth about America was its "equality of condition." America had no king, no aristocracy, no established church—none of the titled landlords and ancient privileges with which democracy contended in Europe. American land was abundant, and it was held in freehold, transferable ownership. American well-being was not a matter of inherited leases and inherited rights but of work, initiative, and individual accumulation. American families were not the upholders of tradition and paternal power that Tocqueville had known in Europe. They were nurseries of self-reliance, held together by freely given affection and not an ancient system of power. American religions taught subservience only to God; in this world, American Christians relied on themselves. Thus Tocqueville's Americans were not feudal underlings but independent citizens who rose and fell through their own efforts. Individual fortunes came and went with dizzying speed. The result was not a class system but a nation of strivers engaged in a social and economic free-for-all. "For an American," said Tocqueville, "one's entire life is spent as a game of chance, a time of revolution, a day of battle."

Tocqueville called this new American way "individualism," a word that he helped introduce into the American language. In his own French, individualism meant pure selfishness: an individualist was a sociopath who took what he wanted and cared nothing for other people. Democratic America produced individualism as a national culture, and the great question was how American society cohered at all. In answering that question, Tocqueville came up with the term "self-interest rightly understood." American laws protected individualists from each other, and they acted uniformly—without special privilege—upon all citizens. Americans obeyed government and the laws, first of all, because they believed that they had made both. They also understood that the laws sustained and governed the individualistic game that they all played. They respected the law and treated each other well for selfish reasons. And in all of this they were sustained by a religion that was separate from government and public life, but that transformed uncoerced individuals into self-disciplined democratic citizens. In the end, Tocqueville said, Americans behaved themselves and respected each other because it was in their interest to do so.

The single greatest danger built into this system was what Tocqueville called the "tyranny of the majority." The United States had the good fortune to be ruled by an undemocratic Federalist elite during its first years. Having stabilized the new republic, the Federalists lost control to Thomas Jefferson ("the most powerful apostle that democracy has ever had"), and Jefferson's party had been winning easily ever since. As a result, there were no fundamental political or ideological divisions in the United States. Politicians simply flattered the majority, and the majority became as omnipotent as any tyrant. "The people reign over the American political world as does God over the universe," said Tocqueville, and the result was that civic and intellectual excellence were excluded from government. For the same reasons, the majority ruled over the minority, restrained only by the laws that the majority made.

Capitalism and majoritarian democracy: it is the two-sided coin that modern politicians call "free society." Indeed Tocqueville's *Democracy in America* is often recommended as the first full description of freedom as a way of life. The book that you are finishing has attempted to tell how that way of life came into being, and how it was criticized and fought over by the Americans who lived it. We have seen that not all Americans—not even all white men—were eager participants in Tocqueville's new world. The whole white South remained committed to the old hierarchies of the traditional family, to slavery, to a traditional economy that discouraged change, and to a reinvented evangelical Protestantism that stood for tradition and not innovation. We have also seen that much of the North and West practiced similarly traditional ways of life. Judged by the results of elections, these men did not welcome Tocqueville's new world of winners and losers. They defended a half-mythical Old Republic—limited government, rough equality, and a community of respect among white men—against what they had begun to call "the Money Power." Thus it is true that democracy and free-market capitalism rose together in American history. But it is not true that they were inevitably in partnership. Indeed in 1830, as in most years since then, they were suspicious of each other.

Many present-day readers are able to ignore such considerations, but even these often find Tocqueville's formulation (or the formulations of those who claim to have read him) a bit too cheerful and finished. Tocqueville's democracy, after all, was exclusively white and male. Women and racial minorities had no voice in it, and that conflicts with our idea of what democracy is. Tocqueville knew that, and he wrote about the people who were excluded from American democracy. On the equality of women, he shared the axioms of the whole European world: men were clearly intended to rule over society and within families. Although Tocqueville and other liberal spirits called for an equitable division of labor and for kindness and respect toward women, and although he saw that the ethos of American democracy could logically extend to women, he stopped far short of endorsing or predicting equality. "One can easily conceive," he said, "that in thus striving to equalize one sex with the other, one degrades them both; and that from this course mixture of nature's work, only weak men and disreputable women can ever emerge." Many things had come into being between 1789 and 1830. But the equality of men and women—even as an idea—was not prominent among them.

The longest chapter in *Democracy in America* discusses the politics of race. Tocqueville was not interested in the experiences of blacks and Indians. Instead, he pointed out ways in which the democracy of white men was affected by the presence of other races. Observing the situation of American Indians in 1830, Tocqueville concluded, as had most political leaders, that they were on the road to extinction. Defeated in war and overrun by settlement, native peoples east of the Mississippi were at the mercy of the white republic. The federal government signed treaties and treated native peoples as separate nations—weak and conquered, but nations nonetheless. Some southern states routinely refused to recognize those treaties. By 1830 the national government, unwilling to make enemies of the southern states, was abandoning its commitments to native peoples. Tocqueville saw the political logic clearly: "it resolves without difficulty to let some already half-destroyed savage tribes perish in order not to put the American Union in danger." It was far from the situation in 1789, when the presence of powerful Indian peoples on the western boundaries of settlement had been among the reasons for establishing a national union.

Tocqueville paid great attention to the place of African Americans within the republic, for it was here that he saw the greatest threat to the existence of the United States. "The most dreadful of all the evils that threaten the future of the United States," he said, "arises from the presence of blacks on its soil. When one seeks the cause of the present troubles and future dangers of the Union, from whatever point one departs one almost always arrives at this first fact." In the half century following the Revolution, northerners had emancipated their slaves, whereas southerners had become vitally dependent on theirs. Tocqueville was quick to point out that white northerners rejected both slavery and racial equality. Anticipating the most recent scholarship on these questions, he noted that the simultaneous rise of emancipation and white democracy led northerners to *create* white supremacy. Free blacks were excluded from the vote, from juries, from schools—from the whole spectrum of public life—in most northern states. Popular racial prejudice was strongest, Tocqueville tells us, in those states. Southerners thought less publicly about race because slavery cemented white supremacy and allowed no questions about the role of blacks in public life. White Americans shared a nationwide racism and a dread of racial mingling. But differing regional histories led to racial fears that were silent in the South, violently noisy in the North.

Tocqueville insisted that the success of American democracy depended on the Union—on the survival of the United States as a unified nation. By 1830, he said, a tyrannical majority threatened to tear the Union apart. Democratic individualism had gone much further in the North than in the South. White northerners relied on their own labor, said Tocqueville, and the combination of self-interest and work generated prosperity and growth. It also produced the busy, ambitious, self-reliant personality that was the principal subject of Tocqueville's book. In the South (Tocqueville seldom got off the main roads in that region) slaves did the work and whites learned to despise labor as they despised black people. The result was the creation of distinct white regional personalities. North and South agreed on democracy and exalted the people, and they both insisted that the United States was the best country and the only true republic in the world. But they were different kinds of people: "The American of the South is more spontaneous, more spiritual, more open, more generous, more intellectual, more brilliant. The American of the North is more active, more reasonable, more enlightened, and more skillful. The one has the tastes, prejudices, weaknesses, and greatness of all aristocracies. The other, the qualities and defects that characterize the middle class. . . . Slavery therefore does not attack the American confederation directly by its interest, but indirectly by its mores." We may agree or disagree with this way of stating the problem, but we must concur that there was a problem.

To make matters worse, the northern majority grew every day. In the North every transaction bred others, and northerners created economic growth and sectional power in the course of their daily lives. And while northern growth produced change, southern growth, dependent on the availability of new land and on the price of cotton in other countries, produced only the expansion of an old economy across space. The differences, Tocqueville noted, were showing up in Congress. In 1790 Virginia had had 19 representatives, whereas New York had had only 10. In 1833 Virginia had 21 congressmen. New York had 40. The greatest threat to the Union, said Tocqueville, was northern prosperity. It was making a northern majority that, in southern eyes, was naturally and permanently hostile to the South.

Tocqueville had it right: capitalism, democracy, and white supremacy were indeed the principles of Americanness by 1830. These three, however, were not the established and eternal pillars of American civilization. They were the principal—and malleable—objects of argument. The "meaning of America" in 1790 or 1830 was not, as some Tocqueville aficionados would have it, a system of agreed-upon rules. It was an ongoing debate. It was not settled in 1830, and it is unlikely to be settled while Americans are still making history.

SUGGESTED READING

—»·◦·«—

The scholarly literature on the early American republic is rich and getting richer, and this bibliographic essay is intended as an introduction for serious students. It also acknowledges the principal books that have shaped my thinking on the subject.

POLITICS

Federalists

Stanley Elkins and Eric McKitrick, *The Age of Federalism: The Early American Republic, 1788–1800* (1993) provides a full and thoughtful account of politics in the 1790s. James Roger Sharp, *American Politics in the Early Republic: The New Nation in Crisis* (1993) is a good interpretive essay, whereas John C. Miller, *The Federalist Era, 1789–1801* (1960) remains a valuable brief account. Specific issues are treated ably in Ralph Ketcham, *Presidents above Party: The First American Presidency, 1789–1829* (1984), Robert A. Rutland, *The Birth of the Bill of Rights, 1776–1791* (1955), Thomas G. Slaughter, *The Whiskey Rebellion: Frontier Epilogue to the American Revolution* (1986), Richard H. Kohn, *Eagle and Sword: The Federalists and the Creation of the Military Establishment in America, 1783–1802* (1975), James A. Smith, *Freedom's Fetters: The Alien and Sedition Laws and American Civil Liberties* (rev. ed., 1967). The rise of Jeffersonian opposition is traced in Lance Banning, *The Jeffersonian Persuasion: Evolution of a Party Ideology* (1980), Banning, *The Sacred Fire of Liberty: James Madison and the Founding of the Federal Republic* (1995), Joyce Appleby, *Capitalism and a New Social Order: The Republican Vision of the 1790s* (1984), and David Waldstreicher, *In the Midst of Perpetual Fetes: The Making of American Nationalism, 1776–1820* (1997). Saul Cornell, *The Other Founders: Anti-Federalism and the Dissenting Tradition in America* (1999) traces localism and distrust of central government from the debate on the Constitution into the early republic. Two good studies of the political culture of these years are Joseph J. Ellis, *Founding Brothers: The Revolutionary Generation* (2000) and Joanne B. Freeman, *Affairs of Honor: National Politics in the New Republic* (2001). There are numerous fine studies of individuals. The best modern rendering of Washington is Joseph J. Ellis, *His Excellency George Washington* (2004). On Hamilton, see Ron Chernow, *Alexander Hamilton* (2004). Madison's activities in these years are insightfully described in Banning's *The Sacred Fire of Liberty*, cited earlier. On Jefferson, Merrill Peterson, *Thomas Jefferson and the New Nation* (1960) and Noble Cunningham, *In Pursuit of Reason: The Life of Thomas Jefferson* (1987) are good one-volume biographies, whereas Joseph J. Ellis, *American Sphinx: The Character of Thomas Jefferson* (1997) is a learned interpretive essay. The principal letters, speeches, and state papers of Washington, Hamilton, Jefferson, and Madison have been collected and published in modern editions by the Library of America.

Jeffersonians

For good introductions to the politics of Jeffersonianism, see Peter Onuf, *Jefferson's Empire: The Language of American Nationhood* (2000) and Peter Onuf and Leonard J. Sadosky, *Jeffersonian America* (2002). Marshall Smelser, *The Democratic Republic, 1801–1815* (1968) is a thorough traditional account; Forest McDonald, *The Presidency of Thomas Jefferson* (1976) is both critical and thoughtful. Henry Adams, *History of the United States of America during the Administrations of Thomas Jefferson and James Madison* (1889–91; reprint 1986) is the classic account, and it is still valuable. Drew McCoy, *The Elusive Republic: Political Economy in Jeffersonian America* (1980) is a fine study of economic ideas and policies. The courts are treated in Richard E. Ellis, *The Jeffersonian Crisis: Courts and Politics in the Young Republic* (1971), Robert Lowry Clinton, *Marbury vs. Madison and Judicial Review* (1989), R. Kent Newmeyer, *The Supreme Court under Marshall and Tawney* (1968), and Charles F. Hobson, *The Great Chief Justice: John Marshall and the Rule of Law* (1996). Opposition to the Jeffersonians is the subject of four good old books: Robert E. Shalhope, *John Taylor of Caroline: Pastoral Republican* (1980), Norman K. Risjord, *The Old Republicans: Southern Conservatism in the Age of Jefferson* (1965), Linda K. Kerber, *Federalists in Dissent: Imagery and Ideology in Jeffersonian America* (1970), and James M. Banner, Jr., *To the Hartford Convention: The Federalists and the Origins of Party Politics in Massachusetts, 1789–1815* (1969).

Diplomacy, 1790–1829

Bradford Perkins, *The Creation of a Republican Empire* (1993) and Reginald Horsman, *The Diplomacy of the Early Republic* (1985) provide overviews of international relations in these years. More specialized accounts include Henry Ammon, *The Genet Mission* (1973), Samuel Bemis's classic studies, *Jay's Treaty* (2nd ed., (1962) and *Pinckney's Treaty*, (2nd ed., 1960), Jerald A. Combs, *The Jay Treaty* (1970), Wiley Sword, *President Washington's Indian War: The Struggle for the Old Northwest, 1790–95* (1985), Alexander DeConde, *The Quasi-War: Politics and Diplomacy of the Undeclared War with France, 1797–1800* (1966), DeConde, *This Affair of Louisiana* (1976), and Lawrence Kaplan, *Entangling Alliances with None: American Foreign Policy in the Age of Jefferson* (1987). On the diplomatic, political, and military history of the War of 1812, the essential accounts are Bradford Perkins, *Prologue to War: England and the United States, 1805–1812* (1967), Clifford I. Egan, *Neither Peace nor War: Franco-American Relations, 1803–1812* (1983), J. C. A. Stagg, *Mr. Madison's War: Politics, Diplomacy, and Warfare in the Early Republic, 1783–1830* (1983), and Donald R. Hickey, *The War of 1812: A Forgotten Conflict* (1989).

National Republicans and Democrats, 1815–1830

Sean Wilentz, *The Rise of American Democracy: Jefferson to Lincoln* (2005) is the most comprehensive study of politics in these (and earlier and later) years. Students should also consult the relevant chapters of Charles G. Sellers, *The Market Revolution: Jacksonian America, 1815–1846* (1991), Arthur Schlesinger, Jr., *The Age of Jackson* (1945), and Harry L. Watson, *Liberty and Power: The Politics of Jacksonian America* (1990). On presidential elections in these years, the best place to start is Arthur M. Schlesinger, Jr., and Fred J. Israels, eds., *History of American Presidential Elections, 1789–1968,* 3 vols. (1971). George Dangerfield, *The Era of Good Feelings* (1953) and Glover Moore, *The Missouri Controversy, 1819–1821* (1953) remain valuable treatments of their subjects. John Lauritz Larson, *Internal Improvement: National Public Works and the Promise of Popular Government in the Early United States* (2001) is essential. William W. Freehling, *The Road to Disunion: Secessionists at Bay, 1776–1854* (1990) provides an interpretive overview of the South and slavery in national politics. Freehling's *Prelude to Civil War: The Nullification Controversy in South Carolina, 1816–1836* (1965) and Richard E. Ellis, *The Union at Risk: Jacksonian Democracy, States' Rights, and the Nullification Crisis* (1987) describe the rise of extreme states' rights positions in the 1820s. Good biographies of political leaders include Robert V. Remini, *Andrew Jackson and the Course of American Freedom, 1822–1833* (1981), Sean Wilentz, *Andrew Jackson* (2005), Remini, *Henry Clay: Statesman for the Union* (1991), Samuel Flagg Bemis, *John Quincy Adams and the Foundations of American Foreign Policy* (1949), and Drew R. McCoy, *The Last of the Founders: James Madison & the Republican Legacy* (1989).

ECONOMY AND SOCIETY

Two good introductory collections on economy and society in the early republic are Melvyn Stokes and Stephen Conway, eds., *The Market Revolution in America* (1996) and a special edition of the *Journal of the Early Republic* (Summer 1996). Still essential are Douglas C. North, *The Economic Growth of the United States, 1790–1860* (1961) and Stuart Bruchey, *The Roots of American Economic Growth, 1607–1861* (1968). For detailed economic syntheses, see Curtis P. Nettels, *The Emergence of a National Economy, 1775–1815* (1962) and George Rogers

Taylor, *The Transportation Revolution, 1815–1860* (1951). On literacy and communications, see Paul Starr, *The Creation of the Media: Political Origins of Modern Communications* (2004), Richard R. John, *Spreading the News: The American Postal System from Franklin to Morse* (1995), William J. Gilmore, *Reading Becomes a Necessity of Life: Material and Cultural Life in Rural New England, 1780–1835* (1989), Kathy N. Davidson, *Revolution and the Word: The Rise of the Novel in America* (1986), and Davidson, ed., *Reading in America: Literature and Social History* (1989).

Northern Farms

For thorough regional studies of northern rural society in these years, see Christopher Clark, *The Roots of Rural Capitalism: Western Massachusetts, 1780–1860* (1990), Martin Bruegel, *Farm, Shop, Landing: The Rise of a Market Society in the Hudson Valley, 1780–1860* (2002) Laurel Thatcher Ulrich, *A Midwife's Tale: The Life of Martha Ballard, Based on Her Diary, 1785–1812* (1990) Carolyn Merchant, *Ecological Revolutions: Nature, Gender, and Science in New England* (1989) and Winifred Barr Rothenberg, *From Market-Places to Market Economy: The Transformation of Rural Massachusetts, 1750–1850* (1994). Jack Larkin, *The Reshaping of Everyday Life, 1790–1840* (1988) is a valuable synthesis of scholarship on material culture, particularly in the Northeast.

The West

Studies of Native Americans in these years begin with the final chapters of Richard White's magisterial *The Middle Ground: Indians, Empires, and Republics in the Great Lakes Region, 1650–1815* (1991). More specialized accounts include R. David Edmunds, *The Shawnee Prophet* (1983), Anthony F. C. Wallace, *The Death and Rebirth of the Seneca* (1969), William G. McLoughlin, *Cherokee Renaissance in the New Republic* (1986), Joel W. Martin, *Sacred Revolt: The Muscogees' Struggle for a New World* (1991), and Gregory Evans Dowd, *A Spirited Resistance: The North American Indian Struggle for Unity, 1745–1815* (1992). White settler societies are treated in John Mack Faragher, *Daniel Boone: The Life and Legend of an American Pioneer* (1992), Faragher, *Sugar Creek: Life on the Illinois Prairie* (1986), Stephan Aron, *How the West was Lost: The Transformation of Kentucky from Daniel Boone to Henry Clay* (1996), Andrew R. L. Cayton, *The Frontier Republic: Ideology and Politics in the Ohio Country, 1780–1825* (1986), Charles E. Brooks, *Frontier Settlement and Market Revolution: The Holland Land Purchase* (1996), Alan Taylor, *Liberty Men and Great Proprietors: The Revolutionary Settlement on the Maine Frontier, 1760–1820* (1990), and Taylor, *William Cooper's Town: Power and Persuasion on the Frontier of the Early American Republic* (1996). Still very useful is R. Carlyle Buley, *The Old Northwest: Pioneer Period, 1815–1840,* (2 vols., 1950).

The South

Mark M. Smith, *Debating Slavery: Economy and Society in the Antebellum American South* (1998) provides a solid introductory overview. Students should also consult Robert William Fogel and Stanley Engerman's controversial *Time on the Cross: The Economics of American Negro Slavery* (2 vols., 1974) and R. W. Fogel, *Without Consent or Contract: The Rise and Fall of American Slavery* (1989). More specialized studies include James Oakes, *The Ruling Race: A History of American Slaveholders* (1982), Oakes, *Slavery and Freedom: An Interpretation of the Old South* (1990), Orville Vernon Burton, *In My Father's House are Many Mansions: Family and Community in Edgefield, South Carolina* (1985), Eugene D. Genovese, *The Political Economy of Slavery: Studies in the Economy and Society of the Slave South* (2nd. ed., 1989), Gavin Wright, *The Political Economy of the Cotton South: Households, Markets, and Wealth in the Nineteenth Century* (1978), and Peter Coclanis, *The Shadow of a Dream: Economic Life and Death in the South Carolina Lowcountry, 1670–1920* (1989). Walter Johnson, *Soul by Soul: Life Inside the Antebellum Slave Market* (1999) brilliantly uncovers the culture-making powers of the slave trade.

On the family culture of southern whites, see Bertram Wyatt-Brown, *Southern Honor: Ethics & Behavior in the Old South* (1982), Kenneth S. Greenberg, *Honor & Slavery* (1996), and Elizabeth Fox-Genovese, *Within the Plantation Household: Black and White Women of the Old South* (1988). Eugene D. Genovese, *The Slaveholders' Dilemma: Southern Conservative Thought, 1820–1860* (1992), demonstrates the pervasive paternalism of southern social thought. On the southern yeomanry, see Stephanie McCurry, *Masters of Small Worlds: Yeoman Households, Gender Relations, & the Political Culture of the Antebellum South Carolina Lowcountry* (1995), J. William Harris, *Plain Folk and Gentry in a Slave Society: White Liberty and Black Slavery in Augusta's Hinterlands* (1985), and Grady McWhiney, *Cracker Culture: Celtic Folkways in the Old South* (1988).

Slavery

Peter Kolchin, *American Slavery, 1619–1877* (1993) is a fine synthesis of the scholarly literature on the slaves. The relevant sections of Ira Berlin, *Many Thousands Gone: The First Two Centuries of Slavery in America* (1998), Berlin's *Generations of Captivity: A History of African-American Slaves (2003)*, and Philip D. Morgan, *Slave Counterpoint: Black Culture in the Eighteenth-Century Chesapeake and Lowcountry* (1998) are essential. The modern classic on slave culture is Eugene D. Genovese, *Roll, Jordan, Roll: The World the Slaves Made* (1974). Students should also consult Lawrence W. Levine, *Black Culture and Black Consciousness: Afro-American Folk Thought from Slavery to Freedom* (1977), Charles Joyner, *Down by the Riverside: A South Carolina Slave Community* (1984), Herbert G. Gutman, *The Black Family in Slavery and Freedom, 1750–1925* (1976), Ann Patton Malone, *Sweet Chariot: Slave Family and Household Structure in Nineteenth-Century*

Louisiana (1992), John Michael Vlach, *Back of the Big House: The Architecture of Plantation Slavery* (1993), and the essays in Ira Berlin and Ronald L. Hoffman, *Slavery and Freedom in the Age of the American Revolution* (1983). On slave resistance, see James Sidbury, *Ploughshares into Swords: Race, Rebellion, and Identity in Gabriel's Virginia* (1997), Douglas R. Egerton, *Gabriel's Rebellion: The Virginia Slave Conspiracies of 1800 & 1802* (1993), Norrece T. Jones, Jr., *Born a Child of Freedom, Yet a Slave: Mechanisms of Control and Strategies of Resistance in Antebellum South Carolina* (1990), and, more broadly, Eugene D. Genovese, *From Rebellion to Revolution: Afro-American Slave Revolts in the Making of the Modern World* (1979).

Race

The classic, aging, study of early American racial ideology is Winthrop D. Jordan, *White over Black: American Attitudes Toward the Negro, 1550–1812* (1968). Edmund S. Morgan, *American Slavery, American Freedom* (2nd ed., 2004) began a study of relations between white freedom and black slavery that includes David R. Roediger, *The Wages of Whiteness: Race and the Making of the American Working Class* (revised ed., 1999), Joanne Pope Melish, *Disowning Slavery: Gradual Emancipation and "Race" in New England, 1780–1860* (1998), Gary B. Nash, *Forging Freedom: The Formation of Philadelphia's Black Community, 1720–1840* (1988), James Oliver Horton and Lois E. Horton, *In Hope of Liberty: Culture, Community and Protest Among Northern Free Blacks, 1700–1860* (1997), and the essays in Michael L. Morrison and James Brewer Stewart, eds., *Race and the Early Republic: Racial Consciousness and Nation Building in the Early Republic* (2002). The limits of southern antislavery in these years are traced in David Brion Davis, *The Problem of Slavery in the Age of Revolution, 1770–1823* (1975), and in the relevant essays in Peter S. Onuf, ed., *Jeffersonian Legacies* (1993).

Religion

The modern scholarly study of religion in the early republic begins with two books: Jon Butler, *Awash in a Sea of Faith: Christianizing the American People* (1990), and Nathan O. Hatch, *The Democratization of American Christianity* (1989). Good studies of white southern religion include Christine Leigh Heyrman, *Southern Cross: The Beginnings of the Bible Belt* (1997), Paul K. Conkin, *Cane Ridge: America's Pentecost* (1990), John B. Boles, *The Great Revival: 1787–1805* (1972), and Donald G. Mathews, *Religion in the Old South* (1977). Religious developments among slaves and free blacks are treated in Albert J. Raboteau, *Slave Religion: The "Invisible" Institution in the Antebellum South* (1978), Sylvia Frey and Betty Wood, *Come Shouting to Zion: African American Protestantism in the American South and the British Caribbean to 1830* (1998), Frey, *Water from the Rock: Black Resistance in a Revolutionary Age* (1991), and the early essays in Paul E. Johnson, ed., *African-American Christianity: Essays in History* (1994). The religion of the North's emerging middle class is the subject of Mary P. Ryan, *Cradle of the Middle Class: The Family in Oneida County, New York, 1790–1860* (1981), Paul E. Johnson, *A Shopkeeper's Millennium: Society and Revivals in Rochester, New York, 1815–1837* (1978), and the early chapters of Carroll Smith-Rosenberg, *Disorderly Conduct: Visions of Gender in Victorian America* (1985). The most thorough treatments of popular evangelism are the works of Jon Butler and Nathan Hatch, cited earlier. Lewis O. Saum, *The Popular Mood of Pre-Civil War America* (1980) is a valuable study of the unsentimental culture of plain folk. Characteristics of plain-folk religion emerge in Curtis D. Johnson, *Redeeming America: Evangelicals and the Road to Civil War* (1993), David L. Rowe, *Thunder and Trumpets: Millerites and Dissenting Religion in Upstate New York, 1800–1850* (1985), Paul E. Johnson and Sean Wilentz, *The Kingdom of Matthias: A Story of Sex & Salvation in 19th-Century America* (1994), and John L. Brooke, *The Refiner's Fire: The Making of Mormon Cosmology, 1644–1844* (1994).

INDEX